Electronic Boy

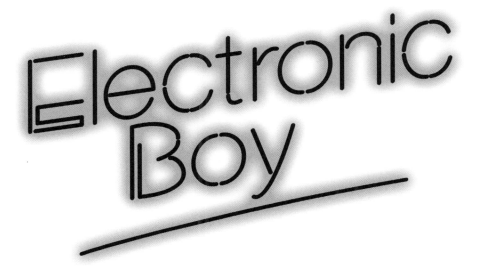

Electronic Boy

MY LIFE IN AND OUT OF **SOFT CELL**

DAVE BALL

OMNIBUS PRESS

London / New York / Paris / Sydney / Copenhagen / Berlin / Madrid / Tokyo

Copyright © 2020 Omnibus Press
(A Division of Music Sales Limited)

Cover designed by Amazing15
Picture research by Dave Ball

ISBN: 9781787601598

Typesetting by Evolution Design & Digital Ltd (Kent)
Printed in Malta

A catalogue record for this book is available from the British Library.

For Brenda & Donald

"Art is anything you can get away with"
– *Andy Warhol*

"Money for old rope"
– *my Dad*

"Suicide the easy way"
– *Alan Vega*

CONTENTS

Prologue
ADOPTION

ACCORDING TO MY *GUINNESS BOOK OF BRITISH HIT SINGLES,* 'It Doesn't Matter Anymore' by Buddy Holly & The Crickets was posthumously number one in the pop charts on Sunday 3 May, 1959, when I was born. Ruth Pritchard – my birth mother – alas, was no Peggy Sue and unlike the girl in another of Buddy's songs, hadn't got married. Until I was one and a half years old I was named Paul Pritchard, shortened from the Welsh, 'ap Richard', so it's possible I may have some Celtic blood in me and not, in the literal sense of the words, be an entirely English bastard.

I never met my real father and lived with my mother and her elderly parents until my crying and the smell of nappies got too much for the old folk and we moved temporarily into my mum's aunt's home in Bridges Cottages, Chester, right by a bridge on the bank of the river Dee, near the Welsh border. This possibly explains why I've always loved being near water.

The stigma of being a single parent (not to mention being an offspring of one) in the post-war, pre-*Jeremy Kyle Show* austerity of Britain in the late 1950s meant times were pretty hard; child benefit wasn't so freely available and social housing was mainly reserved for nuclear families. My mother and I were rehoused in a 'home for unmarried mothers' in Cheetham Hill, Greater Manchester. Her aunt saw the hopelessness of our situation and eventually suggested the unthinkable – that I be put up for adoption.

I'm told my mother desperately tried to keep me but at some point realised I'd probably have a much better chance in life, not to mention of becoming an eighties synthpop star. It broke her heart to let me go and I've often wondered how different things would have turned out if she hadn't...

PART 1

Chapter 1

BLACKPOOL

I WAS OFFICIALLY ADOPTED AT BLACKPOOL COUNTY COURT on 17 November 1960.

According to my new parents, Donald and Brenda Ball, His Honour Judge Holgate's exact words to me were, 'Now, let that be the last time I see you in my courtroom, young man!' He needn't have worried as I wouldn't appear in court until nearly forty years later when he was dead and buried and I was in the divorce court at Somerset House, London.

My adoptive parents met when they both worked for the GPO (General Post Office) – now BT. After doing his national service in the Royal Signals, my dad became a telephone engineer and my mum a telephonist. They married in 1952 and planned to start a family of their own but, as the result of a complicated hysterectomy operation, Mum was unable to conceive. Fostering or adoption were their only options and they chose the latter.

When I was old enough, they told me that, although they both liked the name Paul, as my new surname was going to be Ball, a rhyming Christian and surname like Paul Ball might be problematic for me at school, so they settled with David. Not that it made any difference – with a surname like Ball, I may as well have had a target printed on my shirt anyway.

We lived at number ten, a semi-detached house on the corner of Orkney Road and Falmouth Road, South Shore, Blackpool. It was five minutes' walk from Bloomfield Road football ground and Blackpool's legendary northern soul club – the Highland Room.

In 1962 my parents adopted Susan, who became my sister when she was only a few months old. It was one of my first memories – I have a vague recollection of getting out of a taxi with my parents, and my mum smiling and carrying a tiny baby wrapped in a white candlewick shawl. Susan was also the offspring of an unmarried mother; an 18-year-old girl from Southport who worked as a secretary for a local company until she got pregnant by her middle-aged, married boss. She couldn't keep the baby and the father wasn't exactly overjoyed at the prospect of explaining it to his wife. Needless to say, the unwanted child was promptly put up for adoption.

As soon as they had my new sister safely into the house, my parents celebrated with a glass or two of sherry and played 'Stranger On The Shore' by Acker Bilk in her honour. My mum loved that record. My dad's musical tastes stopped with Glenn Miller. He detested rock'n'roll because his younger brother, my uncle Tony, had been a teddy boy and he and his gang got sent to borstal for slashing cinema seats with flick knives when the film *Rock Around The Clock* was shown. My dad seldom bought records for himself but occasionally surprised my mum with her favourites – *The Sound Of Music*, *South Pacific* and *West Side Story* soundtracks being prime examples. It's ironic that my dad never actually watched *West Side Story* and was blissfully unaware that it concerned The Jets and The Sharks; two rival flick-knife-carrying teenage gangs. Mum and Dad could both agree on 'Stranger On The Shore' and, subconsciously, the associated memory is probably the reason I've always loved the sound of the clarinet and featured it on several of my recordings over the years.

★ ★ ★

A distinctly unpleasant memory I have from my infancy was my parents talking about the Moors murders carried out by Ian Brady and Myra Hindley which were on the TV and in the papers all the time. My mum did her best to explain to me when I asked her the inevitable question: 'Mummy, what's a "Moors murder"?' She told me some children had been murdered by 'very bad people' on Saddleworth Moor near Manchester. I was quite a sensitive child with a fertile imagination and knew Manchester wasn't very far from Blackpool. I'd just gained enough confidence to walk to infant school on my own, then the nightmares about the black-and-white footage of detectives digging up the shallow graves of children on the Moors started. When they published the infamous pictures of Brady and Hindley, the dark, staring eyes of the evil pair were indelibly imprinted on my mind. I knew exactly what 'bad people' looked like and it wasn't long before my mum was holding my hand on the way to and from school again.

There were a few things on the old black-and-white TV that scared me. Lots of my fear was related to noises I heard on the war documentary my dad watched, called *All Our Yesterdays* – wailing air raid sirens, screaming sounds of German Stuka dive-bombers and Japanese kamikaze pilots. The other show that scared the shit out of me and probably most kids in the UK every Saturday evening was *Doctor Who*. Apart from being terrified of the Daleks and the Zarbi, the main thing I remember was the amazing other-worldly title sequence, in particular Ron Grainer and Delia Derbyshire's BBC Radiophonic Workshop's theme music. I think that was possibly the first time I ever heard electronic music, apart from *Sparky's Magic Piano* – although, strictly speaking, that wasn't really electronic as it was a Sonovox talk box that created the voice effect, but it does sound like an early vocoder and, according to my *ELO's Greatest Hits* album sleeve notes, was the inspiration for 'Mr. Blue Sky', so that's good enough for me. (A Sonovox talk box worked in a similar way to a voice box as heard on Peter Frampton's massive seventies hit 'Show Me The Way'. Either the driver of the loudspeaker went into a tube that was put in the mouth of the 'singer' so he/she could shape the words, effectively using the mouth as a loudspeaker cone, or a loudspeaker playing the music was strapped facing inwards to the abdomen of the singer who shaped the words orally. This method didn't last for long as it caused serious damage to the singer's internal organs.)

In 1965 Gloria Jones released the US single 'My Bad Boy's Comin' Home' on Champion Records, with a B-side called 'Tainted Love'. The record was a flop and I only heard that B-side for the first time ten years later, in a northern soul club. On its first release, I was only 5 years old and had just moved up from the infants to Revoe junior school on Grasmere Road, Blackpool. It was quite a rough-and-tumble little school, with a constant nit problem. I had close-cropped hair so I never caught them, although I did catch chicken pox, mumps, measles and rubella in quick succession. One poor girl in my class was taken into care when her single mum was convicted of being a prostitute, which really confused my friends and me because we were all Protestants and we didn't know it was illegal.

There were always fights in the playground but there's one particular scrap I've never forgotten: I punched a boy in the face and, when he looked back at me, to my horror he only had one eye left, with a gaping hole where the other one was meant to be. I thought I'd blinded him until he bent down, picked his glass eye off the ground, licked it clean and put it back in the socket. He wanted to carry on fighting, until an equally stunned teacher intervened. Nobody had known he had a false eye until that day. It freaked us all out, particularly me, and I never punched anyone in the face again.

Chapter 2
VISCOSE AND VELVETEEN

I LOVED SATURDAYS WHEN I WAS A KID AND WOULD GO
to the children's Saturday morning matinee with my friends at
the King Edward cinema, where they showed various cartoons
and British Gaumont and Pathé News and travelogue films. At
the interval, 'Asteroid', the theme for advertisers Pearl & Dean,
would blast out of the speakers and we'd race down the aisle
to buy little tubs of ice cream and cartons of plastic-flavoured
orange juice from the elderly usherette. Once back in our seats,
full of 'E' numbers, the main entertainment would begin: two
hours of Laurel & Hardy, Charlie Chaplin, Harold Lloyd,
Keystone Cops and Buster Keaton shorts interspersed with
various cartoons.

Sunday was by far my worst day of the week; my mum would
force me to get up and put on my Sunday best – brown-tweed sports
jacket, black, flared trousers, brown slip-ons, a purple psychedelic
shirt and a hideous, bright yellow, 100 per cent viscose kipper tie
that my grandma had bought me one Christmas. I was then forced
to accompany her to Holy Cross church as she was going through
some sort of born-again, menopausal, midlife crisis and I was her
unwilling disciple.

One time she even volunteered me to be the page boy for the Holy Cross Rose Queen parade. I had to wear all-white; shirt, trousers and shoes, with a black dickie bow. My job was to present the Queen – an Afro-haired girl called Noelle, who lived across the street from us – with a bunch of white roses and a plastic tiara from Woolworth's resting on a black velveteen cushion. It was almost as tacky as an early Soft Cell video and was in fact my second live appearance on stage (the first was a wise man in the school Nativity play). The Rose Queen and I were flanked by a bunch of squealing ladies-in-waiting while a gang of old crones looked on menacingly, cooing away into their warm sherry, oblivious to the swarm of thirsty wasps buzzing around them. A swaying press photographer drunkenly snapped away for the *Blackpool Evening Gazette*, where, to my horror, our pictures would appear in the centrefold the following week. To complete the ritual humiliation, we had to be driven and displayed around Blackpool in a horse-drawn landau. The horse not only shat constantly – people excitedly ran out of their gardens with shovels and put it on their rose beds – but it had a piss right outside the church while we had our photos taken and, yes, he really was hung like a horse – it was about a yard long.

The closest thing I had to a religion at that time was football, as music wasn't yet my main interest. Blackpool were quite a good side at that point, when the top league was Division One and they'd been in it from 1946 to 1967. Throughout one season I got to see all the players who would play in the 1966 England World Cup squad and many of the other top players of the day, including one of my all-time heroes – George Best.

My dad's views on Best weren't that dissimilar to his views on most male pop stars. He hated flamboyant men, especially if they were successful, had long hair and looked vaguely effeminate (i.e. most of them). Whenever he heard a successful band on the radio, his standard comment was, 'Bloody money for old rope!' One of my few regrets in life is that my dad never lived to see my fifteen minutes of pop fame with Soft Cell. I'd have loved to have shown him my platinum, gold and silver discs – not to mention my bank balance – just to prove he was absolutely right about the 'old rope' bit. Also, to have seen his reaction to Marc Almond would have been absolutely priceless.

One of my most memorable childhood recollections was the 30 July 1966 win for England over West Germany in the World Cup Final at Wembley Stadium. I watched the match on TV at home with my dad and my World Cup Willie mascot. To celebrate the victory, my school splashed out on England football strips for all of us. As I was the goalie I had a yellow top just like the one Gordon Banks wore in the final. I was obsessed with being a goalkeeper but with the true fickleness of a 7-year-old, swapped my football allegiance from Blackpool to Chelsea. The reason was quite simple: my favourite goalkeeper at the time was Peter Bonetti, a.k.a. the Cat, and he played for Chelsea and often wore an emerald-green kit, including matching socks and gloves. Much as I'd enjoyed being Gordon Banks, I desperately wanted to be the Cat. No prizes for guessing what I got for my main Christmas present that year.

A few days after the World Cup Final, my dad and I went to watch it all over again at the local cinema in glorious Technicolor. My dad often took me to the cinema and I saw all the early James Bond films with him: *Dr. No*, *From Russia With Love*, *Goldfinger*, *Thunderball* and *You Only Live Twice*, as well as two non-Bond films: *Born Free* and *Zulu*. My dad may have inadvertently created a lifelong fan of composer John Barry, as he scored the music for all apart from *Dr. No*. Most boys of my age loved James Bond and I had the toy Aston Martin DB5 with all the gadgets – ejector seat, bulletproof shield and machine guns. I was also naively convinced that James Bond didn't wear underpants under his trousers because Sean Connery always seemed to wear a towel round his waist in the bedroom. I even tried wearing a towel instead of Y-fronts under my trousers, much to my mum and dad's great amusement.

My mum also took me to see a few films that made deep impressions on me, notably *Oliver!* and *Chitty Chitty Bang Bang*. My favourite characters were usually the baddies like Bill Sykes and the Child Catcher – come to think of it, they could almost have been the prototypes for a certain synth duo.

Television became an increasingly important influence on my life. I was a huge fan of the American TV series *Batman* starring Adam West. I remember my dad saying to me, 'Let me know when you get bored with being the Cat and I'll stencil some black question marks on your new green strip so you can be the Riddler instead.' I never got to be the Riddler but I did persuade my mum to make me a Batman outfit. One day one of my friends, also wearing a homemade Batman outfit, copied a stunt he'd seen on the show and tried to scale the wall of our garage using his Bat Rope (actually a piece of thick wool). He almost made it to the top before it snapped and he fell about six feet to the ground, smashing his elbow joint so badly he was never able to bend his arm again. The power of television.

BBC2 became available up north in 1967, having only been broadcast in London in black-and-white. We still had our old monochrome set but as a special treat I was allowed to go to a friend's, whose parents had just bought a new television, to watch *The High Chaparral* on BBC2 – the first TV programme I ever saw in colour. My friend's parents were considerably younger than mine and hence a bit more 'with it'. My friend's father had longer hair than my dad and sported a rather dubious Peter Wyngarde/Jason King-style moustache with sideburns. He also wore polo-neck shirts, flared trousers and Chelsea boots. They even drank Nescafé, which was relatively new to Britain at that time – I'd never had coffee until then.

It was a totally different world in our fifties-style household where we only ever drank tea and my dad and I always had Brylcreemed short-back-and-sides haircuts and always wore a collar and tie except in the evenings and at the weekend when I was allowed to wear my Wranglers. Even these fell to my mum's obsession for ironing everything: not just shirts, but socks, underwear, handkerchiefs and much to my annoyance those jeans, which had ironed-in faded creases down the middle of each leg.

Chapter 3
DISCOTHEQUES AND DWARVES

I WAS JUST 10 YEARS OLD WHEN APOLLO 11 REACHED THE moon on 20 July 1969. I remember being allowed to stay up with my parents to watch Neil Armstrong and Buzz Aldrin walk on the lunar surface for the first time and hear Armstrong utter the immortal words, 'That's one small step for man, one giant leap for mankind.' It certainly was a giant leap in our household because my parents splashed out on a colour television especially for the event. A truly life-changing moment, like in *The Wizard Of Oz*, when the film transforms into glorious Technicolor. Life became much more colourful for me in another way too – I went to my first ever discotheque.

During the summer, when there were no Blackpool football fixtures, all my friends from school were allowed to go to the afternoon junior disco at the Mecca on Central Drive – later Tiffany's and since demolished. Going in was really exciting because there was an escalator at the entrance that took you to the first-floor reception area, which led to two big dancefloors:

the Locarno Ballroom, which featured huge illuminated plastic trees, and the Highland Room. The latter boasted tartan carpets around its bar and dancefloor and became one of the most legendary northern soul venues during the seventies. We were always in the other room and I don't recall them ever playing any northern soul. Instead they played 'Groovin' With Mr. Bloe' by Mr. Bloe, 'Spirit In The Sky' by Norman Greenbaum, 'Young, Gifted And Black' by Bob & Marcia, 'Neanderthal Man' by Hotlegs, 'Na Na Hey Hey Kiss Him Goodbye' by Steam and 'Time Is Tight' by Booker T. & The MG's. There's a very good reason I remember those particular tunes so fondly. In a seaside resort like Blackpool, even at a kid's afternoon disco session, the manager insisted there be two 18-year-old 'fembot'-style, blonde go-go dancers on the stage. They always danced to those songs and for some reason, the image of their pert gyrating bodies, in tight, white mini-dresses and platform thigh boots has always stayed with me.

Another incident from those long, hot childhood summers that left an indelible mark on my psyche featured my mum's friend Joan and her son Paul. Mum and Joan had known each other since their early twenties when they were both telephonists. They wanted to catch up without the children under their feet and gave us some spending money to go to Blackpool Pleasure Beach amusement park. As Paul was the eldest, he was deemed responsible for both of us and we had a great time going on all the rides, drinking bottles of pop and eating ice creams. We realised we'd spent all the money.

'Shall we just go home now, Paul, we've got no money left?' I asked.

'No, David, don't be daft, we can sneak onto the miniature railway, just follow me,' he replied. 'Right, keep your head down and jump on now, the man can't see us.' We leapt on board but within minutes we were in the clutches of 'the man who couldn't see us'. He had a very firm grip and I soon realised why he worked on the miniature railway – he was a dwarf!

'Aaah, get him off me!' I shrieked hysterically.

After lecturing us and promising that he'd find us and eat us if we ever did it again, the little man finally let us go. I had nightmares about being chased and eaten by dwarfs for ages after that. It's strange to think that years later I would appear in a banned video, featuring a blood-splattered, chainsaw-wielding dwarf in bondage gear, for a song I co-wrote with Marc, called 'Sex Dwarf' – talk about confronting your demons.

Some of my other memories of growing up in Blackpool during the late 1960s and early 1970s also concern the strange, magical, mad carnival of the Pleasure Beach, a place not dissimilar to Tod Browning's 1932 film, *Freaks*. There was the life-size, laughing clown automaton at the entrance to the Pleasure Beach that bore an uncanny resemblance to my future manager, and at one time there was even a lady with a beard – possibly the stick-on variety from the joke shop. The local people who populated the funfairs and the promenade included families of dwarfs, midgets, Romany gypsies and every kind of entertainer and petty crook you could imagine. There were singers, comedians, trapeze artistes, strippers, clowns, wrestlers, drag artists and a whole array of pickpockets, brawlers, hookers and conmen. One old local guy used to run children's donkey rides on the beach. He had about seven animals and used to keep them all in the stables in his cobbled backyard at night; all except his favourite, which was allowed in his house. I watched outside television broadcasts of Stuart Hall presenting *It's A Knockout* in what now seems like more innocent or unknowing times – long before he was convicted.

One summer, I got a job selling the *Manchester Evening News* on the seafront and on Saturdays I also sold a sports paper called 'The Pink'. Many times some drunk northern blokes would ask me, ''ave yer got a Pink, cock?' causing them much amusement. 'Ha, ha, never 'eard that one before, mate,' I would sneer back.

There was one tragic character I knew called Billy who had the pitch next to me selling the *Liverpool Echo*. I used to think he drank a hell of a lot of milk because he always seemed to be swigging from a glass bottle full of white liquid. One day he asked me to watch his pitch while he nipped to the public toilet on the street corner. He came back with a milk bottle half-full of tap water and produced a hand-sized plastic bottle from his pocket, then poured the contents into the glass bottle and shook it vigorously until the liquid went pure white. It looked exactly like milk. 'What the fuck is that?' I shouted to him.

'Refills – hair lacquer,' he replied matter-of-factly, then swigged from his freshly filled bottle. 'Try some, it gets you really blitzed,' he offered.

'No thanks, mate,' I replied. I'd seen the state of my mum's hair and imagined what lacquer would do to someone's guts. One sunny morning, two weeks later, Billy was found dead in a gift-shop doorway, poor old guy.

The Golden Mile, the stretch of promenade between the north and south piers, was still lined with garishly painted little wooden sheds. They were the retail outlets for traders who sold everything for your holiday needs: rock, candy floss, condoms, hot dogs, kiss-me-quick hats, fancy goods, saucy postcards, fish and chips, fake Swiss watches, ice creams and don't forget keychains and snowstorms. My favourite stalls belonged to the Romany gypsy fortune-tellers with exotic names like Gypsy Rose Lee and Gypsy Petulengro. Their stalls were very ornate with lots of richly coloured velvet fabric, mosaic mirrors and glass beads, all lovingly adorned with framed collections of black-and-white photographs of them posing with the stars of the day who'd appeared at one of the town's many venues. It was like a who's who of the British showbusiness stable of impressario Lord Bernard Delfont – The Beatles, Cilla Black, Max Bygraves, Tommy Cooper, Ken Dodd, Bruce Forsyth, Engelbert Humperdinck, Tom Jones, Bob Monkhouse, Morecambe & Wise, Des O'Connor, Tom O'Connor, Dorothy Squires, Frankie Vaughan and Norman Wisdom being notable examples. Oddly enough, two of the biggest stars that played Blackpool, Frank Sinatra and Jimi Hendrix, never had their photos in the gypsy galleries.

We had some almost-famous neighbours who lived just up the road from us in Waterloo Road and I often used to see them buying sweets in the local tuck shop. I quite fancied one of them. Their family had a dark-blue Ford Transit with a DayGlo orange sign in one of its back windows proclaiming 'The Singing Nolans', handwritten in black marker pen. They were a family group who used to play all the local clubs and the daughters would, of course, become better known as The Nolans. To think I used to fancy one of The Nolans!

It was around that heady, star-struck time that I went to my first live performance at the Winter Gardens, 97 Church Street. It was The Ken Dodd Show, featuring his tickling stick, and was a total sell-out. It had already been a huge hit on television with kids and parents alike; I went with my family and we all loved it. It was possibly the very beginning of my lifelong fascination with showbiz (and dwarfs) – Ken Dodd and his Diddymen have a lot to answer for.

One of the things I really loved about the seaside was Blackpool Tower. I often used to go to wrestling matches with top grapplers of the day, including Big Daddy, Mick McManus, Adrian Street, Jackie Pallo, Giant Haystacks and Kendo Nagasaki. They also had a few female wrestlers, notably Mitzi Mueller, then British Ladies Champion, and the wonderfully named Klondyke Kate. I used to collect wrestling posters, basic red and blue or black on cheap white paper. Like old boxing posters they were very iconic. There were always a few old ladies sitting in the front row of every bout doing their knitting. If they didn't like a particular contestant, they'd jab at them with their needles if they came close. This sort of old lady would, in a previous incarnation, have taken her knitting along when watching public hangings.

The Tower also had a fantastic ballroom where they used to film *Come Dancing* (later updated to *Strictly Come Dancing*) and there was the Mighty Wurlitzer organ that came out of the floor and rotated, usually played by 'Mr Blackpool', Reginald Dixon, and occasionally by the wonderfully named Ernest Broadbent.

The other main attraction was the Tower Circus with the clown Charlie Cairoli and the famous ringmaster, Norman Barrett. I have very fond memories of the circus; the sounds, smells and the spectacle of it. These days I don't really agree with animals being used for the purpose of entertainment, although the ones I saw – lions, tigers, leopards, monkeys, elephants and seals – all looked very healthy and contented. But for all I know, they may have been drugged.

Michael Polakovs was the son of Coco, the most famous clown of all time, and both men used the same stage name. Polakovs' descendants included the half-Russian circus family who lived opposite us in Orkney Road. In his younger days, Sacha – the man of the house – had continued the family clowning tradition (I don't know many people who can say they grew up living across the street from a real Russian circus clown). He and his wife had four sons and a blonde, 18-year-old daughter called Zayna; a real looker and local pin-up girl. One of my more enjoyable chores would be cutting the grass on a sunny day when Zayna was out sunbathing in her front garden wearing one of her skimpy bikinis. Oddly enough, on those days, my dad would generously offer to help mow the lawn, especially the area that overlooked where she was reclining. There was always a bald patch on that corner of our lawn when he'd finished perving over our nubile neighbour. This was the inspiration for my original lyrics for the Soft Cell track 'Frustration' that first appeared on the *Mutant Moments* EP. It was later re-recorded with Marc's additional lyrics for *Non-Stop Erotic Cabaret*. My dad's the reason the *Non-Stop Exotic Video Show* featured me as a middle-aged bloke with stick-on sideburns, cavorting with an ample-bosomed young lady while mowing the lawn, before having a heart attack.

I was playing with my friend in that front garden when my nana arrived back from Africa. She'd been on holiday for three months and stayed with my alcoholic uncle Tony and his long-suffering wife, Maureen, while they were living and supposedly working over there. She brought loads of presents for my sister and me, including a dagger with an ivory handle and two spears for me. I don't know what she was thinking of, giving me weapons, not to mention having no idea how she'd got them through customs. The authentic Zulu spears had pointed, ten-inch steel tips attached to carved wooden shafts and were traditionally used for hunting and killing small mammals.

My friend and I treated the spears as toys and were enthusiastically throwing them at each other on the front lawn, blissfully unaware that we too fit the description of small mammals. All of a sudden there was a hammering on the bay window and my dad's apoplectic face appeared through the net curtains as he yelled something inaudible at us. Seconds later he came tearing out of the front door like Norman Bates and grabbed the spears off both of us. 'You bloody idiots, are you trying to kill each other?' he ranted, snapping both spears over his knee. 'David, go and get that dagger, under no circumstances are you allowed to play with these things, they are not toys!' I handed the dagger to my dad, who threw it into our wooden gate, with all the skill of a knife-thrower. 'Imagine if that had been a person,' he said menacingly. He was completely right, of course, but for once we didn't get the blame; my nana did.

★ ★ ★

That summer, my friends and I all built wooden handcarts out of old planks and pram wheels so we could go 'bagging' and make some extra pocket money. (I must point out that this had absolutely nothing whatsoever to do with 'tea-bagging' as seen in the John Waters movie *Pecker*). Bagging, for the uninitiated, is totally illegal and basically entails hanging out at one of the many coach stations with a handcart on Saturday mornings around nine, when the first of many coaches start arriving.

Boys like me with handcarts were a godsend as we offered visitors an alternative to queuing for taxis or public transport. As soon as I knew where they wanted to go, I'd agree a price, one pound minimum, then load up and wheel the tourist's luggage to the hotel or, more usually, guest house.

Guest houses were never more than ten minutes' walk from the station so I could fit in a few round trips, picking up a return job at the guest house. I always got good tips and usually pocketed about £20 every Saturday morning for two hours' work – not too shabby for an 11-year-old. In fact, that's more than the minimum wage is now and I'm going back about forty-odd years.

Chapter 4

1970

NINETEEN-SEVENTY WAS A LANDMARK YEAR IN POP MUSIC for me. I bought my first-ever seven-inch single or, I should say, my mum did. It was 'Love Grows (Where My Rosemary Goes)' by Edison Lighthouse; it stayed at number one for five weeks between January and February and I loved it. The second single I got was the not so great 'Back Home' by the 1970 England World Cup Squad and, to make matters worse, we lost.

The other big loss that year was Paul McCartney announcing he was quitting The Beatles. I was the proud owner of a plastic Beatles wig and Beatles guitar and I was fascinated because they were so famous. Everyone seemed to be blaming Yoko Ono's relationship with John Lennon for causing the split. Even my mum and dad, who weren't exactly Beatles fans, blamed her. Like a lot of British people who'd lived through WWII, they hadn't even forgiven the Germans, let alone the Japanese, and her ethnicity may well have prejudiced their opinions. My dad's best friend had been a prisoner of war for four years. He hated the Japanese with a vengeance as he'd personally suffered various tortures and beatings at their hands and lost many friends in Nippon POW camps in Burma. He wouldn't allow anything Japanese in his house and even threw away his daughter's Beatles records when they released 'The Ballad Of John And Yoko'.

Yet, funnily enough, when Brian Jones, Jimi Hendrix, Jim Morrison and Janis Joplin died at the same age, joining the '27 Club', my parents didn't say a word about any of their premature deaths. It was further proof of how little interest or knowledge of pop music they had. Apart from The Beatles, the only pop stars I recall my dad ever commenting on were The Rolling Stones, singling out Mick Jagger for loathing: 'He looks like an ugly girl on drugs.' His other pet hate was Tom Jones, scathingly referred to as the 'Welsh Twit' or, when my mum was out of earshot, the 'Singing Penis'. There was definitely an element of male jealousy as far as Tom's tight trousers were concerned.

Unsurprisingly, my dad was a staunch, lifelong, old-school Tory voter and was delighted when the Labour Party were defeated in the 1970 general election and Edward Heath became the new Conservative prime minister. Apart from once shaking Prince Philip's hand, my dad's biggest claim to fame came during the Labour Party conference at the Winter Gardens a few years earlier. As a senior telephone engineer, he was in charge of the confidential phone lines to Whitehall in London. One day he was doing a routine check, inquired who was on the line and was told it was the prime minister, Harold Wilson. Apparently, they had a very pleasant chat – luckily for the PM, politics weren't discussed.

That same year, 1970, was a landmark for me in a much less glamorous way. Somehow, without even cheating, I achieved 98 per cent in my 11-plus exam at junior school. That put me in the top 2 per cent of pupils in the catchment area and automatically guaranteed me a place at a grammar school. I was offered the choice of Blackpool Grammar or Arnold Boys. The latter was far more prestigious in my aspirational dad's opinion as it was then a direct-grant school, which meant it was just shy of being a minor public school. My biggest concern, apart from the lack of girls, was that its sports were rugby union and cricket – no football – but my dad had already made his mind up. Regardless of their sports curriculum, like it or lump it, I was going to Arnold school for the next five years.

Notable Old Arnoldians have included *Blue Peter* presenter Peter Purves, northern soul DJ and record producer Ian Levine and (somewhat ironically, given the lack of football) England/Blackpool player, Leeds United manager and football commentator Jimmy Armfield. Another pupil was Pet Shop Boy Chris Lowe and I've always thought that was such a weird coincidence – what was the likelihood of two 'other ones' from famous synth duos attending the same school in a northern seaside resort? I never knew Chris at school, as he was in a lower year and we didn't usually hang out with the younger boys. I did finally get to meet him and Neil backstage at my friend Sean Rowley's Guilty Pleasures night at Koko in Camden Town many years later. I must say, I was very impressed that he'd kept his Blackpool accent – mine changed quite a lot as I lived in Chester and Salford for a year, Blackpool for sixteen years, Leeds for five and London for the last thirty-seven years, minus a few prolonged stays in Pembrokeshire and New York.

I don't have particularly fond memories of my secondary education; the school had a stuffy, slightly old colonial vibe about it, as if the British empire and the Raj still existed. We had quite a few Asian pupils – there was one boarder called Harjinder, a Sikh who always wore a turban. I always remember him because I was really jealous that he was allowed to grow his hair and beard for religious reasons (not that I could have actually grown a beard, aged 12). At that time, there were only one or two black and Asian families living in Blackpool and Enoch Powell's 'Rivers of Blood' speech was still firmly lodged in the British psyche. Multiculturalism was still a long way off in our town, so I guess my school was fairly cosmopolitan for the time, albeit still very conservative. There was a mixture of boarders and day boys, 99 per cent of them fee payers. Some boarders had fathers serving overseas as officers in the armed forces. In fact, several of the masters were ex-military; we had a retired lieutenant colonel, a major and a few captains. There were also pupils from America and Hong Kong plus quite a few white South Africans from what was then apartheid Rhodesia, when Nelson Mandela was still in prison.

I was really glad I wasn't a boarder – not because I had any deep racial or political convictions but mostly because rumours of homosexual shenanigans in the dormitories were rife. I imagine it was probably the case in most same-sex boarding schools.

As a day boy my principle concern was the vast amount of homework we were given. The school also placed a very big emphasis on discipline; they caned boys and hit us with rulers, blackboard rubbers, gym pumps, rubber tubes in the labs and once – no word of a lie – with a broken chair leg. Other punishments included weekday and the dreaded Saturday-morning detention if we'd done something really bad (I think I had a season ticket).

The headmaster when I first enrolled was a gentleman called Oliver Wigmore. His name comes to mind because of my adoption. Long before I started grammar school, when I was about 7 years old, my parents tried to explain to me what adoption was. I remember them always saying, 'You are special, David, because we chose you' (which almost made it sound like I was Jewish as well). I was happy with their explanation during my junior school years but as I got older I started to feel slightly different to the other lads, most of whom lived with their birth parents. That was compounded one day when the usual teacher was sick and the headmaster took charge of the class. He told us all to do our family trees, quite a tall order for me as I only had adoptive parents, an adoptive sister and adoptive outlaws. I'd never even met my real father and I was only with my birth mother for the first year and a half of my life. I explained this to the headmaster, who was slightly embarrassed by his oversight and said, 'Well, just write about your adoptive family. Don't worry that you can't trace your real family back.' His comment said it all as the words '*real family*' resonated in my head. I did as I was told but from that day on, I always felt like an outsider. Even if I'd been 'chosen', I didn't have a family tree, just a family stump.

★ ★ ★

When decimalisation came in, we were all given a blue plastic commemorative pack containing several coins worth nearly a quid each. I think mine, like most other boys', were commemorated in the school tuck shop at eleven o'clock break time with a week's supply of Mars Bars purchased and consumed before lunchtime. Decimalisation meant that school dinner money was now twelve-and-a-half new pence a day, just enough for a packet of ten Gallagher's Park Drive non-tipped cigarettes. I got way too casual with my new-found allowance and was caught smoking in our garage one evening by my dad. He went ballistic. I was grounded for a fortnight, my dinner and pocket money were suspended indefinitely and I was sent to school every day with a packed lunch of brawn or ox tongue sandwiches and no treats. I tried to reason with my dad. Both he and my mum smoked and I had been breathing in their fumes but he was having none of it. After a long lecture, he repeated the classic line employed by all hypocritical dictators: 'Do as I say not as I do.' The term 'passive smoking' had yet to be invented.

Another memorable lecture my dad gave me was when I reached puberty; it was more of a man-to-boy chat really. My parents had realised I was developing what could only be described as adult-like feelings. I was showing all the signs, the most obvious being my mum finding used tissues by my bed even when I didn't have a cold. Then there was the most embarrassing morning of my life; I woke up in bed with the covers off, a girlie magazine in one hand, my sleeping dick in the other and a piping hot cup of tea on my bedside table. I'm sure my parents had a bloody good laugh about it, whereas I was totally mortified. I couldn't look either of them in the eye for about a week. Eventually, my dad took me to one side, put on a straight face and did his best to explain the facts of life. The way he described the sex act was more akin to an Open University professor explaining how a hydraulic pump system worked. He used all the correct biological/anatomical terminology and made it sound like something you really didn't want to be doing.

Chapter 5

PROG ROCK

MY FIRST VISIT TO LONDON WAS A WEEK-LONG EASTER family holiday in 1971. I decided there and then that I wanted to live in the city. It was around that time that my sister decided she was bored with tap-dancing classes and wanted to do piano lessons instead, which meant two things: she would need an instrument to practise on at home, and we would never again have to endure the terradactylian tones of her descant recorder playing. My parents never considered that I might also want to learn to play an instrument – and possibly more so than my sister. In the Ball household, music was a hobby for girls while boys played football and helped their dad build walls and mend cars. I used to love bashing out tunes on the piano I'd learned by ear but, even though it was obvious I had some sort of natural aptitude for the instrument, my parents never actively encouraged me to become a musician. In fact, my dad used to tell me to shut up whenever I played – something he never had to say to my sister. She hardly ever practised and, after a few lessons, as I'd correctly predicted, lost all interest.

By then I had begun record-collecting. I listened to DJs Tony Prince and Kid Jensen on Radio Luxembourg, Fab 208 on my transistor radio earpiece in bed every night. I would buy one single a week with my pocket money and always asked for record tokens as birthday and Christmas presents to boost my gradually increasing vinyl collection. For my twelfth birthday I got a second-hand Ferguson five-inch reel-to-reel tape recorder from my parents and was able to tape the songs I liked from the Top 40 every week, as well as friends' records.

I started taping myself plonking away on the piano and then I would play along with what I'd just recorded. I taught myself a lot of fundamental stuff while experimenting with that old tape machine – such as how to create electronic feedback by jamming a screwdriver halfway into the input switch and how to make and edit basic tape-loops of my records using scissors and Sellotape. Without me knowing it, a little acorn of an idea was planted in my young mind. Years later, I would use loops, editing and feedback in my work, as well as play along to backing tapes – with varying degrees of success.

At other times, much of my early teenage life was spent trapped on a canal boat with my family and Judy our Alsatian. After holidays on hired boats on the Grand Union and Llangollen canals, my dad was hooked. He bought a reconditioned, clinker-built, WW2 lifeboat that was old enough to have been used in Dunkirk and upgraded to a four-berth, fibreglass cabin cruiser which was slightly less embarrassing, apart from the crappy 15-hp Zündapp outboard engine that sounded like a hairdryer but not as powerful.

Every Friday evening – unless I'd got detention – we'd load up the estate car and head off to Dodd's Farm, Garstang, where my dad rented a mooring on the Lancaster Canal. All my friends in Blackpool would be going off to discos and parties with girls and I was stuck on a boat in the middle of Boringshire with my family. The only respite was the monthly boat-club do, when everyone would get totally pissed, including us kids. Once, aged 14, I drank seven pints of beer then swigged an entire bottle of cheap apricot wine. I staggered down the canal bank and got my leg stuck between a boat and the towpath. What made it really embarrassing was my drunken realisation that I was trapped by my 13-year-old girlfriend's boat and her parents were both on board, peering at me through the porthole and asking if I was OK.

I do think it odd that my dad would never have allowed my sister or me to smoke in his presence yet he didn't mind us consuming alcohol. He was of the misguided belief that if we got used to boozing at an early age, we wouldn't get into substance abuse-related problems later in life. Boy, did he get that one wrong; although I must confess, I've never touched apricot wine since that day.

★ ★ ★

My interest in school and involvement in sport waned while my obsession with art and music started to grow. Historically, the transition couldn't have happened at a better time for me as the seventies proved to be one of the most innovative and exciting decades in pop music. I'd become obsessed with T. Rex and had pictures of Marc Bolan all over my bedroom walls. The first two albums I bought were *Electric Warrior*, which topped the charts at Christmas 1971, and the follow-up, *The Slider*, which got to number four.

I remember there was a weird snobbery with my schoolmates regarding T. Rex. If you were a Bolan fan, you weren't supposed to like Slade because they were still considered to be a skinhead band, which back in the seventies meant racist, violent and thuggish. I'd read all Richard Allen's skinhead/suedehead/bootboy books and then, to confound everything, he wrote a book called *Glam*, so I read that as well. I liked all those books and I liked both bands for totally different reasons and I didn't give a shit about musical snobs either – I was just into quality pop music.

If my dad was in a bad mood, which was more often than not, he wouldn't allow me to watch *Top Of The Pops*, so I had to go to my friend's house. Personal highlights from *TOTP* 1972 were T. Rex's 'Metal Guru' and the amazing performance that everyone of a certain age remembers of David Bowie's 'Starman', along with Roxy Music's 'Virginia Plain' and Alice Cooper's 'School's Out'. They were all brilliant tracks and each band featured at least one androgynous male artist. In my opinion, the stand-outs were David Bowie and Eno, who looked like asexual aliens and confused a lot of teenagers like me. Marc Bolan looked pretty whereas Alice Cooper looked like a psychotic drag queen but neither of them had that alien-esque quality. The main thing was, they were all a million miles away from the 'roadies in make-up' look of acts like The Sweet. But even though The Sweet didn't look quite so good, they still made brilliant records.

I remember some of my own hideous outfits during that early to mid-seventies period; red, green and yellow star jumpers like the ones sported by Wigan's Ovation and various other dreadful garments including budgie jackets, as sported by Adam Faith in the popular TV show *Budgie*; split-knee, flared loon pants; shirts with penny-round collars and, worst of all, multi-coloured platform shoes. I think watching Slade on *Top Of The Pops* may have had some influence on my choice of footwear. The shoes were by far the biggest mistake – I was already six foot in my stocking feet, I didn't really need the four-inch heels as well. With that get-up and my short back-and-sides haircut, I looked like a squaddie on acid or, in the words of a Carter USM track The Grid once remixed, one of the 'Glam Rock Cops'.

Blackpool divided into two distinct camps, so to speak, of fans of Bowie and of Roxy. As both acts had such strong visual presence it was a perfect opportunity for everyone to emulate their heroes. Lads wore their mums' and sisters' clothes and make-up in a sort of new romantic precursor. There were Bowie and Roxy nights in our local disco as I'm sure there were in clubs all over Britain. One floor was full of Bowie clones – male and female. The other was filled with boy Ferry and Eno lookalikes while the girls wore pencil skirts and tried to look like the models on the Roxy album covers, with varying degrees of success. I wisely opted for the Bryan Ferry 'army surplus' look. I liked the clothes and didn't think I'd suit the lack of eyebrows and orange spiky hair – badly dyed – that would result if I went for Ziggy Stardust. Some of my mates did take the Bowie route, often with downright comical or scary results. We must have looked a right state, walking through the town centre at night; underage and pissed on a combination of Australian white wine (that was actually brown wine) from Yates's Wine Lodge and watered-down disco-lager from Jenk's Bar in Talbot Square.

When I went to my first soul club with my cousin Jane I discovered I also really liked what could be considered early disco. Jane was about the same age as me – 15 going on 18. I remember the night clearly because it was the first time I wore the fake sheepskin coat I'd bought at the market. We went to a club called Scoey's (named after the owner and DJ Pete Schofield). It was Funk & Philly Nite – we had no idea what that was about but we went in anyway – and it was a musical revelation I've never forgotten. They played recent funk tracks like 'Sex Machine' by James Brown, 'Wicky Wacky' by The Fatback Band, 'Me And Baby Brother' by War, 'Funky Stuff' by Kool & The Gang and 'Machine Gun' and 'The Zoo (The Human Zoo)' by The Commodores. These were mixed up with the more melodic and softer commercial Philadelphia International tracks by artists including The O'Jays, MFSB, Harold Melvin & The Blue Notes, The Intruders and The Three Degrees, whose 'When Will I See You Again' had just topped the charts. Scoey also added a bit of Barry White and Al Green, as they fit the mood perfectly. From that night on, as new genres came and went, I would always love soul and all types of dance music.

Most of my grammar school mates weren't really into the soul thing and grew out of the glam rock stuff they played at our school discos. Eventually, mainly to fit in, I started getting into rock bands who didn't dress up quite so much. I wore T-shirts, faded blue Levi's or Wranglers and a homemade patchwork denim waistcoat with dirty, white Dunlop Green Flash tennis shoes. I stopped reading skinhead books, replaced my T. Rex posters with a huge *Easy Rider* poster and started reading books about the Hells Angels, most notably *Chopper* by Peter Cave.

I grew sideburns and a bum fluff moustache, but my most rebellious statement, much to my dad's horror, was piercing my own ear. I was sitting at the dining table with my family when my dad first saw the earring. There was a long and stony silence during which he stared at me intently then, in a stern, controlled growl, he asked me, 'What is that metal thing in your left ear, David?' (Another long pause.) 'Have you become a homosexual or something?' I pointed out that it was only gay if you wore a ring in your right ear. My sister convulsed with laughter as my mum, sensing a major argument about to ensue, leapt to my defence.

'Don't be silly, Don, it's just the fashion,' she said. 'They're all wearing them.'

'I don't care who's bloody wearing them,' he grunted, knowing he was beaten, as she'd taken my side. 'He still looks like a right big jessy.'

I thought that was the last I'd heard of it until, a few days later, much to my dad's delight, my earlobe went really septic. 'You see, David, what did I tell you? It's like in nature. Just like women have periods and babies – men aren't meant to have long hair and wear earrings.' My dad wasn't even in touch with my mum's feminine side, never mind his own (I doubt he even had one).

'What about pirates and gypsies?' I asked him. 'Are they all gay?' But by that point, my dad had already become Alf Garnett incarnate. I had to let him gloat, although I got my revenge by playing my Black Sabbath, Led Zeppelin and Deep Purple albums and stinking the house out with TCP for the rest of the week.

I saw my first live rock band on 10 December 1972, at the Blackpool Opera House, where a few years earlier I'd seen Ken Dodd. It was Status Quo on their *Piledriver* album tour. I decided there and then that I wanted to be in a band and I needed a guitar like the one Francis Rossi played (half of my wishes came true – ten years later Soft Cell played on the very same stage, when I was armed not with a Fender Telecaster but a Sequential Circuits Prophet-5 synthesiser). The Quo were a rare treat as very few bands played in our town in the seventies. Musical snobbery affected Blackpool, which was renowned primarily for its family-friendly entertainment, and most 'serious' bands didn't want to risk their credibility. The flipside was that the town's biggest venues didn't need rock bands anyway. A family entertainer with a catchphrase-laden weekly TV show could easily outsell most bands, night after night, week in, week out. The nearest gigs for us rock fans were in nearby Preston or further up the coast in Lancaster. Apart from Status Quo and Queen, the only other acts I recall playing in our town were Slade, Hawkwind, Roy Harper and Smokie, who had a summer residency at Jenk's Bar before they started having hit records.

Other acts I saw were The Rockin' Vickers (featuring Lemmy on guitar), Fairport Convention with Dave Swarbrick, Danny Adler's Roogalator, Racing Cars and Big Jim Sullivan – James Last's guitarist and star of the Bay City Rollers' TV show *Shang-A-Lang*. I was really into guitar-hero music, particularly Jimi Hendrix, who coincidentally had also been managed and produced by Slade's producer, Chas Chandler. I've met Chas's son Tim a few times and he's the only person I know that can honestly say Jimi Hendrix held him in his arms when he was a baby – not a bad claim to fame.

It was during my guitar-god-worship phase that I drifted into prog rock after discovering Pink Floyd's *Dark Side Of The Moon*. I liked their use of found and processed sounds and I was especially interested in their EMS VCS3 synthesiser. I bought Emerson, Lake & Palmer's *Pictures At An Exhibition* album and Walter/Wendy Carlos's *Switched-On Bach* – although it did seem a bit pointless recreating classical music on futuristic Moog electronic keyboards. Then there was *The Faust Tapes* by Faust on Virgin Records. There were two reasons for buying it: I liked the artwork and it only cost forty-eight pence – about the same price as a single. I'd never heard the term krautrock before and I didn't really understand it but this German band were apparently the godfathers. They were a lot more experimental than ELP. Some of the boys in my school, particularly the Rhodesian sixth-formers, got into Yes and Genesis although I never did – probably because the Afrikaaners liked it.

I really liked King Crimson, particularly '21st Century Schizoid Man' from *In The Court Of The Crimson King*. The combination of Greg Lake's mangled voice with Robert Fripp's unique guitar playing was brilliant. I'd later have the good fortune to meet and work with both Fripp and Faust in my own kraut/prog phase.

Music was my main way of coping with the miseries of puberty, adolescence and school – apart from wanking (the ladies underwear section of my mum's Grattan catalogue always came in handy if I was feeling too embarrassed to buy a girlie mag). Much malevolent teenage testosterone was in the air at the time and I was occasionally picked on by older boys, making me very depressed. I couldn't even complain to my parents because my father bullied and hit me too; I was trapped between a rock and a hard place, as they say.

Chapter 6

POP CADET

IN YEARS THREE TO FIVE WE HAD COMPULSORY CCF (Combined Cadet Force) and were all issued with unbelievably itchy, woollen khaki shirts and WW2 battledress uniforms complete with beret, belt and gaiters. Every Friday afternoon we marched around like a bunch of extras from *Dad's Army*. After square bashing for an hour or so we also did weapon training and unarmed combat, i.e. kicking the shit out of each other until home time. In the play/parade ground there were various camouflaged military vehicles belonging to the school parked next to the rifle range and armoury. They had a considerable cache of guns too, including .22 and .303 rifles plus a couple of Bren guns, all complete with live and blank ammunition. I always imagined being in the Lindsay Anderson film *If*, when the boys started shooting at the teachers; unfortunately, that never happened at our school. Even so, I quite enjoyed CCF as it was a chance to piss about with my equally disillusioned mates for a few hours on a Friday afternoon.

My dad, a very strict disciplinarian and a firm believer in national service, suggested I go on two of the CCF camping trips, each a week of military training at real army bases in

Yorkshire and the Lake District. I remember coming home on the coach from the camp near Lake Windermere and loads of us had really bad colic. At first we thought it was because of the potassium bromide they allegedly put in the tea to suppress the lads' sex drives. Then someone pointed out that when we'd got lost orienteering, we'd drunk the stream water running downhill, thirstily unaware of a decomposing sheep submerged in a pool a few yards upstream, effectively acting as a filter and contaminating everything that flowed through it. Sheep were always being killed when the artillery regiment were doing shelling practice. I had a fantastic collection of skulls that I kept on the mantelpiece in my bedroom, much to my mum's dismay – I think she thought I'd become a Satanist.

As well as freaking my mum out, the main thing I enjoyed about CCF was getting away for a week with my mates. I've never really enjoyed family life and, at that time, the army seemed much more appealing, and I even got promoted to the lofty rank of corporal. It was highly disciplined but there was a controlled destructiveness I liked, especially when they demonstrated anti-tank weapons blowing up decommissioned vehicles – I loved the explosions. We also had to take part in a few night exercises in full DPM (disruptive pattern material) camouflage. The downside was crawling through fields full of cow shit, thistles, brambles and stinging nettles in the pissing rain and, as I was the biggest, I always ended up carrying the Bren gun which, unlike an Uzi, did weigh a ton. Our mission was usually to try and sneak into the base of the regular soldiers and steal some classified documents, undetected. Not a chance in hell; we always got ambushed – cue more fake gunfire and explosions. It was great fun, playing dead.

Luckily, the only real fighting we got involved in was with some cadets from Northern Ireland in the NAAFI (Navy, Army and Air Force Institutes). We had a full-on, wild west-style, saloon bar punch-up and, on the day we left, they chucked stones and bricks at our bus; it was like we were in Belfast. They were also in the British army cadets, but it would have been exactly the same if they'd been Scottish or Welsh as they all had one thing in common – a pathological hatred of the English.

On Saturday 16 April 1974, all thoughts of joining the army were forgotten for something much more exciting (if equally nationalistic). I sat at home with my family and watched the Eurovision Song Contest at the Dome in Brighton. The Swedish entry 'Waterloo' was the outright winner. I think that was the first time most people in Britain, myself included, had ever heard of ABBA. They were the best thing I'd ever seen on Eurovision and my sister bought the single the following week. Most boys of my age, and quite a few of their dads, became ABBA fans that night when they saw Agnetha and Anni-Frid. Fuck being a soldier – if the girls looked like that I wanted to be in pop music.

My 15th birthday approached and I desperately wanted a guitar. My dad said I should get an acoustic as I didn't have an amplifier. I was after a semi-acoustic, hoping that I would eventually get one. l spotted a second-hand Hofner Congress in the local paper; it was an acoustic with F-holes and, more importantly, an electric pick-up. The only problem was the guitar was £16 and I only had £15. It was the house rule that we got a pound per year for our birthdays and I had no savings. My parents wouldn't budge so I had to negotiate my first deal. The seller wasn't keen but in the end I think he felt sorry for me. I could see my dad was very pleased that I'd had to haggle. He probably had a point; I think most of the stuff he did was ultimately intended to make me a stronger man, although I didn't always approve at the time.

Now I had my first guitar, complete with fake leather case, plectrum, strap, thumbed copy of Bert Weedon's *Play In A Day* and – tantalisingly – a curly black jack lead for the amplifier I didn't have. To my annoyance, my dad – rightly – insisted that if I wanted to play with electricity, I should know how it works and insisted I build my own amplifier from scratch. After extensively perusing his Radio Spares catalogue, we ordered all the valves, cables, capacitors, transformers and so on for my mega-project. We even ordered an aluminium chassis that I had to drill out by hand. I worked like a German rocket scientist for many nights after school when I'd done all my homework. It took about six months because I had to save up to buy the components in batches by mail order. With perseverance, many minor electric shocks and dozens of soldering blisters on my hands, I created a fully functional, hand-built, valve amplifier.

The first thing I noticed was how quiet it was. I don't mean in terms of hum and hiss or signal to noise ratio, I mean quiet as in barely audible. I had pointed out to my dad before we started building that five watts didn't sound like a lot of power compared to the Marshall hundred-watt stacks I'd seen in my music magazines but he always maintained that it would be more than enough for 'my needs'. The amp worked for a whole fortnight before blowing up. On the upside, I'd learned quite a bit about electronics, but on the downside I was back to acoustic amplification.

I put my dreams of being a rock guitarist on hold – not only did I have no amp but I had no ability to speak of. I thought I'd take the easy option and give DJing a shot; I'd play other people's music. I was not discouraged by the exploding guitar amp and decided to use my expertise in electronics to build a mobile disco system. I was always determined to be involved in presenting music in some kind of live situation. The idea originally came about because I'd seen two old Garrard turntables for sale in a second-hand shop and in one of my impulsive moments I bought them with the savings from my weekend job in the greengrocers'. Carpentry was never one of my strong points but I still managed to build a wooden unit to house the turntables with a four-channel line mixer.

This time I took no chances in building another amplifier but saved up and bought a ready-made, second-hand Pye hundred-watt stereo, valve hi-fi amp with two fifteen-inch Fane hundred-watt disco speakers in black cabinets. I also built a light system with six multi-coloured mushroom lights fixed in two small black cabinets. I couldn't afford a conventional sound-to-light system so I used a mechanical/electrical relay which worked as a multi-switcher and created different random light sequences. I scavenged that bit of machinery from one of the many fruit machines in our garage. My dad used to build one-armed bandits for his friend Ernie, who owned an amusement arcade on the Golden Mile.

Ernie was a right old character, a lovable rogue or small-time crook depending on your legal standpoint. I used to think he was great because he'd give me a free bag of coins to play on all the slot machines while he and my dad talked shop. He'd tell me about the time when he kept loads of cash under his bed and got robbed. He didn't dare report it to the police because he was too scared of the inland revenue finding out about his undeclared earnings. He'd have got sent down for tax evasion, so the thieves got away scot-free with about twenty grand.

I built my random light generator and also acquired a second-hand strobe light. The whole set-up looked pretty smart, considering I'd built and assembled it all myself on a shoestring budget – what was more incredible is that it all worked properly. I called it Smile Disco Show, as smileys were all the rage at the time. I really wanted a glamorous female assistant but after watching my sister's treatment of vinyl, I didn't trust girls with records, so I recruited my schoolmate Tim Rice (nothing to do with Lloyd-Webber's partner) as my associate DJ. I paid £14 for some bright orange business cards with our parents' phone numbers. We gave those out to all the small hotels and guest houses and stuck some in local shop windows. I had a driver in mind – but had to make sure my dad was in a good mood when I asked. I think he admired my sheer determination and enterprising spirit and agreed to chauffeur us in his purple hearse-like Vauxhall Victor station wagon.

Living in a town like Blackpool meant bookings were quite easy to come by as there were so many guest houses and small hotels that had parties and private functions. I got to know some of the landladies and they were brilliant. They were years ahead of the Essex look, with piled up peroxide hair, tons of jewellery, orange make-up with bright-blue eye shadow and they were as hard (and sharp) as their highly polished nails. Always very friendly but you knew exactly where you stood with them. Just think variations of *Coronation Street*'s Bet Lynch and you won't be far off. We also played school discos, my dad's boat club and Masonic lodges and also put on a free daytime disco for mentally and physically handicapped children which they absolutely loved. It wasn't exactly the epitome of showbiz but we had fun, everyone seemed to enjoy it and we made a little bit of extra cash.

Most of the money we made (after we'd given my dad something for petrol and his time) was reinvested in records, including my very first northern soul sides. Thankfully, there were a few labels that put out reissues, remakes and compilation albums of otherwise hard to get and unaffordable tracks. Labels like Pye Disco Demand, Casino Classics, Contemporaries, Black Magic and Grapevine. There was also Spark Northern Soul that put out Wigan's Ovation's cover of The Invitations' 'Skiing In The Snow', a remake of 'Crackin' Up' by Tommy Hunt, not to mention the first cover version of 'Tainted Love', performed by Ruth Swann.

Apart from buying those last three records, we made our worst mistake at one of the boat club discos that we held in a huge barn on Dodd's Farm. We had finished our set and everyone had left; we packed all our stuff into the back of the car and locked up. We went back to the boat to crash out, leaving some of our records in open-topped boxes. After a good night's sleep and a late cooked breakfast, we walked round to the field where the car was parked to make sure everything was OK. It was not. The bright morning sunlight magnified through rear windscreen glass had not been very kind to our exposed vinyl. We ended up with about fifty crinkle-cut seven-inch singles, all totally unplayable. We were a bit gutted but luckily we hadn't brought our expensive northern soul seven-inchers, just commercial dance stuff, and we could survive without the aptly named 5000 Volts' 'I'm On Fire' and The Hues Corporation's 'Rock The Boat'.

No sooner had we recovered from that minor setback than it was time for our next DJ spot, at a party in Arnold school's sixth-form centre for the incoming sixth-formers and their girlfriends. This was my farewell of sorts and I did feel quite sad. Even though I was to stay in Blackpool for the next two years, I wouldn't be seeing my school friends on a daily basis as I had for the last five years. In the summer of '75 I finally left school, aged 16, with just two O-levels (an A in art and a B in English language), my performance having deteriorated in relation to my unhappiness there. Apart from rising to the rank of corporal in the Combined Cadet Force my only other school achievement was winning the special prize for art. I got to choose a hardback book, *Dali By Dali*, which was presented by the headmaster at speech day in the Winter Gardens. The book is the only thing I've kept from my schooldays – for me, the best thing about the place was the day I never had to go back there again. I wasn't in the least bit worried about my future as I'd already been accepted at Blackpool Technical College for the two-year foundation course in fine art.

Chapter 7

ICE CREAM AND NORTHERN SOUL

BEFORE STARTING COLLEGE IN THE AUTUMN, I GOT MYSELF a summer job as an ice cream man with a company called Naventi's, run by four Italian sisters who owned an ice cream factory in one of the many dingy back alleys near the seafront. I didn't drive around the streets with a van playing songs or sell Mr Whippy 99s, but instead served freshly made Italian ice cream from a cream-coloured, rusting caravan that was towed by Land Rover down to the beach every morning – tide and weather permitting. I filled cornets using a traditional wooden spatula between 10 a.m. and 5 p.m., six days a week, having been dropped off at one of their six pitches along the beach. My take-home pay was a paltry £16 for a forty-two-hour week. But apart from the shit wages, I had a brilliant summer and I really got into northern soul.

I was a 16-year-old soul boy with flat, leather-soled shoes, high-waisted Birmingham bag trousers and American-style bowling shirts. There were loads of us in town, the older ones cruising up and down the seafront in their parkas and Crombies on pimped-up Lambrettas and Vespas covered in wing mirrors and pendants.

The most famous of the scooter gangs was the Okeh Crew, named after the Chicago blues and soul label that was home to artists like Billy Butler, Major Lance and Little Richard, no less. I never got around to buying a scooter but the music I got into became part of the soundtrack to my life. Significant tunes were 'Bari Track' by Doni Burdick, 'Come On Train' by Don Thomas, 'Real Humdinger' by J. J. Barnes, 'Seven Day Lover' by James Fountain, 'The Trip' by Dave Mitchell & The Screamers, 'Keep On Keeping On' by Nolan F. Porter, 'It's A Woman's World' by The Gypsies, 'Out On The Floor' by Dobie Gray, 'Supership' by George 'Bad' Benson, 'Are You Ready For This?' by The Brothers, 'Thumb A Ride' by Earl Wright & His Orchestra, 'Control Tower' by The Motown Magic Disco Machine, 'Cochise' by Paul Humphrey, 'Love You Baby' by Eddie Parker and not forgetting 'Tainted Love' by Gloria Jones, of course.

I read somewhere that the term 'northern soul' was originally coined by *Blues & Soul* magazine journalist Dave Godin when he was writing a piece about the music that was being played in various UK clubs north of Watford. The term confused a lot of people – usually the Americans. After the huge success of our version of 'Tainted Love', I'd get asked countless times by US interviewers what part of North America did 'northern' soul come from, even though we weren't actually playing a northern soul version of the song. I could understand their confusion; they thought the term referred to a part of the US in the same way that 'southern soul' referred to Memphis labels like Stax and Volt. To add to their confusion, there were some Stax and Volt records that also got played in northern soul clubs... but that's another story.

The truth was that most of the music came from small and often very obscure labels from cities all over the US – mostly Detroit, Chicago, New York and LA – and I would hear it everywhere in Blackpool. There were also quite a few novelty tracks that got played, although they weren't exactly what you'd call soul music – they just had the right grooves. Memorable examples included

'Sliced Tomatoes' by The Just Brothers (as sampled by Fatboy Slim on 'Rockerfeller Skank'), 'Run Baby Run' by The Newbeats, 'Sea Cruise' by Ace Cannon, 'My Heart's Symphony' by Gary Lewis & The Playboys, a cover version of The Rolling Stones' 'Under My Thumb' by Wayne Gibson, 'One Minute Every Hour' by John Miles and 'Afternoon Of The Rhino' by The Mike Post Coalition. Post also wrote many TV themes including *The Rockford Files*, *The A-Team* and *Hill Street Blues*. I still have one single on Casino Classics that has Barry Gray's '*Joe 90* Theme' on one side and Mood Mosaic's 'A Touch Of Velvet – A Sting Of Brass' on the other side, both performed by The Ron Grainer Orchestra (Grainer composed the theme music for *Doctor Who* and Roald Dahl's *Tales Of The Unexpected*). Another surprising track they played was a cover version of the Doris Troy song, 'I'll Do Anything', performed by BBC DJ Tony Blackburn under the alias Lenny Gamble. Once, as a joke, I even heard a DJ play the *Rupert The Bear* theme tune by Jackie Lee.

I could hear that kind of strange mix of music every day, blasting out of the bass heavy sound systems of the Pleasure Beach on the waltzers, the dodgems and even the wall of death – the sound of Blackpool. I remember the smell of the vinyl in the specialist record shops I trawled for hours, combing racks of US seven-inch soul rarities I could ill afford. It was piped out of the tinny speakers of all the stalls and arcades on the Golden Mile and DJ Poth even played it at the ice rink. Imagine that – Northern Soul On Ice.

Undoubtedly, the top northern soul club in Blackpool – and one of the best in Britain – was the Highland Room in the Mecca building on Central Drive, where DJs Colin Curtis and Ian Levine put our town on the map. In northern soul circles, Levine's record collection was legendary. It was said in reverential tones that he had over 30,000 American soul singles. He would discover new tracks in the US, own the first and only copy in the UK and weeks would pass before any other DJ could find out what it was. It was amazing to think he'd been just another sixth former when I'd started Arnold school.

Other clubs and DJs cashed in on the northern scene. I still remember the club run by DJs Gary Wilde and Baz Stanton at Blackpool Casino, a 1939 art deco-style building on the Pleasure Beach. Gary (not his real name) had a day job running a tobacco kiosk in town and was the town's biggest operator in disco equipment and DJs. He had all the latest kit: Citronic turntables and personalised eight-track jingles, and his were the first rope lights and telephone handset headphones I saw.

When the Radio 1 Roadshow came to town, there was a guest spot from Emperor Rosko, one of the big broadcast DJs. He was a renowned showman and his massive sound and light system was set up opposite the resident DJ's area in a very confrontational way – it was gonna be a battle of the sound systems. The local DJ immediately called in reserve power. On a normal evening he would use about eight Electro-Voice Eliminator bass reflex speakers, which could handle up to two thousand watts comfortably. On that occasion, not to be outdone, he was able to call in some eight extra Eliminators and a load of Sai speakers; he could have easily pumped out about ten thousand watts which, considering the size of the room, would have blown all the windows out – not to mention everybody's eardrums.

In a normal week, I would go every Friday and Saturday night to hear the latest sounds with my mate. He was 17 at the time and bought a blue, second-hand Lambretta. He used to let me drive round his big back yard as I was still too young to go on the road – I'm not so sure that he should have been allowed on the road either. One day he was bombing along behind a VW Beetle when the car made an emergency stop. My friend didn't brake quickly enough and went straight into the back of it, his face smacking into the chrome VW badge and cutting into his flesh. The logo left a perfect VW emblem scar imprinted on his forehead. Happily, that didn't discourage him from occasionally driving the few miles up the motorway to the heart of the northern scene – the legendary sprung dancefloor of Wigan Casino in Station Road. It was run by a man called Russ Winstanley and in 1978, US music magazine

Billboard voted it the best disco in the world, beating Studio 54 into second place. I loved that; a tatty old dance hall in Wigan being cooler than a club in New York with its brand new million-dollar lighting system – I bet that pissed off Studio 54's Steve Rubell and Ian Schrager.

In reality, the two clubs were totally different – in drugs, music and clientele. Studio 54 was a cocaine-powered, mainly gay discotheque that played modern dance records and was populated by various rich and famous jetsetters, whereas Wigan Casino was an amphetamine-fuelled dance club that played old R&B records and was full of working-class folk from all over the UK. The one thing both places had in common was fantastic dancing; equally passionate and energetic. The Casino just had a lot more soul and, what's more, it's hard to imagine Warhol in Wigan.

As the summer and my stint as a soul-loving ice cream man were coming to an end I experienced a musical revelation. I was waiting at the factory with my colleagues because the tide wasn't due to go out for a while, so we couldn't get onto the beach. Usually, that meant we'd have to help with preparing the ice cream or make up cartons of orange juice, using an ancient machine that burned our hands. On that particular day we were in luck and had nothing to do for about an hour. An hour that would have far-reaching consequences for the future direction of my life. One of the other guys who worked there, about the same age as me, had a portable cassette player and put on a tape that blew my mind. It was a million miles from the northern soul I'd been listening to and dancing to all summer. The album had a sleeve design like a blue and white motorway sign and it was called *Autobahn*. The four-piece band from Germany were called Kraftwerk, a German word meaning 'power station', and '*autobahn*' meant 'motorway'. It was like something I'd never heard before and I was a fan immediately. The electronic music had a haunting, otherworldly, slightly scary, yet pleasantly menacing quality, vaguely reminiscent of the sounds I'd heard a few years earlier when I first watched *Doctor Who*. I loved those sounds and wanted to know how to make them.

Apparently, a Minimoog synthesiser cost about the same as a brand-new Volkswagen when Kraftwerk recorded 'Autobahn' and performed it live on the BBC science programme *Tomorrow's World*. I didn't know it at the time but that hour in the ice cream factory was a pivotal moment when two kinds of music I really liked began to fuse in my mind, like a mathematical, algebraic equation or a recipe: northern soul + synthesisers = XYZ? In five years I would have the answer but I realised my future was electronic. In the meantime, I had my first year of art college to contend with. I had a feeling I was on the right path.

Chapter 8
AWAY WITH THE FAIRIES

MY PRELIMINARY YEAR AT COLLEGE REQUIRED ME TO PASS two A-levels: one in fine art, the other in textile design. For the fine art exam I had to paint a still life of one of a choice of subjects: a paintbrush in a jug of water, a bowl of fruit or a vase of flowers. I picked the paint pot because it wouldn't wilt, wrinkle or discolour, unlike the organic subjects (or the tutors). The textile exam entailed making a four-colour screen-print of my own design repeated over several meters of fabric. My tutor suggested I create a geisha girl motif, so I attempted to make the design look slightly Japanese. I'm happy to say I passed both exams with ease rather than Es. I was just 17 and had my results a year before my mates who'd stayed on at grammar school. I felt very pleased with myself – life was getting better every day and my self-esteem had gone up by about a hundred per cent. I didn't suffer bullying anymore and I didn't have to wear a stupid uniform. I was permitted to wear my normal clothes: denim shirt, faded Levi's and a pair of red Kickers. I was even allowed to have long hair, smoke in class and go to the Blue Room pub at lunchtime. To top it all, there were some very nice female students on the course who all wore very tight Falmer blue jeans with the obligatory camel toe, so I was very happy.

Christmas 1975 came and went with no major domestic upheavals, apart from my Grandma drinking a few too many sherries and falling into the Christmas tree, something of an annual tradition in the Ball household. She and my dad – her son-in-law – never got on and I'm pretty sure she did it on purpose to wind him up, which worked brilliantly. The rest of us would be pissing ourselves laughing as my dad got more and more angry, trying to untangle my giggling gran from the still flashing fairy-lights before she got electrocuted. Apart from that, I suppose we had what you'd call a quiet one. New Year's Eve at my aunty's house in Poulton-le-Fylde got us all off to a nice boozy start and everything seemed fine and dandy.

Sadly, that feeling of wellbeing didn't last for very long. One cold, dark and miserable February evening, my dad returned home at around 10 p.m. after his weekly table-tennis league game. He kept complaining that his collarbone was really hurting and thought he must have sprained his shoulder when he was playing. That seemed like a reasonable explanation but the pain persisted for the next few days, so he booked an appointment with our family GP on Lytham Road, opposite my old school. Dr Hickey had a nice, *Cider House Rules*-type manner about him (probably the ether) and always smoked a pipe in his surgery. He prescribed some codeine phosphate tablets for my father and suggested something like Fiery Jack cream or Ralgex for him to rub into the affected area. The medication gave only temporary relief; the nagging pain persisted so the doctor referred him to a friend, the orthopaedic doctor at Blackpool Football Club. My dad loved that, getting treatment at his beloved Bloomfield Road football ground. The only problem was, the shoulder massages also only temporarily alleviated the pain.

Eventually, he was referred to the radiology department of Victoria Hospital for tests. The X-rays clearly showed a fracture in his collarbone. Further investigation showed something much more sinister: dark shadows on both of his lungs. It transpired they were malignant tumours and he was duly diagnosed with carcinoma bronchus, a.k.a. lung cancer. As is often the insidious way with many forms of that disease, the fracture had been a symptom of a secondary cancer; in my dad's case, of the bone. By the time it was discovered the prognosis was effectively a death sentence.

The elders decided it was for the best that my sister and I should be kept in the dark about his mystery illness. I only found out the truth in his final days when I'd already guessed after persistently quizzing my mum until she eventually broke down and told me everything. What gave it away was her lighting up an Embassy Regal during visiting hours – unbelievably, smoking was still allowed in hospitals in those days. My dad looked at her in total horror and wheezed through his breathing mask, 'You're not still on those bloody things are you, Brenda?' She made me promise not to tell my sister about that. I kept my promise, but my sister wasn't stupid and had already figured it out for herself too.

My sister and I were quite lucky in that we had some respite when we were at school and college. My poor old mum, on the other hand, loyally stayed with dad throughout the dreadful ordeal. For a whole year, day in, day out, she tended to his needs and took good care of him as he lay on the sofa, always in various states of pain. We got really worried about Mum. Everyone who came to visit could see the terrible situation wasn't doing her own health any good whatsoever. She looked dreadful. Eventually, her friends tricked her into taking my sister and me to see Dr Hickey and get herself checked out at the same time. He prescribed my mum some much needed vitamin supplements as she wasn't eating properly, if at all. He also prescribed us all Valium, in various doses, to cope with depression.

I don't know if that was standard medical practice in those days but my sister seemed a bit young to be taking Valium. She had one a day before she went to school – she was only 13 years old. Come to think of it, I was only 16 when I used to float into college every morning on my fluffy little Valium cloud. I recall one day, albeit slightly fuzzily, I got summoned in to see the principal.

Some of the tutors and my fellow students had noticed that I was behaving rather strangely and always seemed quite distant – 'away with the fairies', so to speak. I was informed that they suspected I was using illegal substances, probably cannabis. At that point, I hadn't told anyone about my nightmare at home, but once I'd explained the situation with my father's illness and showed them my prescription they were wonderfully supportive. I'm eternally grateful to all my tutors at Blackpool Technical College. Throughout all the doom and gloom they helped me focus on my work and get enough decent stuff together for my foundation course final show. I needed to get through that part of the course before I could even consider applying to an art college to do a Bachelor of Arts degree. The only thing keeping me sane at that point was the thought of going away to study for three more years.

In mid-February 1977 my dad was finally admitted to the cancer ward at Victoria Hospital. It was nine o'clock in the morning, the Streamline taxi was waiting outside and I can still picture him now. He closed our emerald-green garden gate and turned around to kiss and said, 'Goodbye' to my mum and my sister. Then he paused for a moment, looked me straight in the eye and said, 'Make sure you look after them, David, you're the man of the house now.' I remember him once telling me how his father, a merchant seaman, had said something very similar to him as a boy when he left for his ill-fated voyage on the *SS Opawa* back in 1942 and died in a U-boat torpedo attack in the North Atlantic. In that instant, I knew my dad knew he would never come home again, and he never did.

Three weeks later, on 12 March, he lost his fight and passed away in a hospital bed, aged just 52. Later in the year, with my mum's blessing, as we accepted the loss of my dad, I applied to Leeds Polytechnic to do the three-year BA degree course in fine art. I was completely over the moon when, a few weeks after my interview, I received a letter informing me that I'd been accepted and could start in September. To be quite honest, by that point and at the risk of sounding selfish, I was just relieved to be leaving home. I didn't really care where I went. I'd just endured the last year watching my dad die. During those final days in the hospital he was given such high doses of morphine that he frequently shat himself and I had to wipe his arse for him. It had been a weird parent/child role reversal. I desperately had to get away. I needed time to get my sanity back.

Art college probably isn't everyone's idea of sanity but the prospect of going to Leeds suited me just fine. From reading their literature, Leeds Polytechnic fine art department seemed to be just what I was looking for. It was considered to be the most anarchic and self-motivated of all the colleges and was renowned/infamous for its involvement in performance art. The previous year there was a near riot when one of the students had shot dead two caged birds in front of an audience (sadly, the perpetrator didn't turn the gun on himself too). Another student had spent his entire grant on a brand-new Tandberg reel-to-reel tape machine then played a tape and poured a bucket of tar all over the machine until it eventually spluttered to a halt. One of the first performances I saw was staged by a guy called Ian Hinchcliffe; he locked the door, then wielding a pitchfork, threw elephant shit from a local zoo all over his captive audience. To complete his act, he ate a few razor blades and chewed a beer glass. It was all very quasi-dadaist, nihilist, confrontationalist and totally pretentious – nevertheless, I was really intrigued as it felt like everything was permitted. During my time at Leeds I would even do a performance myself with two of my fellow students; they both wore identical plastic Marilyn Monroe masks and played amplified vacuum cleaners and I stood in the middle wearing a postbox-red ice hockey mask and shaved my plastic face with a miked up electric razor – it looked and sounded very industrial but (sadly) that was to be our one and only performance and no recordings exist.

Chapter 9

LEAVING HOME

IN THE MONTHS BEFORE GOING TO LEEDS, MY ARTISTIC sensibilities and musical tastes went through a radical transformation and I put my northern soul and rock records away for a while. I was an angry 18-year-old, I'd just lost my dad and the new music at the time was punk. Full of anger and energy, punk fitted my mental state perfectly. I loved the music and the attitude but never became a fully fledged punk, although I did chop my hair and wear skinny black jeans, pumps, white shirts and thin black ties. I put a few safety-pins in my jacket but I think I looked more new wave than punk. Of course, being a vinyl junkie, I had to feed my habit with this new drug and sought out the coolest sounds. I bought Buzzcocks' *Spiral Scratch* EP, 'New Rose' and 'Neat Neat Neat' by The Damned on Stiff, 'Stranded' by Aussie band The Saints and 'Anarchy In The UK' by the Sex Pistols when they were still signed to EMI. Album-wise, I also bought the first Clash, Damned and Ramones albums, the *Live At The Roxy London WC2* compilation and, once Malcom McLaren sorted out his record company shenanigans, the long-awaited, *Never Mind The Bollocks, Here's The Sex Pistols* album.

One day, Steve Sumner, a friend of mine from tech college, turned up unexpectedly at our house. He'd always worn normal specs and had shoulder-length, thick brown hair complete with centre parting. He kept himself to himself and usually wore denims and Chelsea boots. Suddenly, he was standing on my doorstep with spiky bleached hair, wrap around shades, a ripped, safety-pinned T-shirt, black drainpipe jeans and winklepicker boots. To complete the look he had an army great-coat with chains and an orange net onion bag, inexplicably, on top. I laughed when he told me he'd been chucked out by his mum and dad because they strongly objected to his new look. He wanted to know if he could leave his stuff at our house for a few days until he got a flat sorted out. I asked my mum, who said she really didn't mind, as long as he didn't wear an onion bag when he came over again. As a recent widow she was worried that the two-faced, curtain-twitching neighbours might gossip if they saw punks turning up at our house.

I could just imagine the crap they'd be saying behind her back: 'Ooh, look, that punk with the onion bag's at Brenda's again – you know she drinks a bit since Don died...' Blah, blah, blah... There were certainly enough old *Express* and *Mail* readers in our street who believed all the bad press about the evils of the punk rock scene; not that one actually existed in Blackpool at that time of course (apart from John Robb's band, The Membranes). Some of the old grannies should have been punks themselves – they had much more outrageously dyed hair colours and far more attitude than most of the disaffected local youths.

My friend continued to show up on and off for a while (minus onion bag) until he found a place to live. He would sometimes come round with his new girlfriend, a very intense young woman with a mane of auburn hair. She was always full of big ideas about fashion and it soon became clear that she was responsible for my friend's radical makeover. Her name was Glenda Bailey and she did indeed become a mega-fashionista. The last time I saw her name she was on a television documentary. She got very high up at *Marie Claire* magazine in the UK, then became editor in chief of *Harper's Bazaar* in New York. To top it all, she was awarded an OBE in the 2008 honours lists and she's been with my friend Steve the punk for thirty years. I wish my mum's hypocritical neighbours could have seen *that*. 'Ooh look, it's 'er with the OBE going to Brenda's again.' As George Melly's book put it – *Revolt Into Style*.

★ ★ ★

That summer I got another menial job, working for Blackpool town council selling their lottery tickets from one of several kiosks on the Promenade. That was back in the days before the National Lottery existed. I think the top prize was £1,000 which the lucky winner had to collect from the town hall as we were only allowed to pay out smaller wins of up to £50. It was quite a good little earner if you got a good pitch; the best one was by North Pier opposite Talbot Square in the town centre. In good weather I'd work from 10 a.m. until 4 p.m., weekdays only and make an average of about £40 a day, cash in hand. I managed to save about £800 for college over a couple of months.

One morning I was in the kiosk right across the street from the Tower Circus when a well-dressed but slightly dishevelled man wanted to buy some lottery tickets. I guessed correctly that he'd been in one of the casinos all night, as he was clearly still tipsy from the free booze they plied you with in those places. It turned out he'd had a very good night on the tables and was taking in some fresh air on his way back to the plush Norbreck Hydro hotel on the seafront. He laughingly told me he had thought he was having a really bad attack of the DTs earlier on when several elephants had walked past him. He didn't know about the circus, which exercised the animals on the beach early in the mornings. Before he left, he bought me a ticket and I won a fiver – he was definitely on a winning streak and so, it seemed, was I.

I also got really lucky in the bedroom department and lost my virginity. My dad's facts-of-life talk had largely put me off sex, although I'd had a few knee-trembling blow jobs from my previous girlfriend. But I'd never gone all the way. Suddenly, it was a different story; my dad was gone and so, it seemed, were my inhibitions – I'm sure there was probably a Freudian explanation. One Saturday I met Jackie at a local disco, dancing to her favourite record, the aptly named 'Heaven Must Have Sent You' by The Elgins. We hit it off straight away; she dumped her current boyfriend without a second thought and had a fling with me that lasted all summer.

We used to meet with all our mates at the weekend for a boogie and a booze-up at various local dances, avoiding those in town that were overpriced and full of visitors who were quite often looking for a fight with the natives. The worst time was a two-week period known as 'Glasgow fortnight' when things used to get pretty rough, fists and glasses flying in clubs all over town. When we weren't avoiding the threat of blood on the dancefloor, we'd get together at my house on various week nights. My sister would be in her room watching her portable TV while my mum, by now an alcoholic, would sit in the lounge with her cigarettes and daily bottle of whiskey, dozing in her armchair in a drunken stupor. I'd get busy entertaining Jackie in my room until it was time for me to order her a taxi. She was insatiable and so was I.

Jackie had a weird background. Originally from St Helens near Liverpool, her parents moved to Cleveleys after she got pregnant aged 15. She was quite petite and had a caesarean scar from the birth. The father, a boy of a similar age, had stood by her and they tried to bring up the child together with her parents' help. It seems that they'd been walking through a park one day with the baby in a pushchair when a teenage boy they didn't even know approached them. Totally unprovoked, the boy tried out a kung fu move he'd seen in a Bruce Lee film on her boyfriend. It proved fatal and she was a widow at 16. Her elderly parents were quite well off and let her keep the baby, helping with the child's upbringing and general wellbeing and the all-important babysitting on our nights together. The weeks flew by and our summer of lust came to an end as easily as it had started. We went out for dinner, had our last bunk-up, kissed and said, 'Goodbye', then went our separate ways. No strings attached, no looking back, never to meet again. It was September, nearly time for me to pack my bags, ready to start college and take my first steps towards leaving home.

Shortly after my dad died, my mum decided to get rid of our family car. The Vauxhall Victor estate was a very big car, it must be said. It was about the same shape and size as an old American station wagon and my mum, who was quite a nervous driver, wanted to trade it in for something smaller and more manageable that had no reminders of dad. I was given the job of clearing out all his stuff from the car before we got rid of it. She couldn't have coped with that task as she was still way too upset. I'm so glad I did it too; I don't think it would have gone down too well if she'd found his porn stash in the bottom of the glove compartment. I must admit I was a bit taken aback as I'd never thought of my dad as a sexual being; the idea of him looking at girlie mags never crossed my mind, but I suppose he was only human – sort of.

Once I'd valeted the car, mum traded it in for a second-hand, mustard-coloured Mini Clubman 1100 estate. It was a lot smaller and much more to her liking. I liked it too as it had fake wooden side panels, a bit like you'd get on a synth of the time. As far as Mum and cars were concerned, the smaller the better, so I was pleased she now had one she was happy with, especially as she'd volunteered to drive me to Leeds. Her main stipulation was that we didn't go on the motorway. I knew only too well from trips to Manchester and Liverpool that she hated driving on motorways and in big cities and that trip to Leeds was no different. As we approached the outskirts and the surroundings got less rural and more urban she became noticeably more and more nervous. She physically tensed then snapped at me in her panicky voice, 'Do you know which way it is yet, David?'

'Erm, not really, Mum, I've only been here on the train once before,' I replied as I struggled with the map.

All I could remember was a big building but I'd spent no more than an hour in Leeds when I had my interview. Mum then spotted an imposing building that loomed ahead. 'Maybe that's it?' she thought out loud.

I looked ahead. 'I don't think it is, Mum,' I replied. 'Look at the sign.' She squinted as we approached: 'HM Prison Leeds – Armley'. After some helpful directions from a bemused prison guard, we were back on track. I would be spending the next three years in a Leeds institution but, thankfully, not that one.

Chapter 10

LEEDS

I ARRIVED AT LEEDS POLYTECHNIC FOLLOWING OUR BRIEF detour to the prison and found a locker in the corridor to dump all my art books and materials before we drove to my digs in Seacroft. I could immediately see problems with the commute: the polytechnic was forty minutes away by car. Add in the walk to the nearest bus and it was probably closer to seventy-five minutes each way.

I also didn't particularly relish the idea of getting the night bus to that area every evening on my own. Seacroft was a massive new build, low-rise estate and had a reputation for being a bit rough. A lot of Leeds had a very *A Clockwork Orange* feel to it, especially the Leeds University campus. Near where I was staying there was a grey concrete shopping precinct complete with a health centre and a grim little pub that should have been called The Duke of New York, like in Kubrick's film. The place was so depressing, I only visited once.

My landlady was nice enough herself, but the sleeping arrangements she made were not. There was a smug architecture student called Tim who'd moved in first and bagged the single room. I had to share a double room with an engineering student

– Boring Brian from Birmingham. I never had any trouble getting off to sleep when he started droning on about college work, even though I had to endure horribly sweaty, nylon fitted sheets on my bed. I knew I couldn't stay there for more than a term. I'd already figured I'd move into a shared house nearer college, once I got to know some likeminded fellow students.

I took the bus to college to enrol on the fine art course. There were dozens of lost-looking 18-year-olds, wandering around like zombies, all wearing brand-new Levi's and box-fresh Doc Martens, just as I was. I asked directions from a striking-looking guy – gold lamé jeans, leopard-skin printed shirt and short, punky, dyed black hair. I'd correctly guessed he wasn't studying accountancy but it was sheer luck that the first person I ever spoke to at Leeds Polytechnic was Marc Almond.

As soon as I was enrolled, I set about finding my own spot in the huge studio space. There were partitioned-off areas on the ground floor, where there was also a store room for art materials. In the corner was a huge, blacked-out, performance art area. Upstairs in the mezzanine there were lots of little rooms to choose from and a sound studio. I positioned myself right next to it so I always knew what was going on inside. That audio studio was small and basic but was to be the birthplace of Soft Cell in the not too distant future.

I introduced myself to a few fellow students and members of staff. A bunch of us went off to the nearby student union bar to fritter away grant money on subsidised pints of Stones bitter. I'll never forget the jukebox; throughout my entire first year, it always seemed to be playing the same two records – 'Sultans Of Swing' by Dire Straits and 'Freebird' by Lynyrd Skynyrd. I got so sick of hearing those tracks every time I went to the bar which, I admit, was far too often. Freshers' week was a typical student piss-up with bands, DJs, competitions that invariably involved drinking and lots and lots of drunken dope parties. It was great fun and everyone got better acquainted – some intimately. God, it was so much better than being in the sixth form at school or, worse still, working.

I set out to explore Leeds city centre and stopped for a Cornish pasty in a bakery. In a broad Yorkshire accent, the man behind the counter said, 'Thanks, love,' as he handed over my change. I thought, That's a bit strange and I was called 'love' again by the man in the tobacconist's. All sorts of weird thoughts were running through my head. Did I look like a six-foot-three giant woman with a moustache and sideburns? Was every shopkeeper in Leeds gay? It was obviously a weird Yorkshire thing.

One of the more sinister aspects of the city in late 1977 was the number of Anti-Nazi League posters everywhere. They all carried the slogan 'Never Again' over sepia photographs from the Holocaust. I'd heard that Leeds had possibly the highest number of National Front supporters per capita outside parts of London. There had been race riots in Lewisham in south-east London but not as yet in Leeds. However, people were still protesting in the streets as the threat was taken very seriously – the spectre of fascism loomed large and it felt quite disturbing. Another terrifying threat was the Yorkshire Ripper. He'd already commenced his four-year killing spree in the Chapeltown area of Leeds. As soon as it got dark in the evening, the atmosphere of the city changed. People looked edgy and nervous and most women walked in groups of at least two. If I was walking down a quiet street at night and there was a woman on her own ahead of me, I would cross to the other side, just so she knew I wasn't following her. It was not a very comfortable feeling, knowing there was a serial killer on the loose who preyed on vulnerable women, especially as about half of my new college friends were young ladies. Within three years he was to murder a female student in the city though not, thankfully, anyone I knew.

★ ★ ★

My course started the week after we first arrived. The head of the department, a German called Willy Tirr, introduced all the lecturers and staff. I was to work with performance artist Jeff Nuttall, a key member of the UK underground and founder member of The People Show in 1966. He was also part of the John Bull Puncture Repair Kit group and as a beatnik-cum-surrealist became a friend and associate of author William Burroughs. He also published *Bomb Culture* in 1967. Jeff was a serious toper and a big jazz fan; I often heard him trying to play his trumpet in the performance area on the occasional lunchtimes when the hangover from the day before was too intense and he was trying to abstain – it wasn't a pleasant sound. On his more lucid days he would often rant about militant lesbians being more scary and ultraviolent than the local neo-Nazi skinheads. That was because he'd once made a lewd remark at a gay female student's house party and got a severe kicking from her 'sisters' – although I very much doubt he'd ever attended any National Front birthday parties to prove his theory. He never made it as a musician but did achieve some minor success as an actor on TV and film.

Another one of my tutors was Geoff Teasdale, a painter who'd graduated at the Slade. He always painted still lives with gloss paint in a very slick, graphic style. He was a really nice guy but I don't remember him ever teaching me anything. I believe he later became the head of the fine art department.

My other tutor was an older guy called Anthony Earnshaw. He was, in my humble opinion, a true surrealist. He used to make beautifully handcrafted and totally pointless objects in wood and glass cabinets that looked like bizarre Victorian antiques. He also wrote charming little books of surrealist poetry and stories with gorgeous illustrations, of which I still have two signed copies.

The only tutor who did eventually teach me anything of use was the late John Darling who ran the little recording studio. He had also been part of the John Bull and People Show performance art groups and was in charge of the sound; his particular speciality was weird and often comedic tape effects. He was also known to do 'funny' things off stage as well as on, when he was having one of his manic-depressive bouts. He once transported some equipment across central London in a Ford Transit when some strange voices in his head told him to drive the van into the entrance doors of the Russian embassy – so he did. Not surprisingly, he was sectioned for a while after that.

In one of John's saner moments he assembled the tiny basic studio. Its primary function was to record and edit sound for performance art pieces. It wasn't designed for interlopers like me to try and write pop songs. Another student friend of mine was George Hinchcliffe, a multi-instrumentalist who also wrote quirky little songs in the studio. He went on to co-found and become musical director of the globally successful Ukelele Orchestra of Great Britain.

The studio had two Revox B77s and one Tandberg reel-to-reel, quarter-inch tape machines. The Tandberg was usually used as a tape delay. There was also a basic six-channel line mixer, a turntable with loads of sound effects records and a Shure Unidyne B mic. The audio went through a good sounding Tannoy amp and speaker system. The look was completed with egg boxes and unpainted, perforated hardboard panels on the walls and ceiling for soundproofing. It was just how I imagined an old radio ham's shed would look. Whenever I went in there for a chat, John would greet me with his live jingle for the place: 'Welcome to Radio Hessian – the station with the dark brown sound.'

Chapter 11

SNIFFIN' GLUE

THE LIVE MUSIC SCENE IN LEEDS IN THE LATE SEVENTIES was great, with gigs at the city's polytechnic and the university. In no particular order, some of the bands I saw at those two venues were Ultravox! (with John Foxx), The Members, The Damned, The Tom Robinson Band, The Adverts, Sham 69, Joe Jackson, The Skids, Eddie & The Hotrods, John Cooper Clarke, The Boomtown Rats, Chris Spedding & The Vibrators, The Clash, Gang Of Four, Nash The Slash, The Mekons, Cherry Vanilla and, last but not least, The Undertones. I would often volunteer to be a humper or local crew and as there were always a few guys wanting that job we had to take it in turns. We unloaded equipment from articulated trucks into the hall and packed away afterwards. There were huge flight cases containing PA systems, lighting rigs, stage risers and musical instruments and it all had to be handled with extreme care. We got free admission and if tickets hadn't sold too well, we could sometimes get a mate in for half price too. Quite often we got to watch the soundcheck, which I loved. Only very rarely did we get to meet the band. The Undertones' Feargal Sharkey, having been cooped up on a tour bus for hours, suggested a game of football. We had a good kick about in Leeds City centre for a while between the busy traffic island and the grass bank outside the college until the ball bounced off the window once too often and we got moved on by the ever-watchful janitor.

I also used to frequent the F-Club, owned by John F. Keenan, where the DJ was Andrew Eldritch – vocalist and frontman of The Sisters Of Mercy. It was in a club in a very seedy part of town. Considering the acts that performed there and the clientele, it was quite an appropriate location. There was an underlying feeling of danger, not dissimilar to the vibe at CBGB in Manhattan's Bowery district. Around the corner from CBGB was the New York Hells Angels clubhouse, while a few doors away from the F-Club there was a skinhead pub that was always full of NF supporters. At night the area was crawling with drunks and street girls. Zombie kids sniffed Evo-Stik out of crisp packets in the club doorway, the brown glue dribbling down their chins, completely out of it. (I'm no saint with substance abuse but sniffing glue has got to be one of the ugliest habits ever. Regardless of what The Ramones may have sung about it, I knew two glue-sniffers who both died as a result of their habit.)

I saw countless fantastic gigs at the club during 1978–79, including the original line-up of Wire when my friend Bruce Gilbert was still in the band and the original Human League (Phil Oakey, Martyn Ware, Ian Craig Marsh and Adrian Wright), supported by Pere Ubu. Also, Wayne County & The Electric Chairs, Slaughter & The Dogs, Spizz Energi, A Certain Ratio, UK Subs, 999, Sheeny & The Goys, Adam & The Ants, The Raincoats, The Cure, The Teardrop Explodes, Generation X, The Only Ones, Fad Gadget, Monte Cazazza and the original industrialists and 'wreckers of civilisation', Throbbing Gristle. I loved all of them but I guess the most memorable show at the F-Club was on 24 October 1978: Cabaret Voltaire were on first followed by Ian Curtis fronting Joy Division, playing a lot of the stuff off their *Unknown Pleasures* album – absolutely brilliant.

At the end of October there was an art department coach trip to London with a five-night stay at the aptly named hotel Rembrandt, all of us sharing rooms to keep the cost down. We went to all the big galleries: the Tate, the National, the National Portrait Gallery, the Royal Academy, the Courtauld Institute and a few museums, including the Wallace Collection in Manchester Square, Marylebone, which I knew had an amazing collection of armour and weapons and the original *The Laughing Cavalier* by Frans Hals. My parents had bought me a paint-by-numbers set of that picture, my first encounter with oil paint. They were astonished when I told them I'd finished it after about an hour – according to the instructions on the box, it was supposed to take weeks. Then they came to inspect my efforts and burst out laughing – I'd just filled in the outlines willy-nilly with whatever colour I saw fit. I really wish I'd kept it; not exactly a masterpiece – more of a monsterpiece.

My mate and I explored some of the music and fashion landmarks of London: the punks of King's Road in Chelsea and trendy shops like Sex and Boy. I couldn't afford to buy any of the clothes, but I did buy an issue of Mark Perry's Ramones-inspired *Sniffin' Glue* fanzine, which came with a free flexidisc of a track called 'Love Lies Limp' by his band Alternative TV. We then headed to Carnaby Street, which wasn't anything like I remembered when I went with my mum and dad at the tail end of the swinging sixties.

As we'd already seen the EMI building in Manchester Square, made famous by Beatles album covers, we went to Denmark Street, or Tin Pan Alley, as it's affectionately known. It was mostly full of music shops and the sound of hairy young men trying to play 'Stairway To Heaven' on guitars they couldn't afford. We must have looked in every single shop but I didn't buy anything more expensive than a plectrum. We crossed Charing Cross Road and strolled down Old Compton Street across the parallel streets of Soho – Greek, Frith and Dean – until we arrived at Wardour Street. The four roads made up the cab drivers' acronym 'Good For Dirty Women'.

The Marquee Club wasn't open until the evening so we walked a bit further to a pub I'd read about called the Ship, apparently a well-known haunt for music-biz types, especially roadies looking for work. It was run by an old couple who, back in the sixties, had a very famous lodger staying upstairs, namely Keith Moon, the crazy drummer from The Who. We bought a couple of overpriced beers and sat down at a table to soak up some of the atmosphere and tried to imagine Keith Moon falling up or down the big old staircase. We'd only been there for a few minutes when we got approached by an Irishman who'd obviously had a few. He seemed friendly enough and sat down with us. He kept looking at me strangely and repeatedly saying, 'I recognise you, I know who you are.' My mate and I looked at each other, somewhat perplexed. The Irishman winked at me and said, 'You can't fool me, I'd recognise those eyebrows anywhere. You're Paul McCartney. You've got an office building round the corner in Soho Square.' No matter how much I protested that I couldn't possibly be Paul McCartney as I was only 18, which meant I'd have been about five when I joined The Beatles, it made no difference. He was totally convinced that I was Macca. 'Paul, you don't have to be so modest, just let me buy you and your friend a drink,' he insisted, not just once but about three times. As we were skint students, it was an offer we could hardly refuse. After about an hour and a half of constant beers and whiskey chasers, our new best mate, Rory, finally left after we promised to meet him that evening. Sadly, we didn't make it that night but about five years later, in the Some Bizzare offices above Trident Studios, around the corner in St Anne's Court, a large brown envelope addressed to Soft Cell was delivered by hand from MPL in Soho Square. It contained a book of high-quality photographs of sixties rock stars and on the inner cover was the handwritten inscription, 'We love your music', signed by Linda and Paul McCartney.

Chapter 12
HEADINGLEY

ON RETURNING FROM LONDON, I JOINED A GROUP OF fellow students who'd found a shared house to rent in Headingley, home of the famous Yorkshire cricket ground. It's quite odd but throughout my life I've lived by three major British cricket grounds without having the slightest interest in the game. In London I bought a place in St John's Wood (Lord's). The only wicket I ever took there came during one debauched evening at a private party in the clubhouse when I had a quickie with my girlfriend on an outside table by the deserted pitch. For the last seventeen years I've lived five minutes away from the Kennington Oval, where the most exciting thing I did was watch an Australian rules football match while drinking plastic pints of warm Fosters and being attacked by wasps.

My main concern in moving to Headingley was getting out of my digs and living closer to the city, preferably not in another family's house, especially after the landlady made a pass at me when I'd taken a day off and we were alone (I didn't have a bored housewife fantasy and she really wasn't my type). I had four new housemates – two girls and two boys with no romantic involvement whatsoever: a perfect scenario. Our place was at 29 Norwood Terrace, a rundown back-to-back street (think 'opening sequence of *Coronation Street*'). I had a leaky attic room, complete with electric fire and meter. I painted all the woodwork in emerald green gloss, left over from our house in Blackpool (to remind me of home), and bought some pastel green emulsion for the walls. I've always found green very relaxing and, in fact, my favourite record at the time was *Another Green World* by Brian Eno. That little green room was to be my humble abode for the next three years.

The area was mostly populated by fellow students and many Asian families, mostly of Pakistani and Bangladeshi descent. We had one local celebrity who lived in the area, Seth from *Emmerdale*. He could often be spotted buying groceries in our local shop, Patel's Superette, or collecting his pension in the post office. I was a member of the *Emmerdale Farm* Appreciation Society at college and we once went on an outing to the Woolpack pub in Otley. It was a real pub when they weren't filming, unlike the Rovers Return (*Coronation Street*) and the Queen Vic (*EastEnders*).

I had a lot of fun during my first few months at college and was feeling a bit apprehensive about returning home for Christmas 1977, our first without my dad. It was gonna be a tough one, particularly for my mum. We made sure we had loads of friends and family around and got through it OK, although my mum got a lot drunker than she normally did. I was starting to worry about her dependence on alcohol but Christmas was hardly the time to mention it, especially as I was pissed for most of the festive season too. I spent most of my time and money meeting old school and tech college buddies, and a new romance came into my life.

I'd been on the foundation course with Karen but, over those two years, when we'd seen each other every day, we'd only ever given each other a passing smile and rarely spoke. Everything changed now and we were like two little lovebirds. On one of our first dates a few of us went to the cinema to see the afternoon matinee performance of a new disco film everyone was raving about called *Saturday Night Fever*. We loved the soundtrack but we also still loved northern soul, Bowie and Roxy, Kraftwerk and punk. It was a confusing time musically but there was one thing that linked all of those genres and artists – attitude and energy.

After I started my studies again I'd see Karen in Blackpool most weekends and we'd sometimes go to the Mardi Gras disco where they'd play modern soul and jazz funk stuff like 'Cherchez La Femme' by Dr Buzzard's Original Savannah Band, 'Do You Wanna Get Funky With Me?' by Peter Brown and 'Native New Yorker' by Odyssey, with Roxy and Bowie tracks occasionally mixed in. We also went to the 007 Club on Topping Street. I knew the owner, Brian London, a retired heavyweight boxer who'd fought and lost to some legendary fighters in his day, including Henry Cooper and Cassius Clay before he became Muhammad Ali. The dancefloor at 007 was shaped like a boxing ring, complete with a red cord. There was never any trouble, especially if Brian was around, except for the night when a bunch of off-duty squaddies turned up. They were all quite drunk and one of them made the foolish mistake of trying to impress his mates and took a misdirected swing at the boss. The response was swift and connected with deadly accuracy – I've never seen one punch launch a fully grown man so far through the air before. 'Get him an ambulance,' muttered one of the doormen, pointing at the unconscious sack of spuds who lay bleeding in the gutter, by now surrounded by his mates, staring down in disbelief – their regimental champion knocked out by one hit.

On quieter weekends Karen came to visit me in Leeds and we'd usually get some cheap wine and food and stay in bed to keep warm, listening to my increasingly eclectic record collection. My latest vinyl at that time was *The Second Annual Report* of Throbbing Gristle, alongside another debut album, the eponymous release by New York duo Suicide, produced by Craig Leon on Red Star Records. Suicide were apparently the first band ever to use the term 'punk music', on a New York club flyer way back in 1970. I also had two Pere Ubu albums, *The Modern Dance* and *Dub Housing*; the Eno-produced *Are We Not Men?* by Devo; *Alien Soundtracks* by Chrome and Eno's own *Here Come The Warm Jets*, which I loved. I think the most traditional records I bought at that time were *Transformer* by Lou Reed and *Lust For Life* and *The Idiot* by Iggy Pop, all three produced by David Bowie. I mostly played albums but my favourite seven-inch singles at the time were 'Private Plane' by Thomas Leer, Cabaret Voltaire's *Extended Play* EP, 'United'/'Zyklon B Zombie' by Throbbing Gristle and 'Being Boiled' by The Human League.

The end of 1977 and the beginning of 1978 was a very diverse and interesting time musically; we'd lost two old-school music legends in Elvis Presley and Bing Crosby, we'd done heavy rock, progressive rock and glam rock earlier in the decade and now punk rock and disco were in the pop charts. In the autumn of 1978, Karen moved to Manchester to do her degree in textiles and fashion and we went to a few great shows, including the Two Tone Records tour featuring The Selecter, Madness and The Specials (tickets were just £6), and we saw Devo twice and the Yellow Magic Orchestra. There were many changes in dress, musical styles and attitudes but the music was still mostly guitar and drum-based. Some bands even boasted 'No synthesisers were used on this record' on their album sleeves, as if being a Luddite was something to be proud of. It's true there were many records that featured synthesisers in the overall production but until the late 1970s – apart from a handful of artists like Kraftwerk, Brian Eno, Tangerine Dream, Tonto's Expanding Head Band, Tomita and Walter Carlos – synths weren't generally used as the sole instrument. Now things were starting to change in a way that I found fascinating. I still remember hearing Donna Summer's 'I Feel Love' for the first time when Annie Nightingale played it on Radio 1. I was totally blown away by the synthetic, rhythmical sounds: it was like hearing Kraftwerk with a soul diva instead of a robotic nerd on vocals. After a bit of investigation, I found out it was from her album *I Remember Yesterday* and was produced by Giorgio Moroder, whose credits included an album by Munich Machine and a solo album called *From Here To Eternity*. A few years earlier, another Moog synthesiser-based song of his, 'Son Of My Father', performed by Chicory Tip, had topped the

UK charts, at around the same time as the Moog novelty record, 'Popcorn' by Hot Butter.

'I Feel Love' was most definitely not a novelty record and Moroder was now on my A-list of Synth Dons alongside Kraftwerk, who had just released *Trans-Europe Express*. A few years later the title song would be recreated as the backing loop for the seminal New York electro track, 'Planet Rock' by Afrika Bambaata & The Soulsonic Force, produced by Arthur Baker. In my opinion, the music recorded and produced by Kraftwerk and Giorgio Moroder in 1977 was undoubtedly the starting point for electro, techno and all electronic dance music as we now know it.

My father's legal affairs were eventually settled, and the details of his will were revealed: he left my sister and me a thousand pounds each with everything else going to my mum. I knew straight away what I was going to do with my share. Even though I loved synths I still fancied myself as a guitarist, so I decided to buy the 1972 Fender Telecaster guitar I'd always promised myself, with a classic sunburst body and a maple neck. The asking price was originally £175 but as I wanted a WEM hundred-watt valve amp with a two-hundred-watt bass reflex cabinet plus a Dunlop Wah Wah and a Jimi Hendrix Fuzzface I got the whole package for £400. The effects pedals and leads had been chucked in for free, so I was very happy with the deal, although I doubt very much that our neighbours shared my enthusiasm.

THE ADOPTION (JUVENILE COURT) RULES, 1959

Rule 21

ADOPTION ORDER

In the County Borough of Blackpool

Before the JUVENILE COURT sitting at Blackpool

WHEREAS an application has been made by   James Donald Ball
of 10 Orkney Road,
. Blackpool
(and   Brenda Ball   his wife)
(hereinafter called the applicant) for an adoption order in respect of
*   Paul Pritchard   (hereinafter
called the infant);

IT IS ORDERED that the applicants be authorised to adopt the infant;

AND IT IS DIRECTED that the Registrar General shall make in the Adopted
Children Register an entry recording the particulars set out in the
Schedule to this Order.

DATED the   17th   day of   November   , 1960..

(Signature)........ J.L. Holdgat........

Justice of the Peace for the County Borough first above mentioned.

SCHEDULE

Date and country of birth	Registration district and sub-district	Names and surname of infant	Sex of infant	Name and surname, address and occupation of adopter or adopters	Date of adoption order and description of court by which made
3rd May 1959 England.	Reg.Dist. Salford. Sub.Dist. Hope.	David James Ball	male	James Donald Ball 10 Orkney Road, Blackpool, Post Office Engineer, and Brenda Ball wife of the above of the same address.	17th November 1960. Juvenile Court for the County Borough of Blackpool.

ABOVE: My adoption
certificate, 1960.

Me aged 2 in
Blackpool, shortly
after I was adopted.

LEFT: Mum and Dad — Brenda and Don — on their wedding day, 1952.

The bowtie makes an early appearance at 3 years old.

Me and Mum at the Lexington Hotel on my first trip to New York, 1978.

LEFT: New York City boy, 1978.

In leather in Lyon, France, 1980.

Outside home in Blackpool, aged 21.

ABOVE: Soft Cell's first
piece in iD magazine, 1980.

In my bedsit just after the release
of 'Tainted Love', 1981.

An early Soft Cell press photo, 1981.

LEFT: Soft Cell live at ENTPE, Lyon, France, 1981.

BELOW: 'Leatherman' takes Blackpool pier, 1982.

LEFT: Our first appearance on *Top Of The Pops*, performing 'Tainted Love', 1981.
LFI/PHOTOSHOT

BELOW: And on *Top Of The Pops* again with 'Bedsitter', 1981.
LFI/PHOTOSHOT

Chapter 13
NEW YORK, NEW YORK!

WITH THE FAMILY FINANCES SORTED OUT, MY MUM SEEMED
a bit more grounded and one day asked my sister and me where
we would like to go on holiday – anywhere in the world. My sister
didn't seem that bothered and muttered something about Benidorm
or Corfu. I, on the other hand, had no doubt where I wanted to
go and it certainly didn't involve lying on an overcrowded beach,
stinking of Ambre Solaire.

'New York!' I exclaimed hopefully.

My mum thought about it for a few minutes while she looked
at the travel brochures. When she saw the exchange rate was three
dollars to the pound she decided she liked the idea and said, 'OK.'
I couldn't believe it, we were actually going to New York City. The
closest I'd ever been to abroad was a school trip to the Isle of Man
and now we were going to the island of Manhattan. The only tall
buildings I'd ever seen were Blackpool Tower and the Post Office
Tower in London. It wasn't just the skyscrapers, I was really into
the whole idea of New York – the whole pop art thing, especially
Andy Warhol. I also loved all the music that I'd heard from that
city, both punk and disco. As I'd recently seen *Saturday Night Fever*
it seemed like the perfect place to go (the movie was actually set

in Brooklyn). We went for two weeks in April 1978 on a TWA DC-10 from Heathrow to JFK. It was my first time on an aircraft but, surprisingly, I didn't get too nervous, even when we experienced a bit of turbulence.

We stayed at the Lexington Hotel on Lexington Avenue and 48th Street, Midtown Manhattan, in a family room on the seventeenth floor. Being so high up was great because I had my Eumig Super 8 camera with me and, every morning before breakfast, I managed to get some nice overhead shots of the rush hour, cross-town traffic down below. That footage would be projected during Soft Cell's early live shows and eventually edited and used in the video for 'Memorabilia' on the *Non-Stop Exotic* video, although I never got a camera credit.

We did all the tourist stuff like the Circle Line boat trip around Manhattan, going up the Empire State Building and, more poignantly now, the World Trade Center. My ears popped as the high-speed elevator went up to the 110th floor and I stood on top of one of the twin towers with my mum and my sister. After 9/11 it seems very strange to think we once stood up there, all those years ago. Likewise, we had our photos taken outside the Dakota building when John Lennon was still living there, two years before his murder.

I bought the *New York Daily News* every day during the two weeks we stayed in the city, when it reported on twenty-four murders. The city also had a widespread heroin addiction problem. New York was then considered to be one of the more dangerous cities in America alongside Detroit, which topped the murder rate. The place was in crisis. The city had been officially declared bankrupt and practically disowned by then president, Jimmy Carter (the peanut farmer), until Mayor Ed Koch eventually turned it around. There were potholes on every street and basic services like refuse collection and sewage were not always working. The Philadelphia All Stars' song, 'Let's Clean Up The Ghetto' and Martin Scorcese's 1976 film *Taxi Driver* perfectly captured the vibe of the city the first time I visited. They still had Checker Taxis, steam coming out of the manholes and an all-pervasive sense of sleaziness that was both scary and dangerously fascinating. The place was pretty fucked up but in that strangely glamorous way that only a city like New York can be. Postcards for sale in every gift shop depicted the Empire State Building and the Chrysler Building modified to look like giant hypodermic needles – heroin chic or what?

Times Square and 42nd Street hadn't yet been sanitised and were still full of porn theatres, strip joints, hookers, pimps and junkies. I was once approached by a guy on the street at about ten o'clock in the morning who tried to sell me a gun – I didn't hang around long enough to check if it was a real one! Suffice to say, my mum, sister and I never ventured out at night (it was still a few years before I would pass the velvet rope into Studio 54).

In the daytime I would head off alone to the Museum of Modern Art and the Guggenheim while they went shopping in Bloomingdale's, Gimbels and Macy's department stores. One day I wandered into Woolworth's on Broadway to buy a fake diamante treble-clef brooch I'd seen in the window. It was just like the one Florian Schneider wore in his lapel on the cover of the *Trans-Europe Express* album (I was such a trainspotter even then). As the pound was so strong, everything in the USA was relatively inexpensive, particularly denim and vinyl, so I bought loads of Levi's jeans and shirts and a few records. I asked about the latest tracks being played in the New York clubs and was recommended a funky album called *Bootsy* by Bootsy Collins and a disco release, *Let's All Chant* by The Michael Zager Band. My sister was persuaded to buy the overtly gay *Macho Man* twelve-inch EP by the Village People, a rather curious selection I remember thinking at the time, but she seemed happy enough.

Before I knew it, our two weeks in the Big Apple were over and we were on our way back to Blighty. New York had made an even bigger impression on me than London had – I love big cities and always will. All the way home, I just kept telling myself I'd be back in both places very soon – but next time, without my mum and sister.

Chapter 14

KORG

AS SOON AS I GOT BACK TO LEEDS I PUT TOGETHER A collection of artwork for a joint exhibition in the college's main gallery for my course work. Not surprisingly, my stuff was all based on my recent trip to NYC. It looked sort of punk/pop art and I called my part of the show Art Plastic. It comprised lots of black-and-white photocopies of US magazine ads overlaid with geometric, multi-coloured pieces of clear plastic light gels – not particularly groundbreaking but at least no one laughed.

Now I had a better place to live, I brought my new guitar and amp to Leeds and bought a second-hand Akai reel-to-reel tape recorder, a Melos Tape Echo Chamber and an Electro Harmonix, Deluxe Electric Mistress Flanger for my damp bedsit studio. I also booked some time in the fine art department recording room. My first efforts consisted of rhythmic tape-delayed guitars and a newly acquired Stylophone playing drones – primitive ambient. I was starting to think about the possibilities of going more electronic. The guitar was a great instrument but I still wasn't a great player and I couldn't make the electronic sounds or the music I really wanted to with it. I bought a second-hand twin stylus Stylophone, which was much bigger than the original and had an electric eye filter (a photo-electric cell that controlled the tone not the pitch) and a pulse generator.

During one of my short sessions in the sound room I found a Crumar Compac electric piano. I couldn't resist it and recorded some tracks using the keyboard without the consent of its owner. This turned out to be a third-year student called Frank Tovey, who was rightly pissed off and never forgave me. When he left college he performed under the name of Fad Gadget and released some great music on Daniel Miller's Mute Records. Sadly, Frank had a rare heart condition; he passed away in 2002 and I never really got the chance to apologise properly. As a belated thank-you and by way of tribute, I can say that it was playing his borrowed keyboard, all those years ago, that probably inspired me to buy my first synthesiser.

I'd first had a go on a synthesiser when I was about 14 years old. My gran's next-door-neighbour's son had a dual manual Farfisa electric organ with a little synth on the top. I knew the boy so I was invited round to have a mess about on it and I was immediately hooked. I finally made my move from strings to synthesiser one Saturday afternoon during a visit to see my mum's new house in Blackpool. I took the bus into town to have a good rummage around the local musical instrument shops. I planned to trade in my Fender Telecaster as soon as I found a second-hand synthesiser for the right price. I think the shop was called Blackpool Sound Centre and an interesting-looking electronic keyboard caught my eye immediately. It was a MiniKorg 800 DV duophonic synth, complete with wooden side cheeks; the price was £450 and I wanted it. Duophonic simply meant that it had twin oscillators with separate outputs for each and it also had really interesting controls called travellers that split the individual faders into high pass and low pass on each filter – like an extreme graphic equaliser. The guy in the shop told me he was selling the synth on behalf of the drummer from the band Jethro Tull. That was totally plausible as there was a local connection; their singer, Ian Anderson (who Marc has since worked with) was a local lad and had attended Blackpool grammar school. Using my best negotiating skills, I managed to do a part-exchange deal and swapped my guitar and £300 cash for my first ever synth.

I managed to lug my new toy back in a canvas suitcase on the train to Leeds and couldn't wait to get into the sound room at college and show it off to my fellow students. It was like I'd given birth; everyone popped their heads round the studio door to see how we were getting on and to have a play with it. I persisted and with many hours of trial and error I pretty well knew the machine inside out. Shortly after I bought the Korg, another student got his wealthy parents to buy him a Minimoog. It was a lot more expensive and much trickier to operate than mine but a far superior instrument. Luckily, it wouldn't be too long before I acquired one of those little beauties as well.

Initially, I didn't have a drum machine so I used the LFO pulse to generate white and pink noise rhythms and played everything else manually. I was still using my Stylophones through the flanger alongside the synth at the time to expand my extremely limited sound palette. It was a very tricky procedure because I would record a synth and Stylophone in one pass onto one Revox, then play that back through the mixer into the other tape machine while playing over the top. It was the same approach for the vocals. Everything was recorded in one take. Based on old film footage I've seen, it was very much how I imagined Joe Meek would have recorded although he clearly got much better results. I was just recording strange ultra-low-fi/sci-fi pop ditties and instrumentals entirely for my own amusement.

But I wasn't entirely out of step with what was happening in music. At the tail end of the seventies, there was a new underground electronic scene developing. Many bands still used guitar, bass and drums line-ups, albeit heavily processed, but there were a few people out there like me, who were using only electronics. I felt there was something going on that was not a million miles away from what I was trying to do – there seemed to be a post-punk zeitgeist in the air.

By this time I'd got to know Marc a lot better and we'd become good friends. He'd heard my strange electronic bleeps coming out of the studio and popped in for a cup of tea and a chat one day. I'd seen the beautiful ceramics he made but his main work was performance art. I'd only seen a bit of his work and a short Super 8 film he was in. He said he was working on a new performance piece and wondered if I would be interested in creating some mad electronic music for him to use. I was totally flattered and agreed immediately, thinking how great it would be to hear my music used in context. I remember working on something called *Zazu* and two of Marc's other pieces, *Glamour In Squalor* and *Twilights And Lowlifes*. The last two titles have always stuck in my mind as they summed up the underlying themes of many of our future collaborations as Soft Cell as well as Marc's solo work.

Some of the music we worked on was starting to develop into real songs – 'Fun City' being a prime example. That track started out as an idea for a song about a rent boy for one of Marc's performances and ended up being a Soft Cell B-side on the single 'Say Hello, Wave Goodbye'. It was also released as a Marc & The Mambas track on their first twelve-inch single, 'Sleaze (Take It, Shake It)', which I co-produced with Marc. I was also credited as drummer, Lance Rock. Marc did live performances in Leeds at places like the White Elephant Gallery and one at Manchester University. The latter entailed him smearing cat food all over himself whilst singing something about a pussy cat eating its dead owner. That particular number was received with great disdain from the student audience who thought they were attending a nice Footlights-type affair. I engineered the live sound and our friend Steve Griffiths did the visual projections and lighting. We also doubled up as bodyguards, just in case things turned nasty. Marc's performances were often quite explicit and narcissistic and included such delights as 'mirror fucking'. They could have easily caused offence to the prudish or faint-hearted – at least, that's what we hoped.

When Marc asked if he could rework and, in some cases, rewrite some of my attempts at pop lyrics, I had no problem as, by my own admission, I was never much of a lyricist let alone a singer. I continued on the kit side, buying a Rhythm Master drum machine that had tempo control and about twelve fixed drum patterns, including the usual waltz, tango and bossa nova. They were all pretty useless for my musical needs, although the rock and disco presets seemed to work as they were basic 4/4 patterns. I ended up using one of the more cheesy presets as the rhythm for a song Marc and I had just written, called 'L.O.V.E. Feelings' – a spoof schmaltzy crooner's song like the ones they play in northern working men's clubs, also parodied by Peter Kay in his brilliant comedy, *Phoenix Nights*. (Incidentally, Kay took the piss out of my keyboard playing when he was interviewed by Michael Parkinson.) As it was Marc's brand-new song it ended up on what became the *Mutant Moments* EP, as did a re-recorded version of 'Metro MRX' featuring my new drum machine. The other tracks on the EP, 'Potential' and 'Frustration', were completed before we'd really formed Soft Cell proper and were just my rough sketches as I had no intention of releasing any of my stuff as a solo artist. Those original demo cassettes would eventually be released as very poor-quality CDs on Some Bizzare as *The Bedsit Tapes* – strictly for the completists.

Marc and I were both big fans of cult films and used bits of their imagery as inspiration. At the Hyde Park cinema in Headingley we watched many arthouse films by Andy Warhol and Paul Morrissey like *Heat*, *Trash*, *Lonesome Cowboys* and *Chelsea Girls*. We also loved the George Romero zombie films and his teenage vampire classic, *Martin*, was the original inspiration for a track we released on a bonus twelve-inch with *The Art of Falling Apart* album. The John Waters/Divine collaborations – *Pink Flamingos*, *Mondo Trasho*, *Desperate Living* and *Female Trouble* – were all hugely inspirational as were Russ Meyer's breast-obsessed films like *Beneath The Valley Of The Ultravixens*. We also liked more highbrow stuff like Pasolini's *Salo – 120 Days of Sodom* – a scatological film based on the Marquis de Sade book – and Kenneth Anger's epic *Scorpio Rising,* as well as the German vampire classics *Nosferatu* and *Vampyr.* We also watched *The Cabinet Of Doctor Caligari* and Fritz Lang's *Metropolis*, *M* and *Dr Mabuse.* We were there for the advent of the early slasher films such as *Friday The 13th, Halloween, The Hills Have Eyes, Nightmares In A Damaged Brain, Maniac, I Spit On Your Grave* and the ultimate arthouse-psycho film, *The Driller Killer* – a movie that was a nice, unhealthy mix of trashy, arty, psychotic and gothic. Warped and twisted, it was perfect source material for Soft Cell.

Other tracks we originally co-wrote and recorded at college that eventually became fully fledged Soft Cell tracks included 'The Art Of Falling Apart', 'Martin', 'Facility Girl', 'Persuasion', 'A Man Could Get Lost' and 'The Girl With The Patent Leather Face'. I'd written the music and the basic lyrics to 'Facility Girls' at college but when it went on the B- side of 'Bedsitter', Marc did his own vocal arrangement and changed and added words where necessary. The same was true with all the other tracks that ended up being released. The only time my original vocal appeared was on the original recording of 'Frustration' on *Mutant Moments*, when I muttered the immortal line, 'I'm just an ordinary bloke'. That was probably my best ever attempt. From then on, Marc was the singer and lyricist and I was in charge of writing, playing and producing the music.

Marc left college with his 2:1 degree but stayed in Leeds, working part-time as a barman in Leeds Playhouse at lunchtimes and as a cloakroom attendant at Leeds Warehouse at night. I still had another year of my course to do which meant I didn't have to get a job and we still had access to the studio. We just carried on writing and using the facilities as much as possible, sometimes sneaking in illegally in the evenings as I'd made a copy of the keys. We were a lot more serious about it than we'd ever been before, with the real world outside of college starting to rear its big ugly head on the horizon. Our main objective was to make a decent enough demo to play to record companies in the unlikely event of getting a deal. If all else failed, my mum had foolishly agreed to lend me £400 so we could release something ourselves. For the time being, I kept on trying to improve our sound with the very limited resources I had available.

Chapter 15
SOFT CELL

IN THE AUTUMN OF 1979, THE SAME FATEFUL YEAR Margaret Thatcher was elected prime minister, Soft Cell officially formed. We'd considered other names; I first came up with Man Made Fibres, then Soft Cell and Marc suggested Here's Health, but after the usual debate and straw poll of trusted friends, it was agreed that Soft Cell just sounded right. I'd been reading a stolen library book our visuals guy, Steve Griffiths, had lent me, *The Hidden Persuaders*, by Vance Packard, a scientific study of subliminal messages in American advertising. I had another book on the same subject called *The Clam-Plate Orgy* by Wilson Bryan Key, which I'd acquired in New York. Our name was based on the notions in the books relating to 'soft selling'. We had the idea of someone going insane in a supermarket after being mentally overloaded by advertisements and subliminal voices controlling them and ending up in a padded cell; in our case, a cell with pink and blue neon bars (obviously a Blackpool/Soho influence). It all started out very art school and was intended to be anti-establishment and anti-advertising yet, completely unintentionally, we were creating our own brand.

Marc's idea for 'Persuasion' (the B-side of the 'Memorabilia' twelve-inch) also came from his reading of those books – and not from the unlikely fusion of Jane Austen and Throbbing Gristle, as someone once jokingly suggested. A lot of our material – 'Bedsitter' being the most obvious example – had a basis in our immediate reality and 'Persuasion' also made a reference to the mass looting in Morrison's supermarket in Merrion Centre during an electricity blackout. There was a lot of civil unrest throughout the UK during the late seventies; not just the miner's strike but rioting in several major British cities, Leeds included. We once had a Molotov cocktail explode outside our front door, which was quite exciting but a bit too close to home. One of our local pubs, the Fenton, next to college, had once been attacked by a gang of about twenty neo-Nazi skinheads all wearing black bomber jackets and doing fascist salutes. A pitched battle ensued with various members of the rival Socialist Workers Party. Chairs, bottles and glasses were smashed everywhere and one man lost an eye – it was very scary.

On quieter evenings in the Fenton, around the time we'd decided to be Soft Cell, all the usual Leeds University art history student bands were in there: Gang Of Four, The Mekons and Delta 5. It was their regular haunt and some of them used to rehearse in a room upstairs as the landlord was a fan. We all knew each other but they all used to treat us as something of a joke because we didn't play drums and guitars like everyone else, and they looked down their noses at us because we went to the polytechnic. I knew a guy who was a good friend of those bands but I discovered his secret vice: not only was he also a huge fan of Echo & The Bunnymen but he was also really into synthesisers. He'd even built a synth in an attaché case so I knew he was a genuine circuit head. He and I debated how Soft Cell could play gigs as there was only Marc on vocals and me on synth. We didn't want any more band members but I couldn't play everything at once and we didn't have sequencers, never mind computers. We were at a loss what to do in a live situation. Then it came to me: we'd just have the reel-to-reel tape recorder onstage.

We all burst out laughing when my friend said, 'But you can't have a tape recorder on the stage!'

'Why not?' I replied. 'It's only a machine.'

It was a definite 'Eureka!' moment. We agreed that using backing tapes was perfectly legitimate as a performance device. After all, a lot of the musique concrète composers and krautrock bands had used tapes on stage, as did The Human League, so why not us?

We checked out a few other bands, Sheffield-based acts like Clock DVA, Vice Versa (an early incarnation of ABC) and Cabaret Voltaire. It turned out quite a few of them were using not only tapes but projections too. Steve Griffiths was doing Kodak slides and Super 8 projections for our live shows and was the only other member of Soft Cell. It was pretty much the same set-up we'd developed for Marc's performance pieces, except I was now on stage too. The pre-recorded material was effectively doing the same job as a sequencer, with live vocals and live synth over the top.

This was the advent of the British synth duo and we were going to be the first to have hits in the pop charts! We played our first gig at the fine art Christmas 1979 party in the students union recreation room and it went surprisingly well. Admittedly, there were quite a few shoegazers with mushroom haircuts and greatcoats in the audience but I think they'd come to see MRA (a little-known Leeds band) or some other quasi-socio/political popsters. Most of them were in fact the rebellious Marxist offspring of wealthy Tory bankers and stockbrokers from Sevenoaks. At the gig they were in sombre festive spirit, full of Christmas sneer, but at least we didn't get booed or canned off. It all worked out fine and a big gang of our friends turned up sufficiently pissed and stoned, so we got lots of over-enthusiastic applause. We invited a friend to record the show for us – Marc and I still own the copyright on the unreleased recordings and they may yet surface one day for posterity... you never know.

★ ★ ★

One of the many great things about the Leeds art department was that they would invite guest lecturers from various branches of the arts, such as artist Patrick Hughes and writer/artist Molly Parkin, and I had the pleasure of meeting them. Molly was one of the outside judges at Marc's degree show and took a real shine to him. They could have been related, with their dyed black hair and heavy black eyeliner. She even invited him to stay at her house in Cheyne Walk, Chelsea, made famous when Keith Richards and girlfriend Anita Pallenberg lived there. Another guest lecturer at college, much to my delight, was Scottish composer Ron Geesin; probably best known for his work with Pink Floyd on their album *Atom Heart Mother*. He also worked with Roger Waters on his album *Music From The Body*, when they sampled sounds made by the human body. I bought one of Ron's solo albums of library music, *Electrosound Vol. 2*, when I met him as there was one amazing track I recognised immediately, used during a car chase sequence for the seventies TV cop show *The Sweeney*. I visited his workshop in the studio and he did a fascinating demonstration of creative tape editing and how to distort, manipulate and warp pre-recorded sounds by magnetising random metallic objects strategically placed on the tape. I think you probably had to be there to fully appreciate what he was doing. After lunch, he held an open critique and asked people to play one recent piece each of their own stuff that they were most happy with. I played him our latest Soft Cell track, a darkly industrial number called 'Bleak Is My Favourite Cliché', which featured a tape delayed drum loop, my pink noise topline synth and Marc's brilliant lyrics taking the piss out of the 'post-punk' shoegazing brigade. Ron gave us some very useful advice – 'Give up and get a proper job.' Not really; he actually said we showed promise and to keep working at it – we were very pleased with that and took him at his word.

Another guest lecturer I met was Granada Television's very own Anthony H. Wilson. I'd first heard of him when he called himself Tony Wilson and presented the programme *So It Goes* from their studios in Manchester. We used to get the show in Blackpool and it was the first time I ever saw the Sex Pistols on TV. Tony was always a champion of punk from the beginning even though he himself was a suited-and-booted ex-Cambridge graduate. He gave a short presentation about the power of television and the media. It was all very much based on the theories of Marshall McLuhan, the Canadian intellectual, so he didn't really talk about music – much to the frustration of the audience.

Somewhat ironically, one of my fellow students was a guy called Mike Hannett, whose brother Martin was Joy Division's producer – but the band were never mentioned. At lunchtime Tony said he wanted a drink so I took him to the Coberg pub and, as luck would have it, nobody I knew was in there, so I had him all to myself. After boring him half to death with endless questions about Joy Division and his Factory Records label, I finally got up the courage to hand him a Soft Cell demo cassette. My initial optimism faded as the weeks went by. I heard nothing back from him or his label. That came as no surprise; it was the usual response from sending out demos – absolutely nothing.

I didn't get a single reply from any of the record labels I sent tapes to. It was totally demoralising; I must have handwritten and mailed out at least sixty of the bloody things. The amount of time and money I could ill afford that I wasted on cassettes, postage and packaging, trying to get the attention of some jumped-up, ponytailed A&R man still annoys me. I'm fairly certain that all our demo tapes, like thousands of others, went straight in the bin (although they'd be worth a small fortune to collectors nowadays). I later found out that only the ferric tapes were binned and the chrome tapes were recycled. To paraphrase Marshall McLuhan, the medium was not yet the message, at least not as far as we were concerned.

Later in 1980 I had to start getting my degree show together and write my thesis – a convoluted piece about Nazi kitsch and political propaganda. My show was a multimedia project with paintings, drawings and sculpture with film, music and a strobe light (i.e. the Soft Cell film and slide show with instrumental backing tracks). When I left college that summer, I only managed to get a 2:2. That was disappointing as I'd spent five years studying fine art and, like many of my disgruntled contemporaries, I never bothered picking up my degree certificate. It was just a worthless scrap of paper and would have made no difference whatsoever to the life that lay just around the corner. In just over a year I would be an international pop star, arguably the most successful ex-student of my year, so they could stuff their second-class degree – no hard feelings, of course.

PART 2

Chapter 16
FUTURAMA

I WAS WELL READY TO LEAVE COLLEGE AND AFTER A FEW days of drunken farewells, I cleared out my flat in Headingley and moved back to my mum's house in Blackpool for the summer. I was looking forward to being by the sea with my friends, family and, most importantly, my girlfriend Karen and her three dogs. My first priority was to make as much money as fast as I could; some to live on throughout the summer and some to survive on when I returned to Leeds in the autumn to continue with Soft Cell. My career planning ended there – as long as I had a summer job that paid well, that was all. I found one straight away; stacking shelves with palettes in a wholesale grocery warehouse. Almost overnight, I became Dave the Warehouseman.

There were whole business parks full of these vast, aircraft hangar-like buildings that supplied all the hotels and guest houses in town. When you consider that Blackpool had an annual turnover of about six million visitors every summer, that's a helluva lot of food, drink and cleaning products, not to mention all the personal hygiene stuff like toothpaste, shampoo, tampons and condoms. It was a very professionally run business in terms of the pay, the hours and working conditions. The only drawbacks were the rats. In my limited experience of the catering business, wherever there's warmth and a regular food supply there's usually a rodent problem. The place was kept spotless but if rats know there's food to be had, they'll get to it one way or another. Poison and traps were laid everywhere and we'd find the dead ones by their smell as they rotted underneath the massive steel shelves. That was one of the less enjoyable parts of my job, crawling under the shelves to retrieve and dispose of the bodies in the skip outside. I often found cans that the rats had gnawed into – their jaws and teeth were so strong that they could bite through metal. Apart from being slightly terrified by that thought, I was surprised that they were intelligent enough to know the tins contained food; quite amazing.

At the close of business, I would sweep the floor of the entire warehouse; a task that took about an hour. I didn't know that the dust was making me quite ill and I should really have been wearing a mask. The illness was indirectly caused by rats but wasn't life-threatening like Weil's disease or bubonic plague. It was a vicious allergic condition called giant urticaria. The only way I can describe it is a sensation of being randomly stung by nettles all over the body – and I mean all over. From the soles of my feet to the palms of my hands, even my genitals. I'm told it's not dissimilar to shingles in terms of pain and discomfort.

I first became aware that I had the condition after I'd been out with my girlfriend and her parents one evening and we'd all had prawn cocktails as starters. When I awoke the following morning, my bottom lip had ballooned like I'd been punched and it was unbearably itchy. Later on, my eyelids did the same thing and I couldn't open my eyes. I looked like I'd just lost a boxing match without the bruising – and I was temporarily blind for a day, which was really scary. After a visit to my GP and a course of strong antihistamines, I was referred to a skin specialist unit in a hospital in Manchester where I had scratch tests on my arm. They tested for twelve substances and, unbelievably, I was allergic to all of them. Apparently, it was a genetic problem that sent my immune system into overdrive. The most severe reactions were to shellfish and rodent hair, although not cats or dogs (I am also very allergic to the mites found in household dust, so I have a perfect excuse for not dusting). That was the end of my well-paid, albeit brief career in the wholesale catering industry.

I remember one day, lying in bed, embalmed in calamine lotion as I was suffering a particularly bad attack – I must have looked like Michael Gambon in *The Singing Detective* – when I was really shocked to hear on the radio the appalling news that John Lennon had been murdered by a jealous lowlife outside the Dakota building in New York. I'd visited only two years earlier with my mum and sister and stood on the same spot where he died – a very sad, strange moment.

After a week or so, my medication started working and once the severity of my allergic reactions had abated, it was time for Plan B to kick into action. As we'd had zero response from every record company in the land, I borrowed £400 from my mum and went ahead with getting our own records pressed. I'd done the front cover illustration for the sleeve and label and Marc did the back, the tapes were all spliced together, I got a catalogue number and sent my cheque and all the parts to Island Manufacturing, British Grove Studios in London. That was on the recommendation of a guy I'd met in York who ran his own indie label. I guess he'd never had a problem, but for me, doing business with them proved impossible. My main priority was getting finished copies of the *Mutant Moments* EP delivered from London to Blackpool North station by Red Star Parcels. That became a major pain in the arse that dragged on for weeks. I'd ordered 1,000 seven-inch singles with picture sleeves but 300 sleeves went missing. That meant I couldn't sell them on for the full price and would lose money in the process. The manufacturers let me down consistently, making endless excuses on the phone when they could be bothered to answer. What made matters worse was that I'd paid them up front, with money I'd borrowed from my recently widowed mother. I've never forgiven and will never forgive those assholes – I got no apologies, no refund, absolutely zilch. As far as I'm concerned, they treated me and my family like a piece of shit. If my surname had been Corleone or Soprano, they'd be sleeping with the fishes. They really were jokers in every sense of the word – when 'Tainted Love' was number one all over the world they even had the cheek to send me a fucking Christmas card! A more sinister footnote – I found out some years after Soft Cell became a multi-million-selling, globally established act, that someone, without our consent, was re-pressing copies. Considering that the original record with picture sleeve now sells for more than a hundred pounds, a few extra runs of a thousand would have made a tidy little profit for some thieving bastard. Although I have my suspicions, I've never actively pursued it with our lawyers, although I've often wondered whatever happened to the original masters – I certainly don't have them.

We planned to take the finished records to Leeds to sell at gigs and also make a trip to Rough Trade in London to do a sale-or-return deal with them. They took a hundred off us at trade price, which just about covered our coach fares. As we'd agreed that we were a hundred per cent committed to Soft Cell, I returned to Leeds after saving up a reasonable amount of money to see myself through the months ahead and continue with the band. I didn't have a place to live so I crashed on the sofa in the big communal lounge area of the housing association building at 27 Leicester Grove, where Marc lived. Other residents included Mambas keyboardist and DJ, Anni Hogan, 'Tainted Love' sleeve designer Kris Neate, a young guy called Andy Watson and singer Cyrus Bruton whose band, Dance Chapter, had a deal with 4AD Records. After a few months living out of my suitcase while sleeping on the sofa with mice running round it every night, Jo, the girl singer from the group Girls At Our Best!, finally moved out and I got her tiny room. The area was fairly grim but I quite liked it, the room was warm and dry, my friends were there and it was two minutes' walk from the city centre.

It was there that Marc and I wrote all the early hits like 'Bedsitter' and 'Say Hello, Wave Goodbye' and much of the first Soft Cell album. I recorded on my Akai reel-to-reel machine plugged into my mum's old stereogram with my Korg synth and a rhythm box providing the very basic sounds. My room was very institutional, like a cheerful prison cell. It was on the fourth floor and contained one single bed and a wooden chair with a white enamel hand-basin. The carpet was grey, the walls were emulsioned white and there was a bright red, gloss-painted door and matching window (minus bars), that overlooked a stretch of wasteland on the border of Chapeltown, the ghetto area of Leeds. I once woke up and looked outside and there was a cordoned off police tent where they'd just found the body of another murdered prostitute – the Yorkshire Ripper's latest victim.

Like everyone else in the place – apart from Cyrus who had a proper job – when my savings ran out I was signing on and therefore totally brassic. I'd live on cups of tea with margarine on toast and buy the cheapest fags and booze and just write and listen to music all the time. We were doing gigs most weeks when we'd get food and drink and sometimes a bit of extra cash. I'd go back to Blackpool to see my mum every three or four weeks to get my washing done. That was when I was properly fed and she'd always sub me a few quid which I eventually paid back. She was always incredibly supportive in those days and never showed any doubt in my ambition. I knew she missed me a lot, especially now my dad wasn't around but she was totally accepting when I told her I felt it was vital that I stayed in Leeds if I wanted the band to succeed. I had the room opposite Marc's and would hand him cassettes of ideas on an almost daily basis and he'd go through his huge notebooks of lyrics trying to make things work, intermittently listening to various dance records, usually his favourite: Donna Summer's *Once Upon A Time*. Living in those conditions, most sane people would have called it a day. Not us though, we were two men possessed, with an unshakeable amount of self-belief.

Our confidence was considerably bolstered when, after much begging by Marc, F-Club owner/promoter John F. Keenan gave us the chance to play at his Futurama 2 Festival in the Queens Hall, Leeds. That was another reason I was so desperate to get our finished records; we could have sold the lot at that one gig and repaid my mum. Nevertheless, that show was a massive break for Soft Cell and helped consolidate us as a serious act. The audience capacity was five thousand and we had about half that number watching us play third on the bill in the afternoon. Just before we went on I nearly had a very nasty moment when I slipped on a toilet floor that was six inches deep in piss. My quick reactions caused me a sprained wrist and a wet hand but saved me from what could have otherwise been a very cold, damp and smelly gig – and we had already played enough clubs that were little more than toilets.

The line-up included Hazel O'Connor, Altered Images, Young Marble Giants, Psychedelic Furs, Echo & The Bunnymen, Robert Fripp & The League of Gentlemen, Siouxsie & The Banshees and U2. Apart from having the chance to see all those bands soundcheck and then perform, the bonus for us was that just about every music journalist in Europe would be there, so we hoped we'd get a little mention. I didn't have any finished copies of our *Mutant Moments* EP, so I took some tapes and my one and only test pressing to the gig, just in case. It seemed my luck was in when I spotted the great John Peel. I had to make a snap decision – should I or should I not give him my one and only copy of our record? My prized possession... I did and it was one of those rare moments in my life when it seemed I'd made the right choice. He not only kindly gave us a name-check on his show but played 'Metro MRX' on three separate occasions. We were completely gobsmacked: we'd been on Radio 1 without a plugger, manager, publisher or record company behind us. Yes, we had our own label, Big Frock Rekords, but that wasn't meant to be a serious concern, rather, a means to an end – and in that respect, it did a great job.

That wasn't the only way in which the Leeds show played such a significant part in the Soft Cell story. Our forty-minute set went really well and we even got calls for an encore. On the back of that, promoter John F. Keenan offered us a gig at his F-Club, supporting New Zealand band Split Enz, who'd just had a worldwide hit with their single 'I Got You'. They'd obviously just got loads of money, too, as they had tons of brand new equipment – mostly drums and amps that took up every inch of space. We really wanted to do the show but had to pull out because we couldn't physically fit on the stage; we would have had to play in the audience. All we had was one synth, a tape machine and a mic stand but their roadies flatly refused to move any of their gear and we weren't gonna argue with a bunch of guys who looked like they played for the All Blacks. Frontman Neil Finn's next band was Crowded House – that night was more a case of crowded stage. We left the venue as the owner cat-called after us, 'You'll never make it in the music business. Even The Beatles had to play shitholes in Hamburg when they first started!' I wonder if he came to the 2018 O2 arena show in London?

After John Peel lent his support we got some favourable, if minuscule, mentions in the mainstream music press. We also learned that a London DJ who'd been unable to attend had been asking people if they'd seen any interesting new electronic bands at the festival. He was Steve Pearce, a.k.a. Stevo, and he kept being given our name. Stevo was very influential on the early electronic music scene in London, having started a night called Sci-Fi at the Chelsea Drug Store in the King's Road in 1979 and running surreal electronic discos at the Clarendon, Hammersmith, west London. It was only a matter of time before he made contact with us. Marc spoke to him on the phone and scraped the money together for a coach ticket to meet him at the *Sounds* magazine office where he did his weekly futurist chart. We'd noticed that tracks from our *Mutant Moments* EP were frequently appearing in his Top 10, much to our delight, so we knew from the start he was on our side.

Chapter 17

BAD PRESS

WHILE MARC WAS – UNKNOWINGLY – SECURING OUR future with Stevo in a Covent Garden coffee shop, I was staying at my mum's in Blackpool. I remember excitedly going to the newsagents to buy the first issue of a new magazine called *The Face* which came out around my birthday in May. Founded by a guy called Nick Logan, it revolutionised pop music journalism, taking it in a totally different direction from the more traditional papers like *Sounds*, *Disc* and *New Musical Express*. It was as much about fashion as it was about music, which made total sense as the age of the pop video was just around the corner. What you wore as an artist was scrutinised by every teenager in the land. *i-D* was the other style magazine that emerged that year, initially as a fanzine, founded by Terry Jones, who had previously been a fashion editor for *Vogue*. Marc and I had our picture taken for *i-D* on the wasteland outside our housing association building in Leeds. It was the first ever picture of Soft Cell to appear in the press – albeit printed in black-and-white, somewhat different to the slick glossy that *i-D* later became.

Another lucky break came from Yorkshire Television, who were doing a special feature on the burgeoning new romantic scene.

They had a show called *Calendar* and wanted to film us performing at Leeds Warehouse in Somers Street in front of an audience of local clubbers who were into the scene (basically, all our mates). The presenter was a young Richard Madeley of Richard & Judy fame. He turned up in a dinner suit and dicky bow and wrongly introduced the members of the new genre as 'young romantics'. We didn't consider ourselves to be young, new or romantic but the exposure was good. The only problem was that the girls who worked in the social security office also watched the show and started giving Marc suspicious looks whenever he went to sign on.

Leeds Warehouse's owner, an American guy, Mike Wiand and his mother/business partner, Blanche, quickly realised they were part of this new scene. They should certainly have been pleased with the TV exposure they'd got, considering Marc was still their cloakroom attendant and hadn't yet been promoted to DJ status. Mike started booking more and more bands to make the most of the potential of The Warehouse as a live music venue. It had been a New York-style discotheque, with resident US DJs Danny Pucciarelli and Greg James, frequented by upwardly mobile, well-dressed northern clubbers who danced to Chic, snorted coke and paid for bottles of champagne with expensive pieces of jewellery.

Mike invited us to the Sunday lunchtime sessions when the US disco acts who frequently made personal appearances agreed to do a day slot for extra cash. I saw George McCrae singing his 1974 number one, 'Rock Your Baby', followed by my favourite track of his, 'It's Been So Long', which was number four the following year. He was dripping in gold and wore a full-length mink coat hanging off the shoulders of his ultra-sharp, cream-coloured pimp suit, looking like he'd just stepped off the set of *Super Fly* or *Shaft*. But my favourite lunchtime disco performer was Sylvester singing his 1978 hits 'Dance (Disco Heat)' segued into a twenty-minute version of 'You Make Me Feel (Mighty Real)'. He was unbelievable, literally larger than life, with a vocal range to match. George McCrae had a great falsetto but Sylvester sang like a castrato and was one of the campest guys I've ever met. He was a big man and wore spray-on pink spandex pants and a red, sequin top with silver false eyelashes and tons of glittery make-up. It was like Studio 54 had turned into a spaceship and landed in Leeds for a Sunday lunchtime – New York-shire puddings, anyone? Sylvester invited us all to a party he was throwing that evening in London. Unfortunately, Marc and I weren't yet in a financial position to afford a trip like that on a whim and, besides, he'd probably have eaten us alive.

When The Warehouse became more of a live venue, Mike put on some very good current stuff; Deutsche Amerikanische Freundschaft played when they were still a five piece, before singer Gabi Delgado and drummer Robert Goerl stripped it down to a duo known simply as DAF. Other notable acts I saw were Killing Joke, The Sisters Of Mercy, New Musik, The Bureau (Dexy's minus Kevin Rowland), Thomas Dolby and a very memorable, dirty and funky version of ABC before they'd been buffed up by producer Trevor Horn. The Thompson Twins also played just before they hit the big time; there were about ten people on stage who all seemed to be in the band and they stank the whole place out with what smelled like joss sticks. I also saw a strange band from Dublin that I was destined to meet and produce in the not too distant future. They played a torturous forty-five minute intro loop of the *Coronation Street* theme music before finally performing their set as the Virgin Prunes.

On 23 February 1981, Soft Cell played The Warehouse and were paid the princely sum of £40 for supporting local band The Mirror Boys. This was the first time we ever got properly paid for playing. It was around that time I first met Stevo – in fact, he may well have been at that gig. The way Marc described him proved to be spot on; he was wearing a black jumper with parallel glue marks left by red insulation tape stuck across it the previous night. He had smudged mascara, panda eyes. The overall effect was Gary Numan if he wasn't teetotal and if he had a really bad hangover. Joking aside, Stevo was incredibly enthusiastic about Soft Cell and was probably the only person who'd actually bothered to listen to the demo cassettes we'd sent him. When, in his broad Cockney accent, he said, 'Basically, I wanna manage yous,' we were delighted because we knew he really liked our music. I also think he liked the idea of having us because a rival of his, Steve Dagger, had recently become Spandau Ballet's manager and he didn't want to lose face. I don't think he knew exactly what being a manager entailed but then again neither did we. Without legal advice we signed the contract and hoped for the best.

The other part of his proposition was for us to do a track for a forthcoming compilation album he was putting together. He had a deal with Dead Good Records, an indie label run by two guys based in Lincolnshire and we thought the record was going to come out with them. Unbeknownst to us, their agreement changed and we were signing to the unwittingly misspelt Some Bizzare Records which was now solely Stevo's label. He'd also done a licensing deal with major label Phonogram.

The track we contributed was 'Girl With The Patent Leather Face'. Marc had some fantastic lyrics that managed to combine a car crash, plastic surgery and S&M fetishism into one song. J. G. Ballard was then a very popular cult writer and his book *Crash* had influenced everyone from The Normal to John Foxx and, on that occasion, us. The backing track was one of my typical northern industrial cabaret ditties, partially recorded at college then completed at my tutor John Darling's home studio up in the somewhat incongruously picturesque surroundings of the Yorkshire Dales, where we did vocal overdubs and additional equalisation before the final mix.

During the session, I accidently erased two bars of the track off the master tape. Rather aptly, considering the track's title, I happened to be very good with a razor blade and an Emitex editing block so after a little tape surgery, I spliced the track together and it was absolutely fine. John also managed to sell me another synthesiser; a second-hand Korg Synthe-Bass SB 100 for £150. That turned out to be an extremely good investment as that keyboard was to provide the distinctive Soft Cell bass sound on *Non-Stop Erotic Cabaret* and all the singles. I would first play it on 'Memorabilia' and 'Tainted Love' and also used it to make the twangy guitar sound on 'Bedsitter'.

True to his word, Stevo included our track on *Some Bizzare Album* and, I must say, if he had been an A&R man, he would have probably been voted the best in Britain. At the time we met him he was 17 years old and a dyslexic whose headmaster wrote on his final school report that he'd be lucky to get a job as a dustbin man. His only experience in the music business was working on record company distribution vans and DJing. Considering all the acts on the album were relatively unknown at the time, he had very good ears. He signed a track each from us, Blancmange, B-Movie, The The and the most commercially successful electronic band of all time, Depeche Mode, all in one fell swoop.

Unsurprisingly, the album received lukewarm reviews as most of the music writers were stuck in the transitional limbo period between the end of the seventies and the beginning of the eighties. Scared of change and smugly content with their dusty old rock records, they'd taken punk on board and didn't readily champion any up-and-coming new bands, especially when they played synthesisers instead of guitars (a classic example was the way that Gary Numan got to number one in the charts before the music press even acknowledged his existence). That said, a few of the younger, hip writers did pick out Soft Cell and Depeche Mode as the best tracks on the album. We even had Paul Morley from the *NME* come to interview us in Leeds. We sat in a bar called Amnesia with him, buying him drinks and having what we thought was a good chat and a bit of a laugh. When the piece was published we were very disappointed to see that he'd just used the entire interview to try and take the piss out of us by deliberately misspelling our name – what a waste of time and effort, not to mention our money. I did relish the fact that he looked a bit out of touch, to put it mildly, when we were number one all over the world a few weeks later. Finger on the pulse – I think not.

Chapter 18
MEMORABILIA

WE GOT INVITED TO PLAY OUR FIRST EVER LONDON GIG AT a little club called The Latin Quarter in Soho. It was an arty review night called Cabaret Futura, run by my friend, singer, actor and writer, Richard Strange of Doctors Of Madness fame. I'm pleased to say his club is still going strong at the Paradise by Way of Kensal Green, west London. A few other up-and-coming bands including us, Depeche Mode and The Pogues played some of their first London shows at the original venue. There's even a blurry old photo on the Cabaret Futura website of a very young Shane MacGowan watching Soft Cell from the side of the stage – perhaps they were on after us.

Our next London show was at a disco called Maximus in Leicester Square which we played a fortnight before 'Tainted Love' came out. Between the two gigs we were invited to Rayleigh in Essex to play at a club called Crocs (they had a real, live crocodile in a pool by the entrance). The resident house band from Basildon were our support act, with members Dave Gahan, Martin Gore, Andy Fletcher and Vince Clarke, a really nice bunch of guys and a bit younger than us. I'd heard very good things about Depeche Mode and as I watched their soundcheck, my heart sank. Mute Records founder and producer Daniel Miller had put together a virtual band called The Silicon Teens – this lot were like The Silicon Teens made flesh. I thought, These guys are amazing; confident, slick and really punchy compared to us – how the hell are we gonna follow that? I wasn't wrong either – our show was an absolute stinker. My reel-to-reel machine got knocked over and nearly smashed, our sound was really muddy compared to the support act and Marc looked like he was really struggling up front. I was surprised he didn't walk off, I wouldn't have blamed him at all. There had been a recent article in *Record Mirror* called 'Brave New Face', which featured new bands to watch out for. Depeche Mode and Soft Cell were both singled out, so loads of electronic music luminaries had come up from London to check out the competition. It was probably the most fashion-conscious crowd in any club in Britain that night as most of them were regulars at the Blitz and the Beat Route. There were various members, managers and friends of Visage, Spandau Ballet and Ultravox and their entourages in the audience, chucking pennies and laughing at us – a pair of northern oiks, totally out of our depth in Essex clubland. They may as well have thrown us to the bloody crocodile for all I cared at that moment. It was a total nightmare, possibly the worst, most humiliating gig we ever played but it taught us a valuable lesson – if we were serious about playing professionally, we had to raise the bar or die trying.

On the long, depressing journey back to Leeds in the cold Ford Transit, we talked gloomily about maybe calling it a day but, funnily enough, it seemed the more we talked about it, the more determined it made us not to give up – a quitter never wins, as they say. We had nothing else going on at that point in our sad little lives and, besides, we'd suffered setbacks before and always carried on.

There was actually loads of good stuff happening. It just wasn't happening fast enough for our liking. We always felt like we were on the cusp of something and by the time we'd had cups of tea and bacon sandwiches in the Trusthouse Forte services, we'd formulated a new plan of action. We decided what we really needed to do was sort out our backing tracks and our image and get a single out on Some Bizzare as soon as possible. No sooner did we ask than our wish was granted.

Stevo somehow managed to persuade Phonogram Records to release a single with an option for a further one based on chart performance. The producer we wanted to work with was Daniel Miller and we were slightly concerned as he'd just signed Depeche Mode and was producing their first album, *Speak And Spell*. Maybe he might feel there was a conflict of interests if he worked with us as well but he and the band had no problem as our stuff was so different.

We worked in the Stage One studio, in a basement in Forest Gate, deepest east London. It only had a sixteen-track tape machine with a Studiomaster desk but the set-up suited the minimalism of our music just fine. I was used to recording on two tracks and bouncing them while frantically doing live overdubs and it was a total luxury for every instrument to have its own channel, not to mention EQ and FX sends and returns. I had my two Korg synths and Daniel had a fantastic analogue set-up based around an ARP 2600 semi-modular synth that used to belong to Elton John, an ARP Little Brother sixteen-step sequencer and I think he had a Korg 700S synth and a Roland keyboard plus a drum machine and a Roland Space Echo. Daniel's engineer, Pete Maben, was a total electronics boffin who would go on to be the first guy I knew who could read and write on-screen MIDI code for sound and visuals. The tracks we programmed and recorded included 'Persuasion', 'A Man Can Get Lost', 'Memorabilia', 'Bedsitter' and various other backing tracks off the first album, including a version of 'Tainted Love' that was not released.

It was generally a very productive week, apart from the day of Stevo's 18th birthday, when he insisted on eating an entire box of Rice Krispies for breakfast, substituting a bottle of Gordon's gin for milk – a whole bottle. After about an hour of drunken ranting he threw up all over himself and, thankfully, not the studio. He spent the best part of the rest of the day in the recreation room, asleep on the pool table, covered in his own vomit, pissing in his trousers. On the plus side, it kept him quiet and allowed us to get on.

We were staying at Stevo's family home in Dagenham as we had no money and he kindly put us up in his room for the few days we were recording. The first night we got to the house to find his brother Joe was watching telly. Stevo had, ominously, warned us that his brother was not a very tolerant man. We nervously sat down and said, 'Hello.' Joe just stared intently at Marc, who was wearing his trademark black eyeliner, although he might as well have been totally blacked-up, doing an Al Jolson routine as the atmosphere was so uncomfortable. Just when it seemed things couldn't get any worse, the front door burst open and Stevo's well-oiled father entered the room and surveyed his domain. Totally ignoring me, he also fixed his attention on Marc, saying, 'Gawd awmighty, are you a fackin' man or a woman?' Realising the imminent danger for his new proteges, Stevo quickly suggested we adjourn to the safety of his room and play some music. Phew.

★ ★ ★

We couldn't decide on what to release as the single and, confusingly, settled on 'A Man Could Get Lost' as the seven-inch A-side and 'Memorabilia' for the twelve-inch A-side. The twelve-inch was the more important record at that stage as we were aiming to build our audience through plays at nightclubs, relying on DJ support in addition to playing live. We'd sort of made a conscious effort to become a lot more dance-friendly and, because Marc worked at Leeds Warehouse, he got to hear all the latest New York club tracks every weekend and buy or 'borrow' the best ones. Over the years, various DJs and critics have said that 'Memorabilia' was a precursor to house music, with its repetitive, four-to-the-floor electronic dance groove, monotone-filtered synth bleeps and dubbed out vocals – it was really our take on disco. It's been called the first 'E record' in some circles, although at that time we'd never heard of ecstasy, never mind tried it at that point. The 'E mix' of the track on the remix EP *Non Stop Ecstatic Dancing* was only mixed in New York a year after it was first released and by that time we'd familiarised ourselves with MDMA.

The original version did really well in the clubs and became what was euphemistically known back then as a 'crossover' record. If you've never heard that term, let me explain. At that time in the eighties the music scene wasn't as integrated as it is now and there was a very big nightclub in Leeds that had two dancefloors. One was mostly full of white kids while the other was predominantly filled with black kids. Each room had totally different music policies and the DJs spun entirely different records – except for one or two that got played in both rooms. Those were the crossover tracks and if you got one, you knew you were on to something. 'Memorabilia' was one of those tracks... yet it still failed to make more than a dent on the lower reaches of the official UK charts, reaching a pathetic number 101. However, the good news for us was that it did very well in the club charts on both sides of the Atlantic and in clubs such as New York's Danceteria. We also reached number thirty-five in the *Billboard* US dance charts which, although based only on dancefloor reaction and not sales, was still incredible for an unknown English electro duo – a fact that didn't go entirely unnoticed at Phonogram Records' head office in New Bond Street. With that in mind and cap in hand and after much begging, Stevo eventually persuaded the label to give us another chance and allow us to do a single with a further £2,000 advance for him, Marc and me to live on for the foreseeable future.

Visage/Rich Kids drummer and DJ, Rusty Egan, had witnessed our dreadful appearance with Depeche Mode in Essex and completely changed his opinion when he heard the new recordings. He loved 'Memorabilia' and would play extended mixes of it for half an hour at a time during his DJ sets. As luck would have it, he'd just set up a new independent publishing company under the same name, Metropolis, and had a worldwide sub-publishing deal in place with Warner Chappell Music. His business partner was a gregarious Parisian record producer called Jean-Philippe Iliesco Grimaldi, who was very into electronic club music and had previously produced various records including the French electronic act Space. They had a huge hit with the instrumental track 'Magic Fly'. Once Phonogram confirmed that there was an album deal on the table for Soft Cell, Metropolis offered us a publishing deal that was about average at the time for a new act; 60/40 in our favour, with a nice advance. Publishing deals – which relate to the copyright of the lyrics – can be very valuable because, even after people have bought your records, as the songwriter, you continue to get additional royalties whenever your songs are played on the radio, used in a film, performed at a concert, covered by another artist, and so on. So that was a great move because it meant we were published in all the major record-selling territories: America, Germany and Japan, with the mighty clout of Warner Bros. behind us.

As soon as money was brought into the equation it was necessary to employ an accountant to set up limited UK and overseas companies for all of us and sort out future tax situations. Stevo found a brilliant accountant called Ronnie Harris, who has looked after an amazing roster of some of the biggest and best acts in the business, including the late, great Ian Dury. Ian's final studio album came out on Ronnie Harris Records which I would say is a fair indication of Ronnie's good relationship with his clients. I've been with him for over thirty-five years now and have somehow managed to remain solvent thanks largely to his sound advice, in spite of my reckless philandering. Ronnie wisely suggested that we shouldn't pay ourselves each a lump sum and blow the lot but rather put ourselves on a weekly wage of £90 each until the real money – hopefully – started rolling in.

Slowly but surely Soft Cell was turning into a serious business – despite Stevo's best efforts. He managed to get a clause into our Phonogram contract entitling us to a weekly supply of sweets and rather than attend all meetings, he'd sometimes record a cassette tape of demands, put the tape inside a teddy bear and get a bike courier to take it round to the record company office. His most notable stunt was when he – allegedly – signed the Some Bizzare deal between The The and CBS Records. He arranged to meet Maurice Oberstein, then CEO of CBS, at Trafalgar Square in London and insisted they each sat on a lion to finalise the deal. Initially, all that crazy stuff was quite amusing but the joke started to wear a bit thin.

Chapter 19
THE STOLEN REVOX

WE PLAYED A KEY SHOWCASE GIG AT A NEW CLUB IN Victoria Street called The Venue, owned by Richard Branson's Virgin Group. The Venue was a great place, like a big supper club where you could sit and eat and drink wine, or just have a beer and watch the band. It had the first Eastlake live sound system in London and we were determined to sound right, after our Essex experience in Crocs. Within a very short space of time, with a little cash and a lot of hard work, we'd transformed ourselves into a much better band than we thought we ever could be. We'd reprogrammed the set and got our new backing tapes sorted out with Daniel Miller and we sounded more punchy and danceable, much less northern industrial cabaret than before. We'd definitely raised the bar – the only minor oversight was that our new backing tracks were on ten-inch spools and my old Akai machine took seven-inch tape. I explained our dilemma to Stevo and got him to ask Phonogram if we could borrow a Revox B77 machine for the gig as they had one in every office in the A&R department. He was politely told to 'f… off ' by a Sloaney receptionist who was far too busy polishing her nails to be interested in one of their new bands. Never discouraged, Stevo simply waited until no one was looking, sneaked into an empty office, unplugged and carried a Revox past the doorman, out of the Chappell Music building into New Bond Street, then jumped in a cab with us to Victoria. I must say, I preferred his style of hands-on management to Phonogram's hands-off attitude.

Marc's art school friends, Huw Feather and Liz Pugh from Nottingham, designed our set and clothes respectively. Soft Cell had had a pink and blue neon sign from the time we started, a mixture of influences of Kraftwerk's stage set, the trashy glitz of seaside towns and the bright lights of Soho. Now we had a bit of cash we were able expand on what had been relatively cheap and very effective. Huw was a theatrical designer and created a padded cell consisting of four huge panels – twelve feet by six feet – upholstered in white with one window full of pink and blue neon prison bars. Four neon light boxes in the shapes of musical notes and piano keys were arranged around the stage. Liz made us some nice stage outfits: mine was an off-white, raw silk tuxedo lined with handprinted musical notes and matching dicky bow and a grey shirt. I was still sporting a moustache so I looked like an Italian spiv. Marc wore many different outfits – he had always had his image sorted out as long as I'd known him.

As we were both still living in Leeds we needed somewhere to stay overnight when we played The Venue. After our previous experience at Stevo's it was agreed that it was probably safer for us to find alternative accommodation. Marc and I were booked into one of those grubby little businessmen hotels in Sussex Gardens between Edgware Road and Paddington Station. The area was best known for backpackers and the high number of ladies who rented rooms by the hour. I still remember the twin room we stayed in: really hot with peeling wallpaper and two single beds with bright orange, nylon-fitted sheets littered with dark, curly – possibly pubic – hairs. It was the sort of place where you could imagine finding a dead junkie in the bathroom – if you could find the communal bathroom, that is. At breakfast I had tea, toast and cereal while Marc made the mistake of ordering two boiled eggs.

The surly Asian proprietor brought him a knife and fork while simultaneously balancing two eggs – but no egg cups – that rolled around in their shells on a dinner plate. He left everything on the table and promptly disappeared. It was one of the few times I've seen Marc lost for words – *Fawlty Towers* minus the comedy.

Brian and Josie, a.k.a. Vicious Pink Phenomena, came with us from Leeds as our backing singers/dancers and handed out disco whistles to everyone. The gig looked and sounded great, like a big party on stage. Marc was on top form and we got our first really good review off Betty Page from *Sounds* magazine. She was probably the first person to get what we were about and was to become a very good friend and ally alongside her friend Tony Mitchell, also from *Sounds*. At last, we were gradually starting to win people over and get our first nods of approval from the London trendsetters, tastemakers and scenesters. It seemed that the endless schlepping up and down the motorway in a knackered old Transit, gigging every week, was starting to pay off. We'd built a serious hardcore cult following that continued to grow – at one show at Amnesia in Leeds we had to turn away nearly two hundred fans because the place was so rammed. One time we played a packed-out venue called Retford Porterhouse on one floor and the promoter had the cheek to charge people who couldn't get in – they had to pay full price to watch the show on the downstairs CCTV monitors!

Another particularly memorable gig from that time was Rock City in Nottingham. The venue, as the name suggests, normally played host to guitar-wielding rock bands, ranging from heavy metal to punk. We obviously didn't fit that bill but the promoters clearly knew what they were doing – in fact, we had our first ever stage invasion. About a hundred people threw themselves at Marc, then danced dangerously close to me, spilling drinks all over my electronic equipment. It could have been a very 'live' gig indeed. For the grand finale, one of our over-enthusiastic fans jumped into the twelve-foot padded cell backdrop and the whole thing came crashing to the ground, the neon bars sparking and fizzing as they smashed onto the stage floor. We carried on playing as everything around us fell apart; I guess it must have looked pretty shambolic from the audience's point of view. We didn't get booed off though – quite the opposite. I think everyone was totally gobsmacked by what they'd just seen: a synth duo that rocked. Phonogram never got their Revox back and eventually invoiced us for it, once 'Tainted Love' came out and we started making them and us lots of money.

Chapter 20

LONDON/NEW YORK

'MEMORABILIA' HAD MADE HEADWAY IN THE CLUBS, BUT our A&R man, Roger Ames, on loan from London Records, thought we should try working with a different producer on the next single and bring out the more soulful side of what we did.

Daniel Miller was very much a sequencer-based techno producer – a total genius, years ahead of his time, but much as we loved his work, we decided to go for a less machine-driven feel while still using synthesisers as our primary sound source. The person Roger had in mind was an old friend and EMI colleague of his called Mike Thorne, a New York-based Englishman and Oxford graduate who had previously been the A&R man for the Sex Pistols and Kate Bush at EMI. He also produced one of my favourite post-punk bands – Wire – as well as recording and producing the legendary punk album *Live At The Roxy London WC2* for Harvest Records, a subsidiary of EMI. We thought he sounded like a good choice because he wasn't a known pop producer at that time but had done some really cool stuff that we really respected. He was in London to work on a score for a film called *Memoirs Of A Survivor*, starring Julie Christie, and, on his days off, was working with one of Stevo's other acts, B-Movie (hotly tipped to be the next Duran Duran), on a single called 'Marilyn Dreams'. We were definitely not a priority but were told he had a couple of free days in Advision Studios to record a quickie single so it was agreed between Mike, Roger and us that 'Tainted Love'/'Where Did Our Love Go' should be the next single – a double A-side, no less.

The first time I heard 'Tainted Love' was in 1975 in a northern soul club in Blackpool when I was just 16. I don't know exactly when Marc first heard it but I'm fairly sure it was 1980. I knew he'd heard the version by Ruth Swann on Spark Northern Soul Records and he was probably aware of the Gloria Jones original as she was married to one of his idols, Marc Bolan. I had suggested we do a cover version as he loved the lyrics and I liked the idea of punk-electronic-soul music.

I also thought it would be great to have it mixed into a version of the Diana Ross & The Supremes song 'Where Did Our Love Go' as the two songs made a great couple. I adjusted their respective keys and tempos until the two tracks segued perfectly, they both had similar lyrical themes of love gone bad, and the rest, as they say, was history... It's funny how the unexpected so often happens in the world of pop and a silly little record turns out to be a monster. Over the years, that decision to record two cover versions and not one of our own songs on the B-side was to cost Marc and me about a million quid each in lost writing-credit royalty earnings. It was like the anti-Midas-touch struck from day one, inversely snatching failure from the jaws of success, while writers Ed Cobb and Motown's Holland–Dozier–Holland were, for sides A and B respectively, singing and dancing all the way to the bank. The only gold I got from that record were the gold discs that I hung in my toilet. Our publishers, Metropolis/Warner Chappell, didn't even advise us to record a self-penned B-side just in case the A-side was a hit, costing themselves about a million too – quite an expensive oversight. In all fairness, nobody could have predicted just how big that record was going to be so, consequently, no one bothered explaining to us that the publishing on each side was of equal value. We were two naïve young artists with a totally inexperienced manager and all of us were pretty clueless as far as the world of music publishing royalties was concerned. (On the other side of the coin, we've been quite lucky with people doing covers: Nine Inch Nails covered 'Memorabilia', Carter USM did 'Bedsitter' and, most lucratively, David Gray covered 'Say Hello, Wave Goodbye' on his multi-million selling *White Ladder* album.)

Advision Studios, at 23 Gosfield Street, was legendary; it was where Tony Visconti had produced David Bowie's *The Man Who Sold The World* album and where loads of other amazing albums like Kate Bush's *The Dreaming* and Jeff Wayne's *War Of The Worlds* were recorded. The Human League producer, my friend, the late Martin Rushent, had worked there as both engineer and producer during the early years of his amazing career. We felt like we were on hallowed ground and hoped some of the magic would rub off when we arrived at the studio one sunny morning in late spring with our minimal inventory of electronic instruments for the session; we were very excited and slightly apprehensive. This was the first time we'd set foot in a proper west London recording studio. But the session went very smoothly once we got set up.

I had my battered little Korg SB 100 Synthe-Bass for the manually played basslines with the dirty Soft Cell sound, Marc had two Pearl Syncussion electronic drumpads and a Synare electronic drum that created 'Tainted Love's distinctive 'bink bink' sound when enhanced through Mike's DeltaLab DL-4 on a very short clangorous delay, making it more metallic. I had a Clap Trap and an Electro-Harmonix Syndrum which were used for the electronic claps and the crashing metallic percussion section in the middle. Our Boss Dr Rhythm drum machine was replaced with a Roland CR-78 CompuRhythm, a more sophisticated machine but still only having one output. Our engineer, Paul Hardiman, managed to split the signal with a bit of crafty engineering and gating, enabling us to have separate bass drum and snare tracks. The song had a very basic 4/4 beat so that worked just fine with overdubbed live electronic drums, handclaps and finger snaps.

The real star of the show – apart from Marc, of course – was Mike's incredible New England Digital Synclavier Mk II. It was the first commercially available digital synthesiser in the world, with a prohibitive price tag – £120,000. I could have bought the small house I liked in Marylebone, central London, for that amount in 1981. It wasn't until two years later when the Yamaha DX7 came out that algorithmic digital synthesis became available to anyone with a spare £2,000 – and a degree in physics. Under Mike's guidance, I didn't play more than necessary on his synth. I could easily have been tempted to overegg the pudding but he really needn't have worried. My keyboard playing was always minimally simplistic, mostly due to a lack of technical ability and the fact that all my synths were monophonic. It was a quantum leap from playing two Korg analogue mono synths with loads of little black knobs to a totally digital, multi-timbral, polyphonic keyboard with loads of red LEDs and one big silver metal knob.

In my mind I had the notion that we were making a 'cold soul' record. Both songs were about love gone bad and the Synclavier was the perfect dream machine for creating the icy transparent pads and metallic staccato stabs of 'Tainted Love'/'Where Did Our Love Go', not to mention the vast array of incredibly filmic sounds that we used on our first two albums. The segue slide section, or 'the Lancaster Bomber descending' as I always call it, between the two songs on the twelve-inch single was also created with the Synclavier and a ribbon controller. That piece of kit looked something like a metre-long, thin wooden box with a jack cable sticking out of one end and a strip of black Velcro stuck on top of it that you ran your thumb or finger over. It created a portamento effect that could be controlled by the speed of your hand and I think it was originally a Bob Moog invention. The first time I saw a ribbon controller in action was on *Top Of The Pops* in 1972 when Donny Osmond used one in conjunction with a Minimoog to get the screaming sounds on The Osmonds' rocktastic hit 'Crazy Horses', and I'm fairly certain I've seen Keith Emerson use one as well.

We finished the recording in the allocated two days and were feeling very happy with the results as we bid Mike farewell before he flew back to New York a day or so later to do the final mixdown with his engineer of choice, Harvey Jay Goldberg at Mediasound Studios. When we got the mixes back we were delighted – they sounded fantastic. Contrarily, Roger Ames said he really liked it but thought it was a bit slow for a dance track. We hadn't really thought about that – there was a commonly held belief among certain members of the A&R fraternity, depending on the quality and quantity of coke they'd snorted, that if you increased the tempo of a final mix very slightly with the vari-speed controls, it made the record sound more exciting and more like a hit (not to mention it would also increase the tone, making the track slightly sharp of concert pitch). Whether or not our tempo adjustment made a significant difference to the record will never be known but the twelve-inch white labels and promos of 'Tainted Love'/'Where Did Our Love Go' were in the clubs in early July.

DJs picked up on it straight away, continuing the initial groundswell of 'Memorabilia'. We started getting massive reactions in nightclubs across the UK and it was obvious it was gonna do a lot better than the last record – what we didn't realise at the time was quite how much better. As usual we continued to play UK clubs like the Kirklevington Country Club, Retford Porterhouse and Birmingham's Holy City Zoo and got asked to do another gig in France on 11 July at the ENTPE building in Lyon, supporting The Beat. That was my third time abroad and our last overseas gig before we hit the big time. It was really weird playing outdoors in a field on a roasting hot summer's day surrounded by mountains. We were used to playing dark, sweaty clubs with flashing lights and dry ice. Halfway through our set, The Beat's Ranking Roger joined us on stage and was dancing and scatting with Marc, while Saxa, their saxophone player, started jammin' along too. It was brilliant – Soft Cell meets ska! Many years later I got to know Drummie from Aswad and I suggested recording together. 'Yeah,' he joked, 'we could call it Soft Wad.' Fortunately, it never happened.

In late July we were at home in our Leeds slum when Marc took a call on the communal payphone in the hallway. He ran back upstairs shrieking, 'Oh, my God! I don't believe it!' I knew something amazing had happened. 'The record's entered the charts at number ninety-two and we've been asked to do *Top Of The Pops*! It's brilliant!' We both had to get over the initial shock and phone our mums to tell them our great news and that five years at art school hadn't been a total waste of time and money after all. Then it was time for a celebratory drink and to boast to everyone who'd ever slagged us off in the past. It was great, having the last laugh, particularly at the expense of the moody lefty bands that used to take the piss out of our 'poofy little synth duo'. It would have been disastrous if the record had dropped out of the charts the following week – luckily, it did the opposite.

Chapter 21

TOP OF THE POPS

THE DAY AFTER OUR CELEBRATIONS, BOTH NURSING hangovers, we got several irritating calls from the record company in London. Firstly, they had decided we should have a drummer and a bass guitarist on stage with us. They really didn't understand or like the concept of the synth duo; it was very early days. They also decided Marc should refrain from wearing his trademark bangles, tone down his mascara and not talk to the press about his sexuality as there was still a lot of institutionalised homophobia in the UK. It was as if David Bowie, Elton John and Freddie Mercury had never existed. But we made it quite clear that we weren't going to comply with any requests regarding our line-up or our look and after our *TOTP* appearance, the BBC switchboard was jammed with people complaining about Marc corrupting Britain's youth. Within days, all over the UK, tens of thousands of teenagers, male and female, were copying his look. Sales of chunky bangles, skinny black jeans, black T-shirts and mascara must have gone through the roof.

We had to join the Musicians' Union before we could appear on the BBC show. This meant we had to drive from Leeds first thing on Wednesday morning to Clapham Road in south-east London and register en route to BBC Television Centre in White City. There was no choice – it would be no *Top Of The Pops* appearance (or any broadcast slots) for us otherwise. In those days the MU was incredibly powerful, not to mention actively prohibitive, in my opinion. Whenever anyone appeared on a show like *Top Of The Pops* they had to go into a recording studio for three hours and pretend to re-record their single from scratch, just to make their appearance. That rule was such a complete waste of studio time and money. Record companies and pop musicians spent tens of thousands in top studios all over the world with leading producers and session players to get the best results possible. One very famous British producer apparently once took a fortnight just to get the hi-hat sound right, never mind make a finished track in three hours. All the MU guys knew it was a joke too; whenever we 're-recorded' our tracks, they'd sit in the control room for a while and have a chat, then nip out to get a coffee. On their return, as if by magic, we'd have just finished mixing the track which now sounded uncannily just like the record. That was the tape that got used on the show – with MU approval, of course.

Another crazy thing I found out when I got to the MU offices in Clapham was that I couldn't join as a synthesiser player because they didn't officially recognise it as a real musical instrument! The word 'Luddite' sprang to mind – what decade were we living in, again? I've often wondered what early synthpop pioneers like Kraftwerk, Giorgio Moroder and Brian Eno put down as their instruments back in the seventies. I think the MU thought the synthesiser was the work of Satan and if you played one you were in league with the devil, stealing the jobs of honest and decent working musicians who played real instruments in pubs and working men's clubs. What they failed to understand was that synthesisers don't sound like 'real' instruments, they sound like synthesisers – it was the word synthetic that scared them, I think.

What they should have been really afraid of were samplers. We were still a few years ahead of commercially available samplers – I'd love to know what the MU's official view of them was. The closest to a sampler that I'd played was the Mellotron, the Novatron and the Chamberlin – all tape-loop-based keyboard instruments. The most popular sounds were strings, choirs and flutes like the sound The Beatles used on the famous intro to 'Strawberry Fields Forever'. Those tape-based instruments were also used by The Moody Blues, Yes, Genesis, ELP and King Crimson. The keyboard triggered pre-recorded loops on big wooden tape looms, the loops recorded by real musicians playing real instruments – although I very much doubt that the original players got a repeat fee every time someone used their loop. As far as I'm aware, none of the bands that used those instruments ever had a problem with the MU, although I must admit, I've never heard of anyone joining as a Mellotronist.

Fortunately, while the Synclavier system that we used on 'Tainted Love' had a sampling capability, we weren't yet aware of it and neither were the MU. I don't think many people really knew what sampling was back then – I certainly didn't. I didn't use a sampler until 1982, for the bass guitar sound of a track called 'Martin'. What is amazing is how times have changed. I believe nowadays you can join the MU as a DJ/producer. But I towed the line and registered as a keyboard player/bass guitarist instead of synthesist. Come what may, I had to become a member. We were about to make the first of many broadcast media appearances and begin a good working relationship with the BBC.

Around that time we recorded a Radio 1 session for our ally, Richard Skinner, whose show went out on 26 July. It was a taster of the *Non-Stop Erotic Cabaret* album and featured 'Bedsitter', 'Chips On My Shoulder', 'Seedy Films', 'Youth' and 'Entertain Me'. Everything was falling into place, rather than falling apart – just for a change.

In our second week on the charts, we climbed to number forty-five and during the third, as our midweek position was still going up, we were summoned by the Beeb to appear again. We were picked up in Leeds by a car early on Wednesday morning as the show was always pre-recorded the same day. By the time we reached the outskirts of London, it was 10 a.m., the time at which the weekly chart positions were announced. I asked our driver to stop the car by a phone box and nervously called the record company, keeping a totally straight face as I walked back to the car while Marc looked on anxiously. 'We're in the fuckin' Top 30, it's number twenty-six!' I exclaimed. We couldn't believe it. The following week it just kept going and crept into the Top 10, reaching number nine. The only problem was we didn't have a *TOTP* appearance that week but we knew if the record could just keep going up, we'd definitely be on the show the following week and that could clinch it for us. It did exactly that, reaching number two, tantalisingly kept off the top spot by a nice Scottish lady who called herself Aneka ('Japanese Boy'). A week later, on 5 September 1981, the day after my mum's 51st birthday, 'Tainted Love' finally knocked 'Japanese Boy' off the top of the charts and we made it all the way to number one. It stayed there for two weeks and before one *TOTP* appearance we had the dubious honour of being introduced by prolific paedophile Sir Jimmy Savile OBE, dressed in a rather sinister-looking rainbow outfit.

Whenever we had a *TOTP* appearance we would stay at the Columbia Hotel on Bayswater Road opposite Hyde Park. It was great because everyone who was doing the show would stay there unless they were from London. The bar was like a who's who of the UK pop charts every Wednesday night and there were always a few available good-looking groupie types. I had a short fling with a very pretty blonde German girl called Martina and a couple of one-night stands with a secretary from CBS Records – talk about sleeping with the enemy. The barman was a moody South American guy who always wore dark tinted glasses and looked a bit like Carlos the Jackal.

Inter-band rivalry was kept to a minimum and everyone got on fine and even became pals. I befriended ABC frontman Martin Fry and went to his wedding to Julie some years later. I also got on really well with Adrian Wright, The Human League's visuals guy. Other regulars I used to have a drink with were Jim Kerr from Simple Minds and Julian Cope and Dave Balfe from The Teardrop Explodes. I remember one morning, when Marc and I were having breakfast in the dining room before heading off to do *TOTP*, Julian joined us, wearing a pair of impenetrable black Ray-Bans that he refused to take off; I suspect he may have been tripping as he just kept staring at our poached eggs and giggling as he drank endless glasses of orange juice and cups of coffee before heading off to record the show. One evening, Associates singer, the late, great Billy MacKenzie, was sitting at the bar, testing how many bottles of Baileys he could drink. He'd finish one, run to the gents, make himself vomit, then repeat the procedure, eventually passing out after the third bottle. I think my favourite Columbia Hotel drinking/name-dropping moment was when Marc, Steve Severin, Robert Smith and I sat in the bar drinking tequila sunrises literally until sunrise. All four of us were wearing black clothes and eyeliner which was fine at a gig or in a club but we must have looked pretty strange to all the middle-American tourist families as they came down at 7 a.m. for their early morning breakfasts – it must have looked like a scene from *The Lost Boys*.

One of the weirder aspects of having a number one record was the way it changed people's attitudes towards us. We got a whole range of responses – adoration, hero-worship, jealousy, envy, hatred – and that was just our friends. We were still living in our bedsits and people would super-glue or stick chewing gum in our keyhole on a daily basis out of spite. We used to get dozens of begging letters – I even got one from one of my ex-college tutors. People used to send us nude Polaroids of themselves, male and female, offering sexual encounters, presumably in return for money. It was like we'd just won the National Lottery and forgotten to tick the privacy box. Marc and I were in a department store in The Headrow, Leeds city centre, when we heard a word for the first time that was gonna become very familiar to us over the next few years. It sounded like, 'Zim' or 'Itzim' and was usually whispered in a loud hiss to all the friends of the pubescent schoolgirl who'd spotted Marc first. As we walked around the shop we became aware of a group of about six girls following us, giggling as they pretended to be perusing. Before long, another group of girls spotted us and it continued with little pockets of squealing teenyboppers appearing from everywhere. Marc and I made a decision to head for the nearest exit and legged it through the door with about twenty-five screaming girls in hot pursuit. It was like a mini-version of being in The Beatles – Soft Cell-mania. I've often wondered what they would have done if they'd caught us – probably squealed and ran off. I've been asked if I was jealous of Marc getting all the attention, but I preferred to still use public transport without being asked for my autograph by the bus conductor.

Chapter 22

NUMBER ONE!

SHORTLY AFTER THE HUGE SUCCESS OF 'TAINTED LOVE', Mike Wiand, owner of Leeds Warehouse, used his extensive book of American music contacts again. He knew I was a massive fan of Tamla Motown and one evening asked me and my girlfriend Karen if we would like to accompany him to see The Four Tops, who were playing as part of a sixties soul review show. The answer was a resounding 'Yes' so we headed off to what used to be called Batley Variety Club, newly refurbished and renamed The Frontier. It was a great venue and we really enjoyed the show. After the gig Mike, Karen and I got into the minibus with Levi Stubbs, Abdul 'Duke' Fakir, Renaldo 'Obie' Benson and Lawrence Payton – the original Four Tops line-up – and we were driven to Maximillian's Nitespot in Sheffield. I was in my element, totally star-struck and could barely believe I was chatting to some original Motown legends.

My bubble burst when we were ushered into the club and the over-enthusiastic DJ stopped the music and shone a spotlight in our direction. 'Ladies and gentlemen, please put your hands together for... Dave Ball from Soft Cell!' Then 'Tainted Love' kicked in. I was totally mortified; the ignorant jerk didn't even mention The Four Tops, I doubt he even knew who they were. I was just relieved that they were totally cool about it and laughed at my obvious embarrassment, although it still makes me cringe.

We were bought down to earth with a gentle bump, if only for a minute, when taking the train from London to Leeds and loads of kids spotted Marc and put two and two together and semi-recognised me too. Before long, the first child got up the courage to come and ask for our autographs followed by several more kids, as their over-excited parents encouraged them and smiled and waved at us. After the commotion had died down, an elderly lady hobbled over on her Zimmer frame and said very sweetly, 'Excuse me, I've got no idea who you are but would you be kind enough to sign this for my grandson? Oh, yes, and write the name of your group as well because I'll probably forget it.'

Our record went on to be the best-selling UK single of the year and was number one in seventeen countries including Germany. It reached number eight in the US charts and stayed in the Billboard Top 100 for a record-breaking forty-three weeks, becoming the tenth best-selling single of all time in America. That earned us a place in the *Guinness Book Of Records*. Our closest rival, my uncle Tony's favourite, 'Rock Around The Clock' by Bill Haley & The Comets, spent a mere forty-two weeks on the US chart – my dad would have been very pleased about that. We even won the Brit Award for best single but couldn't attend the awards show to collect it as we were overseas doing never-ending international promotion.

On returning to London, I got an invite from Ed Cobb, the man who wrote 'Tainted Love', to meet in the bar at the Old Selfridges Hotel for cocktails. I accepted and he rightly insisted on buying all the drinks – he could certainly afford it with all the millions in royalties we were making for him. He was a really nice guy and showed up with his business partner Seymour Heller, who also happened to be Liberace's manager. I had a great night getting pleasantly drunk and listening to

American showbiz anecdotes, especially the ones about the excesses of Liberace. There was an interesting moment when Ed made a cryptic remark, hinting that 'Tainted Love' may have been about Jackie Kennedy but I never found out for sure. He told me that he also wrote and produced 'Dirty Water' for The Standells, hinting that Soft Cell could do a great cover version. He'd also produced sixties flower-power popsters The Chocolate Watchband. I got very excited when he told me that he also had a TV company in Los Angeles with Glen A. Larson – the producer of some of my favourite TV shows, including *Magnum P.I.*, *Quincy M.E.*, *Knight Rider*, *The Fall Guy* and *Battlestar Galactica*. It turned out that Ed and Glen had been in a very successful US boy band called The Four Preps many years before getting involved in television.

The next time I met Ed was on his home turf, Los Angeles, when we were playing three sold-out nights at The Palace in Hollywood in 1983. I remember his look of disappointment when I told him before the show that we weren't playing 'Tainted Love' any more as we were sick to death of it. A typically headstrong, stupid move on our part as it was the only song of ours the Americans knew. As it transpired, we were never going to really make it big in the States: unlike our contemporaries Depeche Mode, we just didn't put the work in and keep playing there over and over again. U2 did that in their early career and it's the only way to make it big out there; relentlessly going back and touring. Nevertheless, those were an interesting few gigs, not least because we found out later that the strange guy wearing a brimmed hat and a black raincoat standing in the audience at of one of the shows was none other than Michael Jackson. The King of Pop actually came to see us – unbelievable!

In the middle of our four-day stint, we had a night off and we lent American psychobilly band The Cramps our PA and lighting system. We watched them soundcheck and got the best seats in the house with The Cramps running through their entire set, just for us – it was unbelievably brilliant.

On the third night, a weird, paranoid independent TV producer came backstage. The guy was coked off his face and chopped out huge lines for everybody, myself and my three wannabe groupies included. He then started smashing the light bulbs around the dressing room mirrors, at which point it was clearly time for him to leave. He ran down the metal staircase of the artist's exit down to street level. I was next out and, as I stood at the top of the stairs, he turned and pulled out a handgun and pointed it at me. Everything seemed to go into slow motion – I thought I was gonna die on the streets of LA like something out of a TV cop show. He then aimed the gun over my head and fired a bullet that ricocheted off the metal stairs. Stevo came running down the stairs, said something to the guy and he got into a van and headed off into the night.

Our US tour took in one show at the Roseland Ballroom in New York – the same venue where the Sex Pistols had publicly imploded a few years earlier – another at the Malibu Club in Long Island, a cancelled show in Boston, one show in Chicago and San Francisco and three in LA.

Our main concern at that point was the next single. With the phenomenal international success of 'Tainted Love', we had inadvertently made a Faustian pact with the Devil and it was gonna be a very hard act to follow. Where did you go after number one? Unless you were very lucky or happened to be The Beatles, the only way was down – everything we did subsequently felt like a minor failure to me at that time. Over the following two years we went on to have a few good attempts at the elusive number one spot; the following four singles all getting into the Top 4 in the UK charts. Our best effort was a self-penned song called 'Torch' which got tantalisingly high but no further because of an apparent fuck-up with the chart return shops – we were outselling Adam & The Ants three to one yet we got to number two... which is like a million miles away from number one. We was robbed by a dandy highwayman.

We made the 'Torch' video with director Tim Pope. It started off with me pretending to play the trumpet, then Marc emerged wearing the longest false eyelashes since Dusty Springfield. If he had suddenly turned round he would have almost knocked someone over! The only slight hitch was Cindy Ecstasy – who we had flown over from New York to appear in the video as she does a rap on the song – got very upset when told she had to have a bald head to fit with the sleeve illustration for the single. She got quite tearful as she said it made her think of women in concentration camps and as she is Jewish, not surprisingly, she found it offensive. There is a bit of irony here because the sleeve designer, Huw Feather, is also Jewish. Eventually, Cindy relented and appeared in the video in a sparkling blue evening gown on a rotating rostrum with a bald head with a white gardenia attached. She looked fabulous, although to this day I have never really understood why she had to have a bald head.

Cindy herself decided she wanted to form her own synthpop band and invited me to New York and her apartment in Brooklyn to discuss synthesisers. I think she had seen my Sequential Circuits Prophet 5 and liked the look of it but it was out of her price range. I suggested a Pro One which was basically a monophonic version of the Prophet 5, with the same circuitry, a great sound and it was also cheaper. Once we'd settled on this we jumped into the Chrysler she'd hired and drove across the Brooklyn Bridge into Midtown Manhattan, our destination the legendary Manny's Music store on West 48th Street between 6th and 7th Avenues. She got a little demo of the synth, was very happy with the choice and I carried her purchase back to the car. She opened the car door to release the boot and we stood chatting as she thanked me for taking the time to advise and help her. I suddenly noticed the car slowly moving away. 'Oh, my god!' I exclaimed, 'I think you've knocked the handbrake off.' We chased after the runaway car and I did my best to block it as she jumped in. Synth safely secured, she did go on to get a combo together with B-Movie keyboard player Rick Holliday called Six Sed Red and in 1984 they released a very good electro single called 'Shake It Right', co-produced by Cabaret Voltaire. The last I heard of Cindy she had relocated to Hollywood to become a scriptwriter, presumably under a different name.

Chapter 23
MEDIASOUND

ONCE YOU GET THAT MAINSTREAM MENTALITY, YOU PLAY
to win and second-best just ain't good enough. Even though I'd
never had any ambition to be a star, I had all that kind of shit going
on in my mind throughout our entire pop period. Once I'd had
a taste of success, I wanted more. I became very ambitious and
I wanted all our records to be number one, yet I was wondering
whether 'Tainted Love' had just been a one-off. Many years later,
an old retired public school teacher friend once said to me, with a
knowing wink, 'You know what your problem was, dear boy, you
peaked too soon, ha-ha!' I knew exactly what he meant – I was just
happy it wasn't my girlfriend saying it.

The buzz in the Phonogram Records offices in 1981 was very
upbeat and optimistic and, although I'm sure they'd have been
delighted if we'd decided to make an album of 'Tainted Love's,
they eagerly took up their option for us to record our first album
which consisted mostly of self-penned numbers. More importantly,
our working relationship with our A&R man, Roger Ames, and
producer Mike Thorne was excellent. They allowed us a lot of
creative control, gently guided with their expertise, of course.
They were good times for us. We were lucky enough to have the

wonderful Mariella Frostrup doing our press, long before she embarked on her career in the media as a successful writer, critic and broadcaster. At that point, even Stevo was still a tolerable and, dare I say, likeable eccentric.

Mike Thorne came up to Leeds on one of our increasingly rare weekends off. We met at his hotel and, after a pleasant afternoon of self-congratulatory chat and a few glasses of champagne, it was decided that we should record 'Bedsitter' – the all-important follow-up single – and the rest of our first album in New York. That made total sense as Mike lived in Manhattan with his partner Leila and it was a great chance for us to spend a couple of months there. I'd been there with my mum and sister but Marc and Stevo had never been so the whole idea was very exciting for all of us. Marc and I were both living in bedsits in inner-city Leeds and Stevo was still living in his parents' council house in Dagenham and suddenly we were all off to New York.

We arrived at JFK one Friday afternoon in early summer. The immigration officials asked no questions about my little synth, which looked like a small suitcase. We were picked up by a waiting limousine, not one of the ugly white or pink ones you see in the UK every night, full of hen and stag parties, but a proper, old school, black stretch Cadillac, the sort of car in which a Mafia godfather would have been chauffeured around the mean streets. I remember we grinned like Cheshire cats when the famous Manhattan skyline, a sight we'd seen in so many movies, first came into view as we passed Queens. We drove straight through Harlem as we were staying uptown on West 86th Street where the studio owned a large apartment for visiting artists. That was to be our base for the next two months and Mike was waiting outside the building to greet us. We went out for something to eat and a pre-production chat to confirm that 'Bedsitter' was definitely going to be the follow-up single, featuring a track I'd originally written in college called 'Facility Girls' on the B-side.

We had the weekend to settle into the spacious apartment, which had a huge lounge and sound system to match. We hadn't yet bought any American records, so we found a radio station called Kiss FM New York, as they played mostly mainstream club music. I remember it felt a bit like doing homework, checking out what the competition was doing. The big tunes I really liked at that time by two up-and-coming artists were 'Never Too Much' by Luther Vandross and 'Controversy' by Prince – that track really pricked up my ears. The other big track that Hispanic New Yorkers in particular seemed to love was called 'Everybody Salsa' by UK band Modern Romance. The twelve-inch mix of that track was on the radio all the time and in a lot of the clubs. We did a bit of sightseeing, bought souvenirs, ate burgers, watched the trash and soft porn on Manhattan Cable, then rested up before the gruelling recording sessions ahead. We were under an unbelievable amount of pressure for the follow-up single to be a hit – all our futures depended on it.

At 11 a.m. on Monday morning we arrived at Mediasound, 311 West 57th Street between Broadway and 7th Avenue in Midtown. That part of New York is known as Clinton or more fittingly, Hell's Kitchen, the area between 34th Street, 59th Street, 8th Avenue and the Hudson River. We met Mike for a New York-style eggs-over-easy breakfast in the studio, a deconsecrated Manhattan Baptist church. The big live room was where Marc Bolan's tap-dancing at the beginning of the T. Rex single 'Jeepster' was recorded by Tony Visconti. Lots of big hits by US artists such as Barry Manilow ('Mandy') and Gloria Gaynor (her version of 'Never Can Say Goodbye') were recorded there. A host of other megastars including Simon & Garfunkel, The Rolling Stones, Nancy Sinatra, Frankie Valli and Ben E. King used the studio too. I once walked into the lobby as four guys in jeans were coming out of the door and I didn't recognise them without their costumes and make-up – Kiss. Sadly the studio no longer exists and became Le Bar Bat then a restaurant called Providence Lounge.

Our engineer was Don Wershba and his assistant was Nicky Kalliongis, both really friendly but somewhat bemused by our minimal set-up. They'd seen the drum machine but I think they were still expecting a bassist and a guitarist to arrive. The idea of the synth duo was still very new, even to streetwise, seen-it-all-before New Yorkers. But the first day went really smoothly. Mike's Synclavier and his brand-new Roland TR-808 drum machine were both already up and running. All I had to do was plug in my monophonic Korg Synthe-Bass and we were off. By early afternoon we had the drum track recorded. I played the bassline and a few of the basic guide keyboard parts by hand, as we didn't use sequencers. I always thought of myself as a one-man electronic punk band – synths instead of guitars – one note instead of three chords. We didn't usually record a guide vocal as Marc would always nail it in the first three or four takes and apart from backing vocals and a few drop-ins, we had most of the lead vocals done within a few hours.

The following day, the guide backing track for 'Bedsitter' was almost finished and Mike and I were working on synthesiser sounds, going through his vast library stored on seven-inch floppy disks. At about 3 p.m., we got a call from the international department at Phonogram in London. They had a very urgent request: 'Tainted Love' was still number one in Germany and the biggest pop show over there wanted us to perform the following week. An appearance would guarantee at least another week at number one – that meant a potential 25,000 sales. My initial reaction, as I was engrossed in working on the Synclavier, was, 'Tell 'em to fuck off, we're trying to record the follow-up!' Everybody was equally stressed and I realised that I wasn't being very helpful so we said we'd call them back when we'd figured out what to do. Marc suddenly had a brainwave and suggested getting his friend Dylan in Leeds to pretend to be me. It made total sense: a body double. Dylan was tall, dark (and handsome), albeit a bit younger and slimmer, but the Germans didn't know what I really looked like anyway. As long as they had Marc with his bangles and mascara up front, all Dylan had to do was lurk in the background and mime playing the keyboards like I did. Marc got the next plane back to Leeds, met his friend, they flew to Dusseldorf and recorded the show and no one noticed any difference.

As I had the apartment to myself for a few days, I contacted an American girlfriend, an exchange student from New Jersey I'd got to know back in Leeds, and we carried on where we'd left off. By the time Marc returned, not only had I finished recording the backing track for 'Bedsitter' but I'd had my first New York sexual experience and recorded the backing track for the B-side – 'Facility Girls'. We were still bang on schedule and 'Tainted Love' stayed at number one in Germany for another week – I was feeling very alpha male but not for very long.

Our A&R man called from London when he had listened to 'Bedsitter' and said he didn't like it which, roughly translated, meant, 'It's not "Tainted Love Mk 2".' We had been very happy with it but now both Marc and I sank into deep depressions. It was like one person had taken away our dreams in one conversation. Just as I could see it all slipping away, Marc said he wanted to go back to Leeds and left the studio. I was more angry than depressed because I thought 'Bedsitter' was a great record and so did Mike. He was a seasoned professional and had experienced his fair share of knockbacks and said he'd take care of the situation. It definitely helped that he and our A&R were old mates and, much to everyone's relief, he managed to sweet-talk him into releasing the track.

Marc returned the following day, I think possibly having met Cindy Ecstasy in Studio 54 the previous night, as he was in a much happier mood. Soon we were back on course, our confidence slightly shaken but still determined to make a great album. We worked hard, played even harder and ecstasy became our new drug of choice – little white capsules that cost six dollars a pop and were still totally legal. We flew out our friends Josie Warden and Brian Moss, a.k.a. Vicious Pink Phenomena, to do some backing vocals and add some party atmosphere to the album – it was good for our morale to have some familiar faces around.

One of the greatest things about recording in New York was using the session players Mike knew. We'd always said if we had

143

the budget we wanted a few touches of brass and woodwind on the album. Originally, we asked Motown legend Junior Walker to play sax for us; he'd said 'Yes' but he was on tour in Europe at exactly the same time we were recording in the US so it wasn't to be. Things worked out fine as we got Mike's buddies Dave Tofani on sax and clarinet and John Gatchell on trumpet and flugelhorn. Between them they'd played with some of the biggest names in US music, including Steely Dan, Simon & Garfunkel, Aretha Franklin, Barbra Streisand, Quincy Jones and Frank Sinatra. Put it this way – they knew their shit. The really cool thing about them was they never looked down their noses at us or patronised us, even though they were both top musos and we were just a couple of young upstarts from England.

Gradually, we got our own little New York entourage, mostly female clubbers, and we would trawl the clubs of Manhattan in our hired limo with about eight of us in the back. Cindy Ecstasy was our It girl and Stevo had started seeing a beautiful Hispanic dancer called Elise who always turned up with her flatmate Janet, a Marilyn Monroe lookalike. Sometimes we'd do three or four clubs a night so we'd make sure we had a well-stocked bar and lots of E and high grade coke to take en route. Surprisingly, it was cheaper and a lot more fun to hire one limo than to get separate cabs and it also guaranteed us all VIP treatment. We became frequent visitors at all the legendary New York clubs of the eighties: Danceteria, the Roxy, the Mudd Club, Paradise Garage, Studio 54 and the Red Parrot, with occasional trips to see bands at CBGB, the Ritz and the Peppermint Lounge.

The first gig I saw in New York was Nina Hagen and her band Malaria! at Studio 54. There was the famous big moon suspended over the stage, with a spoon next to it that moved, feeding its nose with coke – it seemed like everyone there had the same idea. Nina came on with a wig, a full head of red hair, and during the first number ripped off the wig to reveal a shaved head, as part of a manic, punky set. Another very memorable show I went to was Tina Turner's 1981 comeback, one of three sold-out nights at the

144

Ritz. Other people in the audience included Mick Jagger, Andy Warhol, Robert De Niro and Diana Ross. Ms Turner was fantastic but only played rock standards as this was before her mega-hits 'What's Love Got To Do With It', 'The Best' and 'Steamy Windows'.

For the darker side of town, we'd go to the Baby Doll Lounge on the corner of Church Street and White Street in TriBeCa, where scantily clad girls danced erotically on the bar and sad, lonely guys stuffed dollar bills into their bras and panties. It was the inspiration for our song 'Baby Doll', from *The Art Of Falling Apart*. I think that was one of my all-time favourite Soft Cell tracks as Marc's lyrics captured the sadness of the place so perfectly and I love the way his voice worked with my music. Nowadays, the Baby Doll Lounge is a wine bar.

The heaviest place was the Hellfire Club, in the Meatpacking District of the city. You had to become a member; once in, all sorts of stuff went on. The barman wore just a baseball cap, lumberjack boots and a leather apron that didn't quite cover the tip of his penis. I ordered a drink and he recognised my accent immediately: 'You're English too. Pleased to meet you, my name's Mike, I'm from Manchester,' he said in a broad Manc accent.

'Hi, I'm Dave,' I replied, slightly more at ease hearing his northern tones.

I went to the gents' toilets, a dimly lit concrete room with a tin bath in the middle of the floor. The bath was half full of piss with a fully clothed man lying in it. I turned to the wall to take a leak and he said, 'Don't piss over there, piss on me.'

I'd never been in a situation like this before. I innocently asked, 'Where?'

'On my chest,' he replied, asking if I'd got any poppers. He took a sniff and beckoned me to empty my bladder. 'Thanks,' he said as I left.

Meanwhile, back at the bar, Al Goldstein, the publisher of *Screw* magazine was now sitting with two busty female porn stars. There was a guy on his knees licking their shiny patent leather shoes and sucking their high heels. He came over to me and asked if he could

145

lick my shoes too. Luckily, he thought better of it when I pointed out that my black suede Hush Puppies might be a bit rough and dry on his tongue. The most extreme sexual act I saw there was two women being voluntarily gang-banged. They were both good looking with good figures, about 30 years old, wearing stockings and suspenders but no bras or knickers. They sat side by side on two armchairs, with a leg over each arm. A guy stood over them and dripped candle wax onto their breasts. After about half an hour of hot wax, they were open for business and one guy after another fucked them. They must have got through at least ten men each and no one was using condoms, as it was still wrongly assumed that AIDS was a gay-only disease. I must say, I was quite shocked; I'd never seen anything like it. Strangely, the next day, I was taking a stroll in Central Park when I spotted two very well-heeled ladies, both wearing mink coats, walking towards their multi-million dollar Park Avenue apartments with their toy dogs. Their faces looked really familiar; the two women from the Hellfire Club.

Chapter 24
PROMO

AT 12.01 A.M., US TIME, SATURDAY 1 AUGUST 1981, A VERY significant event happened in America that revolutionised the way pop music was sold and consumed around the world. I refer, of course, to the birth of Music Television – MTV... cue The Buggles' 'Video Killed The Radio Star'.

I watched MTV every morning in the studio with Marc and Mike as we ate breakfast and discussed what effect the new phenomenon was likely to have on new bands like us. We never even made a video for 'Tainted Love' (not until *Non-Stop Exotic Video*) and yet there we were, recording the follow-up single and, literally overnight, the idea of not making an accompanying video seemed inconceivable. The great thing about MTV in its infancy was that they had loads of spare airtime and not enough content to fill it. If you had a video and the clout of a major record label and publisher behind you, as we did in the shape of Sire Records and Warner Chappell Music respectively, getting playlisted was pretty much guaranteed. In a country the size of the USA, MTV gave bands access to a potential audience in the tens of millions, in the same way that YouTube would do years later. It was like an early version of video streaming but without the interaction. Until that point, only a few rich megastars and supergroups were able to afford promo clips, which were just seen as expensive vanity projects that had no real marketing or promotional value. Those films were normally only screened in the UK on *The Old Grey Whistle Test* or as documentary footage. With the introduction of videotape and fast digital editing, MTV changed all that, totally championing the new video age.

We'd learned from 'Tainted Love' that a hot new act with a new single was in demand with every music programme simultaneously, in every country. When it got into the international charts and became number one in seventeen countries, we would do daily trips to Europe. We'd be driven to Leeds airport at 6.30 a.m., get the first flight to Brussels, do a couple of radio shows, half a dozen press interviews and a couple of television appearances before lunch. We'd get the short flight to Amsterdam and do the same type of schedule there in the afternoon and fly back to Leeds in the evening. This cycle was repeated every day for a couple of weeks, seemingly endless promotion round the whole of western Europe. We'd usually stay in Germany overnight as we'd fly to all its major cities over a two-day period – Germany was the third biggest and most important territory after the USA and Japan. Strangely enough, Soft Cell never went to Japan and I didn't visit there until several years later as half of The Grid with Richard Norris.

The 'Bedsitter' video was our first promo clip, filmed at Carlton Television Facilities, Ordnance Hill, St John's Wood as well as the studio's local tube station, a phone box in Wardour Street and also outside Marc's flat in Brewer Street, Soho. It was to be the first of many that we made with director Tim Pope, who made loads of videos for many other artists including The Bangles, Men Without Hats, Siouxsie & The Banshees, Psychedelic Furs, Talk Talk, The Cure, Neil Young, Paul Weller and David Bowie. We had an excellent working relationship with Tim and producer Gordon Lewis. Gordon had cut his teeth working with TV pop svengali Mike Mansfield on a music show called *Supersonic*; Marc and I appeared on that show twice. Gordon set up his own company, GLO Productions; they oversaw everything we did video-wise and, with the help of his cheeky assistant Kirk Field, the process was always very relaxed and usually good fun. I was very touched when Gordon told me that his mum loved our song, 'Say Hello, Wave Goodbye' so much that it was played at her funeral. The last I heard of Gordon was that he was living in Brazil and had written a book called *Secret Child*, which I have yet to read.

One of the final appearances Soft Cell made on UK TV to promote 'Tainted Love' was on the now legendary kids' show *Tiswas*. I have to say, apart from being interviewed by a latex puppet in a leather jacket on a Swiss TV show with Richard Norris in Zurich some years later, *Tiswas* had to be the most stupid TV show I ever appeared on. We were filmed on a Saturday morning in September in Birmingham and, as it was live and largely/totally unscripted, it involved endless cigarettes and cups of coffee for breakfast and lots of hanging around. It was the typical 'hurry up and wait' scenario. We were forewarned that we would probably end up in the 'swamp' and were shown a wardrobe room where we were offered a selection of clothes to wear if we didn't want ours to get drenched and possibly ruined. I remember Marc and I looked at what was available and burst out laughing. We didn't think the world was quite ready for Soft Cell in floral shirts and denim dungarees – it was like The Wurzels' dressing room. We decided to wear our own clothes and sent Stevo out to buy some black jeans and T-shirts from the local shopping centre.

The other guests on the show that day made quite an odd mixture, including Chas & Dave, Ultravox, Rick Wakeman, Suzi Quatro, Rick Parfitt from Status Quo, John Taylor from Duran Duran and a rugby team. Funnily enough (not that I'm suggesting for a minute that there was any victimisation going on), I don't recall anyone else apart from us – and the rugby team – being forced into the swamp. I managed to get out quickly before I got crushed but Marc wasn't quite so lucky; he looked like he was about to be drowned. There were eleven rugby players in the swamp and four of them were standing on him as he thrashed around gasping for air at the bottom of the pool. It was a truly horrible experience, particularly swallowing – or inhaling – the water, which was icy cold and consisted largely of detergent, leaves and soil.

After that experience, Marc and I vowed never to allow ourselves to be publicly humiliated on TV again just to sell records. There had to be a limit. We weren't that desperate. Heavy rotation of videos on MTV meant loads of international airplay and exposure without the need for quite so many personal appearances everywhere at the same time. Records could half promote themselves. We were able to work out timetables that realistically suited everybody's schedules. There was still a lot of international promotion but we cherrypicked a bit more when possible and limited our live personal appearances to what were considered to be the most important shows, i.e. they either had the highest viewing figures – which guaranteed sales and pop chart positions – or they were considered to be what were known as tastemakers, with lower viewing figures but an audience of cooler, more savvy and slightly older kids. The equivalent in Britain was the way Channel 4's *The Tube* was seen as the cred show and *TOTP* the not-so-cool pop show, even though many of the same artists would appear on both shows.

Although there was a lot of hard graft involved, European TV promotion had quite a few memorable moments. The scariest was a flight from London to Nice, on the way to record an appearance on a TV show called *Gray Street* with fellow guests Depeche Mode. The show was owned by an Italian company called TMC and was broadcast in Benelux, France and Italy, which was great because it meant a simultaneous appearance in five European countries. We left Heathrow on a British Airways flight and about halfway there, the plane dropped about a thousand feet. If ever I was worried about turbulence, I'd always look to the air hostess for gentle reassurance; that time, it wasn't forthcoming, as the terrified woman fell over. Amazingly enough, I didn't shit my pants and the plane soon stabilised. The hostess regained her composure and the captain's smooth voice came on the PA, like an old Rothmans cigarette commercial. 'Sorry about that, folks, we just hit an air pocket, everything is fine now.' As everyone on board breathed a collective sigh of relief, Mute Records boss Daniel Miller, cool as a cucumber, turned round to us and said, 'Wow, that could have been an expensive crash couldn't it?'

Gray Street was high camp and Marc wore a peaked Tom of Finland-style leather cap. The presenter of the show was none other than disco queen Amanda Lear who, after a nervous interview with us, sung in the diva style of Marlene Dietrich on wonderful tracks like 'Follow Me' and 'I Am A Photograph'. In her spare time, Lear was the muse of Salvador Dali, the model on Roxy Music's second album cover and a jet-setting regular at Studio 54. No one we knew was a hundred per cent sure of her gender but she was incredibly beautiful. Serge Gainsbourg was also a guest and he had coffee with us in the canteen. He was wearing some rather ill-fitting ladies' sunglasses which he said belonged to the married woman he'd been caught *in flagrante* with the previous night. To prove it, he took off said shades to reveal a very nasty looking black eye – legendary.

Another much more English legend I had the pleasure of meeting on my European travels was Dennis Waterman. His 'I Could Be So Good For You' – the theme from *Minder* – was a huge hit all over Europe at the time. Soft Cell were on the same bill to record 'Tainted Love' for a pop show in Vienna. It was set up like a rock concert and was being filmed in an Olympic-sized sports stadium in front of 17,000 screaming kids. Dennis was top of the bill as he was number one everywhere and we were on just before as we were number two. We flew out with Stevo, a publisher friend and his Mary Millington lookalike blonde groupie. We all checked into the same hotel and around lunchtime Stevo summoned us to his room, where the door had been left slightly ajar. He was in bed with the blonde, who asked if we wanted to join them. We politely declined and beat a hasty retreat. Later that day Stevo proudly told me that while we were in his room talking, his dick was up her arse. Sometimes I wondered what exactly we were paying him for – he behaved more like a decadent pop star than we did.

The show itself was supposed to be totally mimed, which in itself didn't make any difference for me, except the 'synthesiser' they'd hired was a wooden church organ that looked like it belonged to the Salvation Army – it even had pedals and stops. I complained to the production team but to no avail and decided it didn't really matter that much as the main focus was going to be Marc. His problem came when, as usual, he sang along to make it look more convincing but as the broadcast began he realised the mic was switched on and the balance was totally wrong with really bad reverb. It was turning out to be quite an eventful day and it got even sillier. Stevo, minus groupie, met me in the hotel bar for a few drinks after the show with Dennis Waterman, who was also staying at the same hotel. As Stevo and myself were both from tough working-class backgrounds we were quite in awe of Mr Waterman's on-screen hard man image in both *The Sweeney* and *Minder*. We'd also heard that he liked a drink, not unlike ourselves. After a few steins of lager we decided to start on the schnapps – we were in Austria, after all. It soon developed into an impromptu drinking contest and the schnapps was going down like it was going out of fashion. At some point, Dennis stood up and said he had to go to bed, shook both our hands and promptly fell over backwards onto the black-and-white marble floor, knocking himself out in the process. The barman came rushing over to help us get him into the lift and up to his room where we lay him out on the bed. No permanent damage done but if my own hangover was anything to go by, I bet he had a very sore head the following morning.

★ ★ ★

With the promotion for 'Tainted Love' at an end, 'Bedsitter' – the dreaded follow-up single – was released and it was a great relief when it got to number four in the charts – at least we knew we weren't just one-hit wonders. As expected, it wasn't the monster hit to match the previous single, but still went silver in the UK and sold over a million worldwide. The track didn't have the universal appeal of 'Tainted Love' because the subject matter was so English. Most people outside the UK wouldn't know what a bedsit was. I think it was one of our best pop songs; it was certainly one of the most honest, as Marc's lyrics described exactly the life we were living at that time and the words and music were both written in our bedsits.

The other world we inhabited was the seedy world of Soho in London's West End. We decided to call our debut album *Non-Stop Erotic Cabaret*, after a neon sign on the Raymond Revue Bar in Brewer Street. Marc and I sometimes used to go to a porn cinema next door called Naked City Cinema to soak up the sleaze and he even bought a flat across the street. Nowadays, Paul Raymond, the King of Soho, is no longer with us and the Revue Bar is gone, as the property developers got their greedy hands on it and destroyed yet another London landmark.

The album was released in December 1981 and reached number five in the UK charts. Not quite the number one we'd hoped for, but it did well enough to tile a bathroom with gold and platinum discs from around the world and did get to number one in Canada. What was also great was that we'd hear our album blasting out from all the strip clubs while the girls danced to our music. That album was really a celebration of Soho so it seemed totally appropriate. We ended that year with a silly festive photo of us on the cover of *Flexipop!* magazine, complete with balloons, streamers and party hats. It came with a free flexidisc that featured a re-recording of 'Metro MRX' by us and 'Remembrance Day' by Some Bizzare label mates, B-Movie. Nineteen-eighty-one was most definitely a very good year for Soft Cell; we'd been the busiest we'd ever been and Christmas came at just the right time, with a whole two weeks off.

Early the following year, 'Say Hello, Wave Goodbye' made it to number three in the UK. There was a bit of a panic when it came to making an extended version of the track for the twelve-inch single. We'd recorded and mixed the song with vocals for both the album and the A-side of the seven-inch single. An additional instrumental version was recorded in New York, featuring Dave Tofani on clarinet, for the seven-inch B-side. The problem was combining the two versions for the twelve-inch single, as each had been mixed on separate occasions. Mike Thorne had to bolt the differing vocal and instrumental versions together in a sort of 'Frankenstein edit'. I think we got away with it because all the splices were so obvious they sounded intentional. We made a very camp video with a Parisian beatnik nightclub set designed by Huw Feather and costumes designed by his partner Liz Pugh. It was the first video we made that featured dwarves; at the end there are a couple drinking champagne outside the club. Again, we worked with director Tim Pope and the same production team as we'd been very happy with the previous promo video. However, we did make one video featuring a dwarf that wasn't quite so commercial and caused us a huge problem, although ultimately it did our notoriety a world of good…

The video in question, of course, was for 'Sex Dwarf'. The title was lifted from a *News Of The World* headline Marc spotted: 'Sex dwarf lures hundred disco dollies to life of vice'. How could we resist making a mutant disco track based on that? We'd decided to make a video album of all the first singles and a few choice tracks and paid for the videos that weren't singles as they weren't promotional items. Between us we put about £60,000 of our own money into the project. For the 'Sex Dwarf' video we hired Kelly, who was transsexual, and two ladies and a dwarf found in Soho.

The video was pretty full-on: the two ladies wore miniskirts and no knickers and Kelly was totally naked so there were some very risque camera angles. I had a chainsaw and wore a rubber butcher's apron whilst Marc and the dwarf wore black fetish wear, with the dwarf wearing a leather rapist's mask. The video was never going to get shown on *Top Of The Pops* and bootleg copies were reputedly changing hands in Soho for £30 each. Word got back to the *News Of The World* and before we knew it, we were in the headlines; the thing had gone full circle.

Our activities didn't go entirely unnoticed by the Metropolitan Police either and the vice squad popped into Some Bizzare for a quick raid. Nothing came of that and there were no prosecutions. The downside was that W. H. Smith and all the other high street retailers informed us they would not stock our video unless the offensive material was removed. We had no choice but to comply; after all, we had money invested in the video and wouldn't be able to sell it unless we self-censored. To the huge disappointment of the fans, we shot a new video with Marc conducting a school choir and all of us wearing suits. Several years later I was very pleased to see we were in the Top 10 banned videos of all time in the UK and nowadays, you can watch the original on YouTube, albeit in rather poor quality.

Chapter 25

DANCETERIA

OUR NEXT SINGLE WAS 'SAY HELLO, WAVE GOODBYE'. WE appeared on several TV shows including *Top Of The Pops* and a brand-new programme filmed in Manchester called *Oxford Road Show*, hosted by Radio 1's Peter Powell. The premise was a cutting-edge, streetwise mixture of politics, humour, fashion and music. Presenters included BBC London's Robert Elms, the man who'd introduced Spandau Ballet to the world, *The Face* magazine's golden boy of the time. There was also a new comedian called Ben Elton who provided the 'in your face' ranting lefty monologues. I would never have believed that he'd go on to co-write the Queen musical *We Will Rock You*. We also appeared on *The Old Grey Whistle Test* on 4 February to play 'Youth' and 'Sex Dwarf'. The presenter was Annie Nightingale (somehow I doubt that 'Whispering' Bob Harris would have been a big fan of ours). Apart from actually being on the *Whistle Test*, I found the strangest thing was there was no audience, just the presenter, camera crew and a few technicians. Speaking as a fan of the show, I always liked it because you could see what the bands you liked were actually doing without all the showbiz trickery. From a performer's point of view, it felt like doing a soundcheck or a rehearsal – but on TV. I certainly noticed that our credibility increased as a result of doing that show. People in the business started to take us much more seriously and give us a bit of respect as an album-making band, not just some trivial pop floozies. With that in mind we decided to make a mostly instrumental electro-dance mini-remix album, drawing on our new-found clubbing and drugging experiences in Gotham City for inspiration.

Electronic dance music and remixing was starting to be taken more seriously rather than being dismissed as some gimmicky pop fad. We must have been tapping into the zeitgeist because, totally unknown to us, The Human League and producer Martin Rushent were reworking their *Dare* album material into what was to become the excellent *Love And Dancing* mini-album under the name The League Unlimited Orchestra. I'd also heard some brilliant ABC remixes done with their producer Trevor Horn. It seemed that everyone with access to a mega-producer and fuck-off technology – Synclaviers, Fairlights, MicroComposers, LinnDrums etc – was at it. We flew out to New York in February, when it was at its coldest for thirty years. I had a suite at the Mayflower Hotel on Central Park West, which was one of my favourites because of its location. Apparently, a lot of big Mafia drug deals had been done there during the seventies, which gave the place a sinister appeal. On a more practical level, with Manhattan thick with snow, it was by Columbus Circle, just around the corner from the studio on West 57th Street.

Our main concern was to record a follow-up to 'Say Hello, Wave Goodbye'. As we'd already had three tracks off the album it was decided that we needed a brand-new song and a B-side. I was given the keys to the studio for the weekend and locked myself in the control room with the Synclavier, a Roland TR-808 drum machine, a coffee machine and a gram of white lady for inspiration. When I needed to record an idea I just buzzed the assistant engineer in the next studio on the intercom to operate the multitrack tape machine while I played. By the end of Saturday afternoon I had the chords, bass and topline ideas for 'Torch' very roughly in shape. I was back in the studio on Monday morning to play Marc and Mike my new piece. I wasn't totally happy with my drum programming so we re-recorded that until the beat sat really tight. Apart from that, they seemed to like what they heard and Marc immediately had an idea and suggested we get Cindy Ecstasy to do some vocals with him. She'd already done some rapping on *Non Stop Ecstatic Dancing* which sounded great so Marc thought we should use her again on the new tune. It worked a treat, with her Brooklyn drawl sitting coolly with my filmic synth pads – perfect, as the song was inspired by Billie Holiday.

Within a few days we had the music and vocals nailed and got John Gatchell to play Marc's melody idea on the flugelhorn. That was the icing on the cake and just sounded so jazzy, cool and classy. When we finished, John's buddy, Alfred 'Pee Wee' Ellis, sax player and musical director from James Brown's band (he arranged 'Cold Sweat' and 'Say It Loud, I'm Black And I'm Proud' and also sometimes worked with The J.B.'s) came by. I was very impressed and he loved the horn part. He said, in a fantastically deep voice, 'Wow, man. That's mighty purty.' Inspired by Pee Wee, for the B-side I wrote some music that had a sort of cool-yet-hysterical New York feel to it and Marc rapped about insecurity on 'Insecure Me'.

When we recorded the overdubs and oversaw the mixing of our *Non Stop Ecstatic Dancing* mini-remix album with Mike Thorne and engineer, Harvey Jay Goldberg – who eventually became the live engineer on *The David Letterman Show* – it was a bit like a party in the studio. We stripped out or dubbed most of the vocals and added some more horns on 'Memorabilia' and 'Chips On My Shoulder'. Mike also brought his analogue Serge modular system to the studio which we used for generating sequential triggered synths and noise patterns. That was the same pulsating synth we used on the single 'Torch' that can be heard clearly at the beginning of the track and all the way through the B-side. I loved that piece of kit; originally designed by Serge Tcherepnin in the seventies, it looked like a load of homemade aluminium boxes linked together with dozens of patch cords and it generated fantastically dirty, random chaos and the synthetic scratch sounds which just added to the intensity of the album. After all, the album was meant to encapsulate the atmosphere and influences of all the clubs we went to, the music we danced to and the drugs we took during our nights out in New York – the most obvious being cocaine and our recent discovery, ecstasy.

It was during those halcyon days in New York that I got to meet Marianne Faithfull; Harvey Goldberg and I had become good friends during our time in Mediasound and one day he said he was going to a rehearsal studio a few blocks away to check on how sessions were going with Marianne's band, as he was going to produce her next album. I couldn't resist the opportunity to meet such a legend and Harvey was more than happy for me to tag along. I was very excited – Mick Jagger's ex, *Girl On A Motorcycle* and *Broken English* – I was a massive fan. Her band were on top form and sounded great, then they stopped when Marianne saw Harvey. She came over and gave him a big kiss and a hug then turned to me as I was introduced. I involuntarily recoiled as she moved in for a kiss and I saw a huge cold sore on her top lip. 'Don't worry, darling, it's not herpes,' were her immortal words as she pecked my cheek.

Anyway, back to the plan, which was to do some US promotion for the *Non-Stop Erotic Cabaret* album. The 'promotion' we had in mind was a huge album launch party at our regular haunt – Danceteria on 21 West Street, the legendary club that featured in the Madonna film *Desperately Seeking Susan*. Before she signed to Sire Records, the same label as us, we knew Madonna as a regular at the club and she would always put on little dancing shows. Our launch there was the hottest ticket in town. Everybody from the scene turned up, including Cookie Mueller from the John Waters/Divine films, Dianne Brill, some of the Warhol crowd and various musicians including Bryan Ferry's guitarist Chris Spedding and Mick Jones from The Clash, who came over to me and told me he really loved our music. I was totally blown away by that, as you can imagine. We hired a load of strippers and erotic dancers who performed a no-holds-barred stage show in front of a DayGlo backdrop that just said 'Non-Stop Erotic Cabaret' with other sexy slogans painted everywhere – from what I'm told and what I can remember, it was a fantastic night, even by New York standards.

RIGHT: Original poster for *Mutant Moments* EP, designed by me, 1980.

LEFT: The cover of the sheet music for 'Tainted Love' was designed by Kris Neate, who also designed the

RIGHT: For the sheet music for 'Bedsitter', we used a photo by Peter Ashworth on the cover.

LEFT: Huw Feather retouched a still from the 'Seedy Films' video to create the sheet music cover for 'What!'

Huw Feather, one of Marc's art school friends,
designed this sheet music cover for 'Say Hello,
Wave Goodbye', as well as some of our record

With Suicide's Alan Vega, who described Soft Cell as 'Suicide the easy way'. Taken at the Garage, London, 1998.

With one of my heroes, Andy Warhol, at The Factory, New York, 1982.

RIGHT: With Divine at
the legendary Danceteria,
New York, 1982.

LEFT: With Terry Hall at Bar Negril,
New York, 1982.
SOURCE

RIGHT: Reuniting with Mute
Records' Daniel Miller at an
Erasure show, the Roundhouse,

'The Art of Falling Apart' live in Liverpool – the fans were trying to steal Marc's jewellery!

On se
video
LEV/UC

...ube, 1983. Jim 'Foetus' Thirwell joined
...n of Suicide's 'Ghost Rider'.

Chapter 26
CHANCE MEETINGS

AT THE DANCETERIA I WAS CHATTING TO 'SUGARCOATED' Andy Hernandez of Kid Creole & The Coconuts when I noticed a very elegant lady in a big hat, sitting alone at the end of the quiet bar sipping a cocktail. She was Anita Sarko, a DJ at the club.

Unknown to me, she was the top female DJ in New York and also played at Steve Mass's famous Mudd Club at 77 White Street in TriBeCa, where I'd once seen Was Not Was perform. I don't know if it was my cute English accent or my youthful good looks but when I went on the charm offensive and asked her for a date, she foolishly accepted. We agreed to meet the next day for drinks in a little bar she knew in the West Village. Later on, we walked down Bleecker Street back to her apartment on Jones Street. I told her about the new legal wonder drug we'd discovered called ecstasy which, to my surprise, she'd never heard of, even though she was a seasoned clubber. We each took a capsule, drank some tequila and waited for it to come on. Sure enough, within half an hour, the tell-tale tingles started, the petting got heavier and we got all loved-up, as they used to say.

For a year or so, on and off, whenever I was in the city, which was quite often, I stayed at Anita's apartment. Jones Street was made famous by the sleeve of Bob Dylan's 1963 album *The Freewheelin'* *Bob Dylan*, where he is pictured with his girlfriend walking down the street. I loved Greenwich Village, the fantastic little delis and bars and the great bookshops and clothes shops. There were also a couple of quirky little outlets, such as the Erotic Bakery where they made cakes that looked like naughty bits and a sex shop that was run by a weird religious sex cult.

Anita took me to a place called David's Pot Bellied Stove for brunch on Christopher Street, the gay street of the West Village. She recommended the eggs benedict; it was the first time I'd ever had it and I was totally hooked. As we walked back, we became aware of a peaceful demonstration on the corner of Bleecker Street. There were lots of men, mostly 'clones'– cropped hair, moustaches, white vests, leather and denim – all waving placards that bore the slogan, 'What is the gay cancer that is killing our brothers?' It was just at the beginning of the AIDS epidemic in north American cities, when no one seemed to know what was going on and panic and hysteria were starting to set in. At that point I'd only met one barman who used to talk about his boyfriend having the 'gay cancer'. There were all sorts of wild rumours circulating at the time: it was really green monkey disease; it was caused by inhaling amyl nitrate; it was a plot by the CIA to kill Haitians, haemophiliacs, heroin addicts and homosexuals – or anything that began with 'H'. Eventually it became known as 'GRID' (Gay Related Immune Deficiency, nothing to do with my band The Grid), until the biologists accepted that viruses don't actually have sexual preferences and heterosexuals were equally at risk of acquired immune deficiency syndrome. 'Tainted Love' took on an altogether more sinister meaning.

Out of sheer curiosity, Anita and I once went to the Mineshaft club (a New York gay club) and, unbelievably, I found Freddie Mercury standing next to me at the bar. The first thing he said was, 'So David, tell me, are you and Marc lovers?' When I explained I was straight and was with Anita, my girlfriend, he gave me a slightly confused look, bought me a bottle of Beck's and flounced off. Shortly after that chance encounter, I looked in the mirror one day and decided that the moustache had got to go; I looked like a clone – I usually dressed head to toe in black leather and was clearly putting out all the wrong signals for a straight guy.

Anita was a bit older than me but that made no difference to either of us. She was a party animal, just a lot more clued-up, and she became a kind of mentor to me. One night I went to the Mudd Club with her when we'd taken some opium rolled into little balls in cigarette papers. Halfway through the evening, my pupils were like pinholes and I felt so fantastically nauseous that I had to vomit outside the club, out of sight of the doorman. It was the most enjoyable chunder ever and when I went back into the club to catch the last of Glenn Branca's *The Ascension* set, I told her I felt absolutely marvellous. She obviously knew I enjoyed experimenting with sex and drugs and turned me on to lots of relevant literature, including *The Naked Lunch* and several other books by William Burroughs, and what became one of my all-time favourites, *Diary Of A Drug Fiend* by Aleister Crowley. She also gave me a signed copy of a book entitled *The Correct Sadist* written by her dominatrix friend Terence Sellers, a.k.a. Mistress Angel Stern. Terrence was even kind enough to let us use her Midtown dungeon one afternoon, which was very interesting. I was particularly intrigued by all the oversize baby costumes and little girl outfits in the wardrobe. Apparently, lots of her clients – usually high-powered businessmen, senior bankers and politicians – enjoyed being dressed up as children, chastised and spanked or otherwise humiliated to alleviate their executive stress. Call me old fashioned but the dressing up thing never did it for me.

Anita had been a radio DJ in Detroit and was very knowledgeable about music. Her apartment had long wooden shelves stacked with thousands of original, old seven-inch singles and twelve-inches – alongside her vast collection of original 1920s and 1930s hats. I'd go through the records, spending hours playing them on her twin decks in the lounge but I also got to hear a lot of the new music coming out of New York. At Paradise Garage on King Street and Hudson Square, DJ Larry Levan used to spin some great music. One standout track was 'Don't Make Me Wait' by The Peech Boys on West End Records, which I think was connected to the club – that was a massive club hit in Manhattan.

Then there was 'The Message'. Anita's friend Lisa Rosen, a model for Italian *Vogue*, came bursting into the apartment clutching a twelve-inch single on Sugar Hill Records, exclaiming, 'You gotta check out this record!' We were blown away by Grandmaster Flash's piece of rap genius. We'd seen Grandmaster Flash & The Furious Five at the Roxy Roller Rink alongside other Bronx rap acts like Fab Five Freddy, Funky Four Plus One and The Treacherous Three so we were quite clued up on the commercial end of the rap scene. I'd even seen Kurtis Blow play 'The Breaks' at a little place called Bar Negril on 8th Street and 2nd Avenue one night where I met Terry Hall from The Specials, but 'The Message' was something extra special. It just summed up the vibe of the city at the time, it was totally urban.

Anita also played a seminal part in introducing Marc and me to the Manhattan art, music and club crowd, including Jim Fouratt, who'd been hired by Danceteria owner Rudolf Piper as the booker for the club. I got quite chatty with Jim and was very impressed by some of the names in his contact book. One evening, I chanced my arm and naively asked him, 'So, do you know Andy Warhol?' He confirmed that he did and before I could speak, asked if we'd like to meet him. A few days later, Jim called me with the time and address; Monday, 6 p.m., Andy Warhol Enterprises, 860 Broadway, at the north end of Union Square. I couldn't believe it, I was going to meet one of my all-time favourite artists at his studio, The Factory. I told Marc, who was equally excited, as were our designers Huw and Liz, and we promised to take them too.

We arrived dead on time that Monday and got into the elevator. One of Andy's assistants was waiting to greet us and took us into the huge studio. There were about four young people making screen prints and Warhol was sitting at his desk wearing a sleeveless, dark blue Puffa jacket, talking on the phone. We were taken into the boardroom where there was a large antique oak table and chairs and a moose head mounted on the wall above a TV monitor with video player. An assistant brought us all cans of Coca-Cola and put on some of Andy's cable TV show for us to watch while we waited. Eventually Andy came in and it was just how I'd always imagined it would be.

He quietly introduced himself, 'Hi, I'm Andy,' followed by the limpest handshake I've ever felt. It was like visiting a very pale-looking old person in a hospice and I think the conversation was mostly about how we liked New York. He switched on a micro-tape machine and took out an instamatic camera and started to click away, so I did the same, which he didn't seem to mind. We gave him some signed records and in return he gave us signed first editions of his book, *From A To B And Back Again – The Philosophy of Andy Warhol*, complete with a black marker pen drawing of a Campbell's soup can on the inner sleeve. In total, we were probably only there for about an hour. On our way out, I noticed large industrial bins filled with reject prints. I thought about nicking a print but without his signature – or should I say brand name? – they were worthless.

I thanked Jim Fouratt profusely for arranging everything. It was not long afterwards that he departed from Danceteria to be replaced by Ruth Polsky, who had approached Soft Cell about promoting us when we already had a deal. She was the first to champion many up-and-coming Brit bands in New York, including The Smiths, Echo & The Bunnymen, Simple Minds, The Teardrop Explodes and New Order. She died in 1986, in a bizarre accident that wouldn't have looked out of place in one of Warhol's Disaster paintings. She was standing on the steps outside the Limelight club on West 20th Street in Chelsea when a yellow taxi collided with another car and spun out of control, fatally pinning her to a wall. Even the most hardened and cynical Manhattan clubbers I knew, who were used to accidental ODs and the growing threats of herpes and AIDS, went into shock, as did all those UK bands who knew and worked with her. She was well-loved and sorely missed by a lot of people in the music business. Another person who is missed is my old flame, Anita Sarko, who sadly took her own life in 2015.

Chapter 27

NY TO LONDON

WHEN I WASN'T IN NEW YORK, I WAS IN LONDON QUITE A lot and I'd got to know a guy called David Claridge who set up a record label called The Mobile Suit Corporation. They went through Phonogram Records.

David had his first hit with 'Ever So Lonely' by Monsoon which featured the vocals of Sheila Chandra. I'd just put an act together with our friends and Soft Cell backing singers, Josie and Brian, a.k.a. Vicious Pink Phenomena. After a day of doing Soft Cell international press conferences with Marc at the Carlton Tower hotel in Knightsbridge, I met up with David in the bar to discuss a deal. After several drinks he agreed to release their first single, 'My Private Tokyo', on his Mobile Suit label for us. He was also having a very successful television career. He'd invented the puppet character, Roland Rat, Superstar, which had pretty much saved the ailing *TV-am*.

He was also involved in a new nightclub that went under the name of Skin Two. It started off at a place called Stallions in Falconberg Mews, round the back of the Astoria, opposite Centre Point. The venue, as the name suggested, was normally a gay club but on Skin Two nights it was a fetish club. The patrons were a mixture of pop stars, fashionistas into the leather and rubber look and a few genuine fetishists. Marc and I were there one night with our sax player Gary Barnacle and his girlfriend, singer Kim Wilde, who looked fantastic in black leather and fishnets. We'd met her once before, backstage at one of our gigs. I'm pretty sure that various members of Siouxsie & The Banshees may have gone there too. I once went with Genesis P. Orridge from Throbbing Gristle when some guy was after him and wanted to knife him. There was one old bloke who used to walk around with a girl on a dog leash and a gag in her mouth and I distinctly remember a rubber-clad, male nun wandering about. It was all very weird and wonderful. Among the current electronic club tracks, the DJ always mixed in Michael Nyman's baroque-style music from Peter Greenaway's film *The Draughtsman's Contract*. Though not an obvious choice for a nightclub, for me it became the theme tune to the evening; it fit the atmosphere perfectly.

I'd started working on my ill-conceived solo album, *In Strict Tempo*, and I wanted to do a track based on David's club. I'd decided to call it 'Second Skin' as an obvious point of reference. I asked him to write a monologue/soliloquy, documenting and detailing a typical evening's proceedings and invited him to the studio to record it as a voiceover as he was primarily an actor, after all. A few weeks after completing the recording, I got a very panicky phone call from him telling me that under no circumstances was I to use his voice or words on my album. He explained that the tabloids had found out that the man behind the television puppet on *TV-am* was also running a fetish night in a club in London's Soho – the redtops would have had a field day.

Chapter 28
CALIFORNIA SOUL

AS 'TAINTED LOVE' WAS STILL HIGH IN THE *BILLBOARD* charts we were asked by our US label, Sire Records, to fly to Los Angeles to perform on two TV shows. Being English I'd never heard of either show but I was assured that *The Merv Griffin Show* was the second biggest chat show in America after the Johnny Carson show and that *Solid Gold* was the US equivalent of *Top Of The Pops*, with legendary dancers.

The promotion obviously worked because by September, 'Tainted Love'/'Where Did Our Love Go' was the tenth best-selling twelve-inch single of all time in the US. Back in London I'd bought a new grey leather suit in the King's Road and my first chance to wear it publicly was to celebrate the news. We flew out with Stevo, arriving at LAX airport on a Saturday afternoon where we briefly met Black Sabbath (minus Ozzie) on their way back to England. The guy from Warner Bros. was waiting for us, our chauffeur for the week, and we walked to the car park and got into the blue Rolls-Royce with the number plate 'Music 14'. We stayed at the Sunset Marquis Hotel in west Hollywood which was and still is a rock'n'roll hangout (nowadays, the hotel even has a recording studio in the basement where everyone from Stevie Wonder to Justin Timberlake have worked).

Our American A&R man, Michael Rosenblatt, invited us to his family home. His father, Eddie, was also a major player in the American music business but he wasn't home. Michael's grandmother lay on her sun-lounger, occasionally peering over her magazine to watch us three excited, pale-skinned, young Englishmen. It was a typical baking hot Californian day and Marc, Stevo and I – all minus sunblock – wasted no time jumping into the huge swimming pool, drinking beers, taking various stimulants and unwittingly getting sunstroke and really bad sunburn in the process. Michael was a great host and the man responsible for convincing his boss, Seymour Stein, to sign an unknown singer called Madonna to Sire Records, alongside LA rockers Mötley Crüe. Sire was a very diverse label with great taste in music aimed at the mainstream US market. Our American label mates also included Talking Heads and The Ramones so we were in excellent company.

The following day we were driven over to Warner Bros. headquarters in Burbank to meet people that were working our record for Sire. Warner's record division was the parent company of Sire, and Warner Chappell Music also published Soft Cell worldwide. We went into one room and were introduced to Crusaders singer Randy Crawford who gave us some of her birthday cake. Then another nice lady who worked in promotion gave me Mötley Crüe's first album and all of Prince's early albums and kept talking about his development deal, correctly predicting how massive he was going to be in the not-too-distant future. The one thing I really noticed about the US company was just how upbeat and positive everybody seemed compared to some of their European counterparts – particularly the English.

We did *Solid Gold* and *The Merv Griffin Show* which went fine – although I could hardly move in my new suit with my really bad sunburn. We had to sit with Merv Griffin for an interview and he looked exactly as I'd imagined – perfect teeth, dazzling white smile and an orange-tanned, world-of-leather in make-up face. He seemed to like Marc, so I didn't have to say a word as Marc nervously chatted away. The rest of the day I stayed in bed to get over my sunstroke. I was really dehydrated and had a dreadful headache but felt fine the following day.

We had lots of free time so we had to make our own entertainment (making sure we were covered in block before going in the sun again). We saw Godley & Creme at our hotel, sitting in the shade by the pool, studiously reading and discussing what I imagine were video treatments. Rather than doing something intelligent like that, Stevo and I took some tabs of 'California sunshine' acid we'd acquired and sat on the other side of the pool, ordering pitchers of tequila sunrise. When the drinks arrived, the stuff was starting to kick in and it all got very silly. Swimming under the influence of LSD was quite a strange experience in itself but it was when we tried to drink our cocktails then smoke cigarettes under water that it got really weird. It's a miracle we both didn't drown or worse, get told off by 5cc (half of 10cc).

On more sensible days, we did all-important promotion which was, after all, the purpose of our visit. One day we'd just finished an al fresco interview in the garden of a restaurant whist sipping a few cocktails. An English gentleman at the next table turned to us and said, 'Pardon me, I couldn't help overhearing your accents, are you in a band?' We told him who we were and he replied, 'Pleased to meet you, my name's John Mayall.'

We got near other celebrities, driving around LA in our Rolls-Royce looking at all the fabulous houses of the rich and famous including Hugh Hefner's *Playboy* mansion. Hugh obviously had very good electronic security because a voice from a concealed speaker in the stone wall outside soon told us to move on unless we had official business. We also visited the usual places like Rodeo Drive, Hollywood Boulevard, Grauman's Chinese Theatre and the Griffith Observatory, mainly because James Dean filmed one of the scenes from the teen angst classic *Rebel Without A Cause* up there. The main thing I remember was the beautiful pink haze over the amazing panorama of Los Angeles, until someone pointed out that it was actually traffic pollution.

A lot of the big stars have beachfront homes in Malibu. Marc, Stevo and I took a stroll along the shore, chatting with the record company guy, and Stevo said he was going to take a dip in the ocean. We carried on walking and temporarily forgot all about him swimming along parallel to us, in his new cream-coloured linen shirt and trousers. There were lots of bikini-clad California girls sunbathing on the beach when Stevo emerged from the ocean, fully clothed and dripping wet. He walked straight towards the girl in front of him and stopped, then in his broadest Cockney accent, politely asked, "Scuse me, is this America?'

'Yes,' the bewildered girl nodded in disbelief as he thanked her and walked off.

★ ★ ★

We flew to New York after the surreal week in LA to do some more recording with Mike Thorne, including a stopgap single. We chose to do a cover version of the 1968 Judy Street song 'What' written by H. B. Barnum and another song that had been big with northern soul fans. At that point, I think the pressure and possibly the lifestyle were starting to get to both of us and Marc and I fell out whilst staying at the Mayflower hotel. When it came to recording, I went into the studio without Marc and recorded the initial backing track, then left while he recorded his vocals. I'd go back alone, record some overdubs and percussion then leave again, so Marc could do his backing vocals. By the end of the week's recording we were speaking again but it was a difficult time. We'd been so successful very quickly, in constant demand and therefore always together – living out of each other's pockets. I don't think any relationship could have endured that pressure so things were occasionally bound to get a little fraught.

Chapter 29
FALLING APART

WHEN 'WHAT' WAS FINISHED, I LEFT NEW YORK. I FLEW back to England on Concorde – three hours and fifteen minutes from JFK to Heathrow – and got the train from London to Leeds. Due to signalling problems, the last part of my journey took over four hours – longer than it took from New York to London.

Once back in Leeds, officially for a few days off, I wrote 'So', the instrumental track on the B- side of 'What'. The Box was a sixteen-track studio in Heckmondwike where I'd previously co-produced Marc & The Mambas' first single, 'Sleaze', and the first Vicious Pink single, 'My Private Tokyo'. 'So' was the only track on which I played the tenor saxophone, basing my attempted freeform style very loosely on that of James White, a.k.a. James Chance, who I had seen in New York.

When Marc returned to London we went back to Carlton Television Facilities in St John's Wood with director Tim Cooper and made a pop art-style video for 'What'. It featured a cameo appearance by 'Neasden's Queen of Soul', Mari Wilson, reclining regally on a chaise longue. The single did well, selling half a million copies and reaching a healthy number three in the UK charts. My old friend Captain Sensible was just ahead of us at number two with his coincidentally named 'Wot'. To this day, I still don't know where he got the idea for that title from or who tipped him off.

Later in the year we started recording our second album, *The Art Of Falling Apart*, again at Mediasound in New York with Mike Thorne at the helm. We weren't getting on too well with Mike, not to mention Phonogram Records. We'd recorded demos for the album at Point Studio in Victoria, including 'Numbers', a song loosely based on a book by John Rechy about casual gay sex. Not surprisingly, the record label weren't totally enamoured with the subject matter, considering it was the beginning of the AIDS epidemic – not exactly conventional marketable pop fodder, I suppose. We desperately wanted to go back to our roots and make a darker, heavier album without thinking about commercial success, but the record company screamed out for more hits.

When the single 'Numbers' was released after we completed the sessions for *The Art Of Falling Apart*, the record company started double-packing it with a free copy of 'Tainted Love' to hype the new record. This so incensed Marc and Stevo that they went straight to Phonogram's offices in New Bond Street and set off fire extinguishers and smashed all the platinum, gold and silver discs that adorned the corridors. They were absolutely furious and rightly so; if I'd been with them, I'm sure I'd have joined in. The record company showed they had no confidence in 'Numbers', which, as expected, wasn't a chart-topper, but we didn't care about that as we were trying to mature as artists. The disc smashing perfectly symbolised our feelings towards the music business at that time and was the inspiration for the video for 'Soul Inside'. The song was about being trapped and trying to escape to freedom, so in our case trapped with a record company and escaping pop stardom that perhaps we couldn't handle. The only problem was, when we made the disc-smashing video, somebody mistakenly picked up an armful of Status Quo's discs, which they weren't too pleased about.

We were feeling quite jaded by the idea of being pop stars; apart from the constant partying, it was bloody hard work keeping up the pretence – answering the same dull questions, over and over in boring interviews and posing for the press and TV cameras. Everything had happened so fast in a way we never intended or even expected and we'd lost control of our situation.

Mike was caught in the middle and tended to side with the record company, which in retrospect made total sense; our success wouldn't last forever and selling hit records was our lifeblood. We never made any money from touring because we didn't play enough gigs – we even turned down being special guests for David Bowie because we didn't think we were good enough. We were at a point in our fledgling careers when we could have really benefitted from having an older, sober and more experienced manager to give us a bit of guidance, maybe even to suggest taking a holiday, but it never happened. I know I certainly felt very lost at that point and needed a break – I'd got into freebasing cocaine (rich people's crack) and had dabbled with crystal meth and ketamine, so I wasn't exactly thinking straight, if at all. I was mostly just reacting to situations.

I had even considered asking Phil Ramone to help us. Over yet another intoxicated evening in a London hotel, Jean-Philippe Iliesco, our sub-publisher, had introduced me to Phil as Billy Joel's producer. He'd just flown in from New York and, being a pop music fan, I was totally enchanted by his producer stories. He'd been in the music business since the sixties and had produced everyone who's anyone: Barbra Streisand, Rod Stewart, Paul McCartney, Burt Bacharach, Elton John, The Carpenters, Frank Sinatra and even John Barry's *On Her Majesty's Secret Service* James Bond score. I wondered to myself if Phil might produce Soft Cell in his famous A&R studios in Manhattan, to give us a more American sound – whatever that was. The next day, nursing a JD-and-coke hangover, it occurred to me that he'd probably replace me with some shit hot session players and just keep Marc. Eventually, I came to my senses and decided to stick with Mike; I liked him and his work but, more to the point, I didn't want to do myself out of a job. I was just frustrated by my ambition to be a producer and wanted more involvement in that side of things. Looking back now, I'm glad we stuck with Mike as I think *The Art Of Falling Apart* was a great album.

I was particularly happy with the bonus twelve-inch featuring the 'Hendrix Medley'. The idea came when Marc and I arrived at JFK. We jumped into our waiting limo, put on the FM radio and picked up a rock station that just happened to be playing 'Purple Haze'. We looked at each other like we'd telepathically had the same thought and, there and then, decided to do our tribute to Jimi. The perverse idea of a synth duo doing covers of the world's greatest ever rock guitarist greatly appealed to our sense of irony – we'd also been dropping quite a lot of window pane acid and mescaline microdots at the time.

Twelve-inch singles were very important to Soft Cell and we always aimed to make the B-side as good as the A-side. As well as 'The Hendrix Medley', *The Art Of Falling Apart* sessions at Mediasound, New York, gave birth to two memorable twelve-inch B-sides, most notably the flipside of 'Numbers'. 'Barriers' is a slow piece of Synclavier II and Prophet 5-based melancholia with lyrics about the fragility of relationships, complete with the mournful, meandering oboe solo. The track on the back of 'Where The Heart Is' is 'It's A Mug's Game', an upbeat dance groove complete with John Gatchell's wailing New York horn solos whilst Marc wryly evokes memories of teenage angst in northern England with one of his funniest Soft Cell lyrics ever.

I'd had my first proper royalty check by then and I splashed out on some new equipment. My prized acquisitions were a Sequential Circuits Prophet 5 Rev. 3 polyphonic synthesiser that cost £3,000 at Rod Argent's keyboard shop in Denmark Street in London. I also purchased an Oberheim DMX drum machine at a shop in Chalk Farm Road that set me back a further £2,000. I put together the first of many electronic racks that included Korg and Ibanez digital delays, a Roland SVC-350 Vocoder, an MXR Pitch Transposer and graphic equaliser and two Fostex multi-track cassette machines at a total cost of £4,000. All in all, quite a nice little techno shopping spree.

I transported the new synth to New York, taking careful precautions with the equipment – which was in a way going all the way back where it came from, as Sequential Circuits was actually made in San Jose, California. I covered my flight case in 'Fragile, Handle With Care' stickers which a baggage handler apparently thought meant 'Throw, Kick And Drop Randomly'. I remember looking out of the window of the JFK arrivals lounge and watching in horror as a musclebound oaf picked up my flight case and casually chucked it to his equally dense-looking colleague, who just stood by smoking as it crashed to the ground. Thank God they weren't air traffic controllers. When we arrived at the studio, my beloved new synth was totally fucked and had a cracked motherboard. After many official complaints to the New York airport authorities, we finally got them to admit negligence and pay up on the insurance.

With much officious bullshit to get through, it took two weeks to get the synth repaired – I got it back halfway through recording the album. In the meantime, we had to hire a Prophet 5 but we could only get a Rev. 1, which was a totally different and, in my opinion, inferior machine. It didn't have anything like the same control surface or any of the presets that I'd spent hours carefully modifying and resaving, not to mention the new sounds I'd programmed specifically for the album. At least we still had the mighty Synclavier and also hired in Linn and Oberheim drum machines, so we had enough new buttons to press. We used the studio's Steinway grand piano, a Mellotron, a Chamberlin M4 and a Celeste. We also had sets of timpani and congas and various other percussion that both Marc and I would bash about on. Plus, I played bass and guitar on a couple of tracks, so it was a little less exclusively synth-based than the first album. It was the first time samples appeared on our records, Mike sampling my bass guitar and television voices with the Synclavier on 'Martin' and the beginning of 'Baby Doll'.

Chapter 30
SOUND AND VISION

A LOT OF OUR FANS WERE WORRIED THAT SOFT CELL WERE about to split because Marc and I had both been working on outside projects. Marc had been doing stuff with The Mambas and also performed two gigs under the name The Immaculate Consumptives with Nick Cave, Lydia Lunch and Jim Foetus in the USA. I spent all my time in various recording studios and produced three albums in a very short period of time.

I did one album for an electronic trio from Nottingham called Sense that came out on French label Carerre, and Virgin Prunes manager Ian Cranna asked me to produce his group's second album, *The Moon Looked Down And Laughed* for Parisian indie label Baby Records. We spent quite a bit of time in Dublin, the band's home town, initially in U2's rehearsal room, getting the songs into shape, before recording the bulk of the album in Windmill Lane Studios with Flood engineering. I also did a couple of gratuitous Fairlight overdubs in a little place called Keystone Studios. We then relocated to Rockfield Studios in north Wales and recorded some additional guitar with Malcolm Ross from Orange Juice before returning to London to mix the album at Trident Studios.

On my days off I was working on my solo album, *In Strict Tempo*, which featured guest vocals by my friends Genesis P. Orridge and

Gavin Friday from the Virgin Prunes. I recruited Marc to design the sleeve and he got Peter Ashworth to take a great photograph of our friend Bee strapped to a timpani while Jhon Balance from Coil beat him. I also worked on the soundtrack of a German film called *Decoder* with a cast that included William Burroughs, Christiane F. and Genesis P. Orridge.

I wrote and recorded a score for the Tennessee Williams play, *Suddenly Last Summer* with my future wife Gini playing violins alongside my synthesisers to create a weird, quasi-orchestral sound. We recorded it in Wessex Studios on Highbury New Park, north London and Thin Lizzy were recording overdubs for an album in the studio next door. I used to occasionally chat with the guitarists, Brian Robertson and Scott Gorham, in the kitchen. When they were bored they'd come and hang out in our studio and check out what we were up to. According to my engineer, John Walls, who'd also worked on the Lizzy sessions, all was not well in the next room as Phil Lynott was constantly nodding out on smack. Apparently, he once dozed off with a lit cigarette between his fingers; when it burned down to his skin, the shock woke him with a jolt and he and his revolving studio chair tipped over backwards and he landed on the floor – not a good look for a rock star.

I wasn't much better; although I never nodded off because I was a manic workaholic, fuelled mostly by amphetamines, cocaine and black coffee, living on a multivitamin pill and a Mars a day – not exactly work, rest and play. I was very underweight and sometimes didn't sleep for five days at a time. With that amount of sleep deprivation I'd usually start hallucinating by day four, so with the aid of a few strong spliffs and a bottle or two of white wine I'd finally crash out and go into a semi-comatose state for about eighteen hours.

All this effort for the score for the play was really a labour of love, as I'd always wanted to write soundtracks. It was also a bit of a tax loss; rather than pay the Inland Revenue more than I needed, I decided to give some of my new-found wealth back to the arts, which was, after all, where I started. I financed the entire project, paying for the venue, recording studio and equipment hire as well as buying materials for costumes and stage sets, not to mention paying everyone's wages. Huw Feather was put in charge of set design and he recruited the stylist Judy Blame to assist – he is sadly no longer with us. Between them, they created a minimal and beautiful stage set from a bunch of fabric that looked incredible under the lights. We got great reviews in *The Times* and *The Guardian* and the show ran at the New End Theatre in Hampstead, London, for two weeks. I went on the last night, as I was too nervous to go to the opening, and was very proud of our efforts. With outside backing, we could have moved the production to a small West End theatre but I didn't have the knowledge about the theatre business to make it happen.

Later that year, I played with Cabaret Voltaire on two tracks, 'Just Fascination' and 'The Crackdown', on their *Crackdown* album, recorded at Trident Studios in Soho. They'd just signed to Some Bizzare, I was a big fan of the band and I liked Mal and Richard, so Stevo asked me if I wanted to play with them. The album reached a very respectable number thirty-one in the UK charts, their highest position. I must point out that I take none of the credit for that – later that year, my solo album was released and didn't even make a dent in the charts, although it did finally sell over 25,000 copies, over a painfully long two years, and eventually got reissued.

On 5 December, Marc hired the Theatre Royal on Drury Lane for a one-off performance of his solo album *Untitled* as Marc & The Mambas. Just before the set finished, I was suddenly told that they had a backing track and a keyboard ready for me and as an encore, just for the fans, we were going to do a surprise version of 'Say Hello, Wave Goodbye'. My instinct was to refuse and leave but I didn't, I just said I'd do it. The Mambas came off to rapturous applause from the capacity audience, then the stamping for more started and the compere announced a special surprise guest – cue mass hysteria. When the two of us walked on stage the screaming sounded like Beatlemania and thank God it did. They weren't joking when they said a 'surprise' version. Not only was the keyboard out of tune but the backing tape was blasting out of the PA system – backwards! Thanks to the deafening crowd noise, no one noticed and we quickly reversed the tape and I just mimed along. A few weeks later, in the much more controlled environment of BBC television studios, we performed Soft Cell's latest single, 'Torch', on *Top Of The Pops'* Christmas special, which was as tacky as ever. I was just relieved that we'd scraped through another crazy year.

After a well-earned seasonal break, we returned to London and recorded a Radio 1 session at their studios in Maida Vale with producer and ex-Mott The Hoople member Dale Griffin. On 13 January 1983, our tracks were broadcast on David 'Kid' Jensen's show. He, Richard Skinner and John Peel were always my favourite Radio 1 DJs. We played 'Soul Inside', 'Her Imagination' and 'Where Was Your Heart (When You Needed It Most)'.

The new material just wasn't as poppy as the first singles and wasn't getting as much radio play as we'd hoped. If I'm totally honest, I don't think my melodies were cutting through or were even good enough and I was playing way too many chords. On the first album I'd mostly played single-note synths with occasional digital pads. The other key element was the drum machine. I had replaced the Roland TR-808 – which had a really zippy, crisp sound – with the Oberheim DMX and LinnDrum Mk 1 and 2, sample-based machines that sounded sluggish and lumpy by comparison. We'd changed because the DMX and the Linns were more fashionable, but I don't want to sound like the proverbial bad workman blaming his tools. When I think about it now, the difference was that an older song like 'Bedsitter' might have fairly bleak lyrics by Marc but the synth toplines and vocal melodies made it a very catchy little pop song. The new songs were a lot darker than anything we'd done before and maybe just too depressing. Some journalists even suggested that we'd lost our pop supremacy to new acts like Culture Club – after all, in 1982, we had been the second-biggest selling chart act in the UK. We were in a strange dilemma because we'd never set out to be a pop group and had become one only by accident. It was becoming too easy for us to get wrapped up in the user-friendly, sanitised world of TV and radio appearances and soundbites. It was time to face our audience and play some live shows.

Mostly to restore our faith in ourselves, we needed some sort of reality check. That check began in a rehearsal room we'd booked at the Nomis Studio complex in Shepherd's Bush, west London. It was once owned by pop impresario Simon Napier-Bell, who had managed Wham! and co-wrote the lyrics for Dusty Springfield's hit 'You Don't Have To Say You Love Me' with Marc's US manager, Vicki Wickham. Loads of big acts used to rehearse at Nomis – when I set up our minimal equipment in one of the more modest rooms it was sandwiched between Status Quo and Motörhead. I couldn't fault the quality and efficiency of the soundproofing of the studio walls but once in the corridor, I could immediately tell the doors weren't one hundred per cent effective as baffles. When both bands were thrashing away it was how I imagine the sound would be if you stuck your head inside a jet engine on take-off. Not just earsplitting but brain-crushing.

We recruited four of the Mambas/Venomettes as backing vocalists: Martin McCarrick, Billy McGee, Anne Stephenson and Gini Hewes, with Gary Barnacle on saxophone. We also had occasional guest vocal duets with Jim Thirwell, a.k.a. Foetus. Marc wanted to play 'mammoth tremolo arm-blitz' feedback guitar during the wilder sections of our shows and one day turned up with a second-hand Watkins Rapier 44 guitar which, as the name implies, had four pick-ups. It was an original 1960s model; it looked fantastic (and sounded horrible, but that didn't really matter). I think the most important technical detail for Marc was that it was red. Motörhead frontman Lemmy popped his head in to say 'Hello' and when he saw the new guitar he genuflected like he'd just seen the anti-Christ and made a cross sign with his fingers – it appeared that Marc had unleashed a Monster of Rock.

On 7 and 8 March 1983, we played two sold-out, three thousand-capacity shows at Hammersmith Palais followed by a few nights dotted around the UK. The set was divided into two fifty-minute sections; the first half lighter and poppier (although we still refused to play 'Tainted Love') and the second half darker. The interval enabled us to change clothes and freshen up. I'd chain-smoke, have a few lines of coke and large JDs on the rocks while the spools on the four Revox backing tape machines were swapped and the stage sets and lighting effects were readjusted.

It was a different story off stage. While we considered every miniscule detail when it came to the presentation of our performance, we never had a properly thought-out strategy to the business side of touring. It was yet another example of managerial weakness and general lack of financial acumen. It actually cost us money to play as we never played enough consecutive dates to break even and the merchandising was shambolic.

Chapter 31
DIVA ESPAÑA

FOLLOWING OUR SHORT RUN OF UK DATES IN 1983, FOR some inexplicable reason, we did a one-off gig in Brussels, then embarked on a mini-tour of Spain. I've always had my suspicions about the Spanish tour; I think it was partly a working holiday and also a chance for Marc to soak up the Latino vibes and work on ideas for his next Mambas album, *Torment And Toreros*.

I got off to a bad start at Heathrow. We had a guy called Mike working for us as a tour manager. He was always way too eager to please and had that kind of overpowering enthusiasm that made me never trust him. The first helpful thing he did was inadvertently check in not only my suitcase but also my hand luggage containing my passport, my wallet and, most importantly, my cigarettes. I had to go through all sorts of bullshit and sign loads of forms to prove I wasn't an illegal immigrant or an international terrorist just to get through customs and board the plane without a passport to hand. The journey itself was full of other surprises, not least when a member of our team and his girlfriend disappeared together to the toilet to join the mile-high club. They got quite a surprise when they unlocked the door and a Spanish nun was waiting to use the loo. When they got back to their seats, giggling like two naughty school kids, I noticed the girlfriend had a dark curly pubic hair stuck between her front teeth.

After our first date in Madrid we were booked to play a few shows in San Sebastián, Malaga, Valencia, Alicante and Barcelona. For whatever reason, we were very popular – in fact 'Bedsitter' had done even better than 'Tainted Love' in Spain. All the shows were sold out, with average crowds of between one-and-a-half to three thousand. The electricity supply proved to be a problem for us, particularly as some of the venues were outdoor and we were reliant on knackered old diesel generators which could cause the electrical current to fluctuate. That often resulted in our equipment (my synthesisers in particular) randomly switching on and off during the gig – not very amusing.

The venue in Alicante was normally used as a bullfighting ring and the stage was unsafe – it apparently consisted of vats of bull's blood covered by a makeshift floor made of big chipboard panels that might or might not take the combined weight of us and our equipment. I had visions of it collapsing during the gig, Marc in the spotlight, drenched in blood, like in *Carrie*. As far as we were concerned, that was that, the gig was cancelled and we all piled down to one of the quayside bars for a nice drink and a day off. It turned into a classic case of too much sun, sea and sangria. Marc had his Super 8 camera and Stevo's girlfriend kept flashing her minge under the table while he was filming, much to our amusement and the disgust of the holidaymaking families in the bar.

Eventually, we were asked to leave by the management, who were threatening to call the police if we refused. The next thing was we got a message from Marion, our assistant, to say that the promoters, a bunch of Spanish gangsters, were holding our tour manager at knifepoint. They were demanding that we go to the venue immediately... or else! We had to rouse Marc and drive to the venue and try and appease them. They were making all sorts of wild threats – if we didn't do the gig they would smash up all our equipment or cut our throats or shoot us. Then they went back on that and said they would simply have us arrested for breach of contract. We were locked in a dressing room and some menacing blokes with iron bars stood guard. I was half-expecting Tony Montana to walk into the room at any minute. They were very unpredictable, totally coked off their brains, so we just kept schtum. A deal was eventually brokered and we were released unharmed in return for a suitcase of cash (£9,000) which seemed to have done the trick.

We still had to get out of the venue in one piece as there were two thousand angry young Spaniards outside, whose night had just been ruined, rightly demanding their money back. We had to get in the back of a big van and lie on the floor while fans jumped on the roof and others kicked the van from every angle and threw bottles and stones. As soon as there was no one in front of us, our driver hit the accelerator and we were out of there like a shot. On our return to England, we reported the incident to the Spanish embassy and received an official apology for our mistreatment.

★ ★ ★

A few months after the tour, I got the news in the Some Bizzare office that one of my Manhattanite friends, Klaus Nomi, had died of an AIDS-related illness on 6 August 1983. I think he was the first person I knew to be struck down by that terrible disease. I first met him in New York about eighteen months earlier. He'd relocated from his native Germany some years earlier and got involved in the East Village art scene, subsidising his musical ambitions by working as a pastry chef. I remember one typically humid summer night on the rooftop of Danceteria, drinking ice-cold margaritas with him. 'I fucking hate that company!' he exclaimed, as he pointed to the big orange neon sign on top of the RCA building. He wasn't happy with the way they were marketing his records. In fairness to them, it has to be said that he was unique, which possibly explains why label mate David Bowie adopted his triangular dress style on a US performance that featured Klaus on *Saturday Night Live*.

I once took Klaus to CBGB. Apart from all the brilliant bands that played there, it was also famous for having possibly the most disgusting toilets in New York City. Let's just say you wouldn't even want to have a shit in there, never mind snort a line. Alan Vega of Suicide was playing a solo show and as I knew him I introduced Klaus backstage before the show, which was sort of mutant rockabilly. I loved it but I looked over at Klaus and he seemed totally ill at ease in that dirty, dark, punk club, although he was probably the weirdest-looking person in the place.

★ ★ ★

In 1983, after falling out with the record company and the music business in general, the amount of chaos in our private and public lives (some self-inflicted, some caused by the negative influence of outsiders) all got too much. Marc and I decided to disband Soft Cell amicably after recording our third album, self-produced in London where there were fewer outside temptations than in New York. We worked in Trident and Wessex studios but mostly in Pink Floyd's Britannia Row Studios in Islington, north London. To me *This Last Night In Sodom* was the sound of two people who'd taken too much of everything and lost control.

I was still consuming vast quantities of speed and coke but I just immersed myself in the music. I had my usual array of synths and the studio's erratic Hammond B3 organ and Leslie cabinet at my disposal as well as my new toy, a PPG Wave 2.2 analogue/digital wavetable synthesiser made by Palm Productions of Germany. It was designed by Wolfgang Palm, who also built customised equipment for Tangerine Dream and Klaus Schulze, and with a price tag of £4,000 it was more than the Prophet 5.

Apart from being very excited about recording with my new synthesiser, knowing the album was to be our last added a hell of a lot of passion. It was a time of very confused and powerful mixed feelings, not least because my pregnant girlfriend, Gini, was singing backing vocals. I think the intensity really comes across on the recording which, though not technically perfect, is raw, heartfelt and brutally honest.

Once we'd finished, we went out to play to more than six thousand people over two sold-out farewell shows at Hammersmith Palais. Those, too, were very emotional and I think most of the audience were in tears. I'd snorted so much coke that I couldn't even feel my face, never mind any emotions. Both gigs were total triumphs and I can still remember the PA's bass bins vibrating as I cranked up bottom C on my Prophet 5 synth on the final chord of the last number until the whole building shook to 'Say Hello, Wave Goodbye' – the perfect send-off if ever there was one.

The Sun newspaper kept phoning the Some Bizzare offices. They didn't want to ask anything about the band but just to find out if the rumour that I was about to get married to Gini was true – and was she pregnant? Jane Rolink, the only sane person in the office at that time, managed to put them off the scent, although they did print two photos of us individually that looked more like the Moors murderers than a happy couple. The rumours turned out to be true: on 26 November, I did 'the decent thing' and married a heavily pregnant Gini at Marylebone registry office. We had no big ceremony because we didn't want lurid pictures in the tabloids. The only guest was Linda Rowell, a photographer friend who was doubling up as a witness. The officials said that we needed two witnesses so we had to ask the window cleaner to do the honours. We went to a bistro in Marylebone High Street for a nice lunch with champagne and had a party for two, then went home to sleep.

On 28 January 1984, our son James was born at Middlesex Hospital. I was very confused by the idea of being a father and not being in a band; big-time culture shock.

My life was being affected by seismic changes. *This Last Night In Sodom* was released in March and surprisingly reached number twelve in the UK charts. We released one last single; a cover version of Jack Hammer's aptly named 'Down In The Subway', which reached number twenty-four in the UK. The video was shown on *Top Of The Pops* but we didn't appear live on the show, although we did perform the song on Mike Mansfield's *Supersonic*. I watched us on TV and realised I was now an unemployed musician, recently married and a father of one. In some ways it felt great – not being involved in the chaotic world of pop music any longer – but the change was to prove too dramatic and at 24 I was way too young and irresponsible to settle down.

We lived in a nice little one bedroom flat at 12 Bulstrode Street in Marylebone, London, for years, while I played at being the devoted, loving husband and father. My main problem, apart from boredom, was my addiction to cocaine and amphetamines and increasingly, alcohol. When I tried to keep off the whizz and charlie I'd substitute spliffs for cigarettes, just to keep myself sedated. I smoked about twenty joints a day at one point and kept myself hydrated with bottles of dry white wine and Holsten Pils. I was basically substituting one cliched addiction for another – the story of my life.

.

PART 3

Chapter 32
WILDERNESS YEARS
1984–88

I AMICABLY PARTED COMPANY WITH MY MANAGER STEVO and his record label as I felt there could have been a conflict. Marc remained with him for a few more years and I put my musical ambitions on hold for a while until I got the urge to do some more recording.

I put together a little studio band called Other People with my then wife Gini and guitarist Andy Astle, a friend I knew from Leeds Poly. It came about totally by accident through a drummer friend of mine, Nick Sanderson, who at that time was playing with the Sheffield band Clock DVA. He introduced me to his manager, Terry McLellan, a part-time market gardener based in Tufnell Park.

Nick was interested in me producing Clock DVA whereas Terry had other ideas and wanted me to think about working with one of his other artists, Howard Devoto, founder member of Buzzcocks and Magazine. I was a fan of both bands and was intrigued by the idea. I met Howard one evening in the local pub in north London and we had a nice chat but at that time he didn't seem too interested in music and was more into books. I think he was actually working as a librarian or an archivist at the time, so nothing came of it.

Terry did release one insignificant single by my band, 'Have A Nice Day', with 'Another Day, Another Dollar' on the B-side and I produced two singles for another of his acts, Jih, a Scottish singer-songwriter. Yet again, I don't think anyone noticed and the records disappeared without a trace. The last time I saw the young wannabe singer, we were chasing the dragon together in his flat in Fulham Road – probably not a great career move for either of us. I stopped doing that shit just in time, before it got a real hold on me and I hope he did the same.

One of my only other contacts with the music business at that time was Genesis P. Orridge, to whom I introduced Terry. In fact, I think Gen suggested the label name Arcadia (which unfortunately was also the name of Simon Le Bon's new band project at the time). I frequently visited Gen at his house in Beck Road, Hackney, where he kept the Throbbing Gristle archives and his vast collection of camouflage uniforms. Also there was a strange little room called The Nursery that I don't think was intended for children. He and I had become close friends and as Gini and I were also parents and musicians we had quite a lot in common with Gen and his wife Paula. They had two daughters, Caresse and Genesse and a dog, Tanith. Our families would often have a veggie Sunday roast together and when they moved to Stamford Hill we kept in touch. That was quite strange, Gen living with his wife, daughters, Tanith the dog (who was by then stuffed) and a pet python in an area that was mostly populated by Hasidic Jews – he didn't half get some funny looks in his gold Doc Marten boots.

I once introduced Gen to my little old mum when she visited from Blackpool and she asked quite matter-of-factly, 'So, Genesis, why are you wearing gold bovver boots?' It was the only time I've ever seen Gen lost for words.

I already knew that my mum couldn't be fazed. One day she was taking Bosley, her beloved little black American cocker spaniel, for his daily walk on Marton Mere in Blackpool and this young flasher showed her his tiny erection. Mum just said, 'You need help, here's a number, call them.' She later got a thank-you letter from the wannabe sex offender, via the Citizen's Advice Bureau where she worked, thanking her profusely for helping to cure him. My mum was a star.

I was invited by Genesis to DJM Studios in Theobalds Road, Holborn to hear what he was up to with Psychic TV (PTV) bandmates Alex Ferguson and Paul Reeson. I think he just wanted an outside opinion and possibly a bit of keyboard dabbling. They were working on a project called *Thee Starlit Mire*; funnily enough, that's probably where my head was at the time. The title was inspired by Austin Osman Spare, an artist and occultist from Lambeth, south London. I know Gen had at least two of his beautiful paintings and I bought one at the London Art Fair in the Royal College of Art when a dealer friend of mine had one for sale.

The studio was the home of Dick James Music, who'd made millions from the early works of Elton John. The place was opulent, solid marble everywhere. It had previously, and somewhat appropriately, been a bank and the studio was in what used to be the vault, although it felt more like a dungeon, particularly when there was an internal power failure and we were trapped for about half an hour with just emergency lighting. There was no way out because the lift wasn't working. We all got really claustrophobic and the minute the power came back on we were out of there like a shot, heading to the relative safety of the Yorkshire Grey pub for beers and several large glasses of Scotch.

I was a sort of honorary member of PTV and Gen and I collaborated occasionally on various projects, including scoring an arthouse film for Derek Jarman. He came over to DJM studios, read some notes and talked us through live improvisation. We recorded everything and, within a couple of hours, Derek happily left the studio with an improvised Ball and P. Orridge soundtrack. He'd shot some handheld Super 8 footage in Moscow and St Petersburg that became his short film *Imagining October*. We met him again a few weeks later in George Martin's AIR Studios above what is now Nike Town, overlooking Oxford Circus. He was filming a guy dressed as a Russian soldier having his portrait painted and wanted to incorporate the sound of the paintbrush on canvas into our soundtrack.

The completed film was screened at the ICA and played at various international film festivals. As Derek had no budget to speak of, he offered us each one of his small, black and gold, diamante paintings in lieu of payment. Normally, they sold for about £400 each but that was irrelevant, I was more than happy to have a piece of his art. We were invited to his flat opposite Foyles bookshop in Charing Cross Road to choose one. I must say, the flat might as well have had a turnstile instead of a door. The number of gay skinheads and Nick Kamen lookalikes coming and going was unbelievable. Unfortunately, Derek was to be the second person I knew to die of an AIDS-related illness.

Psychic TV had a Christmas show coming up and Gen asked me to play synth for him alongside Icelandic keyboard player and occultist Hilmar Örn Hilmarsson. I was really excited when he invited me to rehearse in Martello Street, Hackney, the site of the original Throbbing Gristle studio or the Death Factory, so named because it was built on the site of a plague pit. Gen was very keen to demonstrate his bass guitar going through his Gristleizer box, designed by bandmate Chris Carter. It produced an instant Throbbing Gristle sound. He handed me the bass and said, 'Have a go.' It was totally out of tune so I asked him if I should retune it for him. 'Yeah, that would be nice,' he said. 'It hasn't been tuned since I bought it about ten years ago.'

I played synth for Psychic TV at a sell-out show at Heaven in Charing Cross on 23 December and we had a real problem with the safety inspector from the London fire department. After watching our crew set up the lighting rig and PA system and the band perform a forty-five-minute soundcheck, Inspector Jobsworth, clipboard in hand, smugly informed us that we needed to move the huge speakers and lights by a foot each side. We had to comply as he had the authority to close down the venue.

The set that night was completely different to the rehearsal. I didn't know any of the songs and just made it up as I went along. No one seemed to notice, no one heckled (or laughed, which would have been worse) and the venue didn't catch fire. All said and done, we got off pretty lightly and suddenly Christmas 1984 was upon us.

I'd been writing loads of stuff and recording demos in my home studio with Gini on vocals. We had about an album's worth of material but I was at a loss what to do with it. She had a long-term working relationship with producer Mike Hedges and over the years worked with many of his artists, including The Cure, Siouxsie & The Banshees and Marc on his solo stuff. Gini played our stuff to him and he very generously said he had a free month and studio time in Bavaria in September. All we had to do was pay for everyone's flights to Munich – Great deal, I thought. Tonstudio Hilpoltstein was a small annex of a much bigger, state-of-the-art studio called Hartmann Digital close to Nuremburg, in the Black Forest. Hilpoltstein was a beautiful medieval German village surrounded by farms and little breweries in Bavaria. The state was completely idyllic except for having been the birthplace of National Socialism. We'd often see armed American troops in camouflage, hiding in rose gardens as part of NATO peacekeeping exercises in the area. One evening we were in the studio and suddenly the whole building started shaking like an earthquake. We ran to the door that opened onto the old cobbled street outside to see what was going on. About a foot in front of us a huge convoy of American tanks rumbled past, destroying the medieval road surface. It came as no surprise that the locals despised the Yankee troops and used to play 'chicken' with them, driving full speed straight at their Jeeps.

The sessions went well enough, although the marital and parental side of things proved to be a bit of a challenge. We had a huge row when I accepted Mike's invitation to Oktoberfest. Gini didn't want to go even though it was for just one night and a four-star hotel room was included. I explained that it was a totally family-orientated event and not just a huge piss-up but she was having none of it, so I went anyway as I needed a break. I was starting to realise that having a baby around was not just all-consuming, it sometimes made trying to work impossible. We'd be in the middle of recording a vocal and the baby alarm would go off and the session would grind to yet another halt – it was very frustrating to say the least. I could deal with singers having tantrums but not screaming babies.

Most of the time the experience of working in Germany was great and I got to meet some interesting people. One of my favourite German bands, DAF, were recording in the big studio and Mike suggested we go and say 'hello'. We ended up having dinner and a few drinks with them. Singer Gabi Delgado also came down to our studio to hear what we were up to. He said he was bored because they were having big problems with the Oberheim sequencer they were using on their new album. Apparently, it sounded really sluggish and his colleague Robert Görl was trying to fix it. I suggested they should go back to the triggered monosynth they'd used with producer Conny Plank on tracks like 'Der Mussolini'. Rusty Egan once introduced me to Conny at Trident Studios when he was in London working with Ultravox. He was an avuncular German hippy and announced that he needed to get some cannabis as it made him 'feel like a woman'. I gave him a knowing look as we were in Soho, then felt stupid when I realised what he meant. He was talking about being in touch with his feminine side – not at all what I had in mind.

Another familiar face I met in Bavaria was my old friend Steve Strange. I hadn't seen him for about three years, when we'd spent a night with my German girlfriend, Martina, doing coke and watching videos at his rich baroness friend's house in Chelsea. Visage had split up and he was now working with his new band Strange Cruise, although all he talked about was Freddie Mercury's 40th birthday party in Munich. He said it was amazing – dishes of cocaine everywhere and whatever else you wanted readily available. I'd only met Freddie the once and I didn't imagine he was a man who skimped on any of life's pleasures. I must admit, I did feel a pang of jealousy – the thought of all that free coke.

The recordings were finished and sounded OK but not outstanding. Once back in London, the free studio time suddenly turned out not to be free and the Bavarian studio owner tried to charge me. I said I wasn't paying and he refused to hand over the masters. I was thoroughly depressed – the recording had been a complete waste of time. But that was where we left it: somewhere out there in the Black Forest is an unreleased Dave & Gini Ball album, produced by Mike Hedges.

There was better business news the following year, when Ronnie Harris, my accountant, said we should audit Phonogram Records. I'd never really understood the concept of auditing. I couldn't believe it when I got a rather large cheque for unaccounted royalties.

Talking of business and art, on 22 February 1987 I heard the news that one of my heroes, Andy Warhol, had died during a routine operation in a hospital in New York. Someone immediately quipped, 'You've met him – how could they tell he was dead?'

★ ★ ★

I came out of a year-long depression after the failed recordings and formed yet another ill-fated band. English Boy On The Loveranch featured Martin Fry's younger brother Jim on vocals, Nick Sanderson on drums and me on synth. Nick was quite in-demand and was also playing for The Gun Club and The Jesus & Mary Chain. We released our first single, 'The Man In Your Life', on Parisian label New Rose. I persuaded my old friend and soon-to-be mega-producer, Flood, to do some mixes and they sounded great, as I knew they would. The track was very electro/hi-energy and the San Francisco-based label, Razormaid, did a great US club remix. It featured on one of their DJ-only mix EPs which also had tracks by Depeche Mode and The Eurythmics, so we were in very good company.

The band rehearsed once a week and we did a few gigs, one at a seedy little disco on Oxford Street where promoter Sean McCluskey hosted the Wrong Club and another one at a dodgy music pub in Brighton. The most memorable moment of that gig was when the backing tape slowed down then sped up in the middle of one song, yet our drummer managed to keep time and it sounded intentional. The real highlight of our brief career was on 30 September, when we played at an all-day festival called the Fabulous Feast of Flowering Light at the Hackney Empire in Mare Street. The event was organised by Genesis P. Orridge and Psychic TV headlined. We were on after New York feminist writer Kathy Acker read one of her monologues. While she was on, I was silently programming my synthesiser in the background as we were on next and didn't have time for a soundcheck. When she'd finished, she stomped over and punched me in the shoulder. I asked her why she did it and she claimed I was distracting her audience, to which I replied, 'Oh, sorry for keeping them awake.'

Around that time, I'd also been collaborating on an Anglo-Icelandic project with Rose McDowall from Strawberry Switchblade, Hilmar Örn Hilmarsson from PTV and Einar Örn Benediktsson, one-time member of The Sugarcubes. We went under the collective name Ornamental and released a twelve-inch single, 'No Pain', on the Icelandic label Gramm Records. I did another one-off with Gen called 'Papal Bull', an electro backing track with various vocal samples from American Catholic ceremonies spun in. We recorded that with producer Ken Thomas at Jacob's Studio on a Mitsubishi thirty-two-track digital machine because Gen had blagged some free time. Even though none of those records were obvious chart-toppers, they were great fun to make.

My only chart entry at all that year was Soft Cell's *The Singles*, which only reached a disappointing number fifty-eight – I was feeling very depressed again. I was also feeling the huge burden of responsibility that is fatherhood and not dealing with it very well emotionally. Our son James was by then a toddler and Gini gave birth to our daughter, Victoria, on 10 September 1987. In preparation, we'd moved into a three-bedroom flat I'd bought in Carlton Hill, St John's Wood. It was just off Abbey Road, a tantalising five-minute walk from the renowned EMI studio and the zebra crossing made famous by The Beatles. I freely admit I've always been a bit of a fame-obsessed fan and one of the reasons I love living in London is it's great for star-spotting – it's really just a glamorous version of people-watching. I don't take photos or ask for autographs but I still get a twinge of excitement whenever I see a star or a celebrity.

My top star-spotting moments were seeing Terence Stamp three separate times in one day (I promise, I wasn't stalking) and Michael Jackson, en route from Madame Tussauds in Marylebone Road, getting out of his stretch limo and going into Blunderbuss, a military antique shop at the end of my street, to buy some authentic army tunics. The shop isn't there any more but the Hellenic Restaurant on the corner is and the owner still talks about how surprised he was the morning Jacko popped his head round the door one day and asked to use the bathroom.

One of my many drinking buddies in Marylebone was the record producer and co-writer of all Gary Glitter's hits Mike Leander. He lived on the High Street and he and I would occasionally get pissed together in what was then the Prince Alfred and is now another victim of gastropubitis. Our evenings would invariably end up with me asking him how he got the Glitter Band sound – which I'd always loved as it was truly unique. He once explained it, after much alcoholic coercion, but I've never felt the need to replicate it.

I kept my one-bedroom flat in Marylebone and Ronnie Harris suggested I rent it out, especially as there was now another hungry mouth to feed. My first tenant was a graphic designer from New York, followed by an elderly American jazz musician by the name of Bulee 'Slim' Gaillard. He was a very dapper, tall black gentleman with a white beret and beard and was a regular performer at Ronnie Scott's jazz club. I first came across Slim on a TV documentary, when he was talking about vout speak, a kind of jive talk, jazz lingo that he'd invented. I don't know if he ever got paid royalties but he did originate phrases that became very famous song titles, most notably 'Tutti Frutti' and 'Reet Petite' – sung by Little Richard and Jackie Wilson respectively.

Shortly after vacating my flat, Slim passed away and everything of his was taken away, apart from various letters that I took the liberty of opening. They were all from a debt collection agency, full of the usual threats. I took great delight in phoning them and a rude woman with a sarf London accent answered. I gave her his name and address and before she could say another word about 'repossession' I casually mentioned that he had died and it might be difficult for them to recover anything as he was being buried in the USA. It seemed so wrong that someone so inarticulate should be pursuing a man who had been so eloquent. I'm glad to say, I never heard from the debt collectors again.

Chapter 33

A NEW DIRECTION

IN 1988, MY BAND ENGLISH BOY ON THE LOVERANCH released follow-up single 'Sex Vigilante', again on the Parisian label New Rose, and like our previous release, it sank without a trace, effectively signalling the end of the band and of my wilderness years.

The two other members, Nick Sanderson and Jim Fry, would go on to form World Of Twist and then Earl Brutus – both bands I produced. I briefly found myself once again at a musical loose end until I got a phone call from my old friend and collaborator Genesis P. Orridge. He'd met Richard Norris, who worked for reissue label Bam Caruso and also wrote freelance for the *NME*. They chatted about a new genre, acid house. No one really knew what it was because nobody had heard an acid house record. They were both into acid rock and psychedelia and assumed it must be connected and decided to do their version of what they thought it should be.

Gen and Richard trawled through psych and spoken-word records for freaky soundbites and noises and reassembled it all using the latest technology – samplers, sequencers, drum machines and Atari games computers running basic Steinberg Cubase software. This was pre-audio and VST (virtual studio technology) software and was then only capable of controlling midi sequencing and mix automation. Derek, an electronic music equipment salesman, had a little studio called Time Square in the basement of his house in Chiswick, west London, with two young engineers, Richard Schiessl (a relative of the Schweppes drinks family) and Richard Evans. I was among various guest musicians called in. As luck would have it, I'd recently invested in midi technology for the first time, including a Casio FZ-1 sampling keyboard that I'd expanded from 1 mb – megabyte – to a (still unbelievably small) 2 mb of monophonic memory. That machine used Sony 3.5-inch HD floppy discs which cost £60 for ten discs – by contrast, today I've got a SanDisk Cruzer Edge 128 gb (gigabyte) memory stick in my wallet which cost me just £25. I'd also purchased an Alesis MMT-8 eight-track sequencer and the complementary HR-16 drum machine. They were both made in California, as proved whenever the little yellow LED screen would flash up in irritating geek-speak, 'Bummer dude, memory full!'

The session itself was quite fraught, with small children and dogs running around everywhere – like a bunch of new age travellers had taken over the studio. It reminded me of the sessions many years earlier when Flood was recording the acts for The Batcave album (*Batcave: Young Limbs And Numb Hymns*) at Trident Studios, although that was more of a goth production line and there were no dogs, just lots of vampiric people dressed in black with strange hair and make-up.

Gen repeatedly urged me to use only an hour to record each of three tracks with various collaborators but I managed it in five hours. They appeared under band names used for the occasion – 'Only Human' by Nobody Uninc, 'Balkan Red Alert' by Alligator Shear and 'Meet Every Situation Head On' by M.E.S.H. The last track was my first joint effort with Richard Norris and I think the single even got into the indie charts. The finished album was released under the name *Jack The Tab – Acid Tablets Volume One* on Richard and Gen's label, Castalia Recordings, and though not a huge commercial success, it did attract the attention of hip DJ/producers like Andrew Weatherall. I had a feeling that my work with Richard Norris would soon be continued.

I booked some time for myself in Time Square Studio and spent a few days a week trying to get some ideas together for a solo project. An Indian guy called Harry also frequented the studio and he had an independent label specialising in the up-and-coming bhangra scene. He asked me to record a techno track with Nusrat Fateh Ali Khan & Party. I thought it was a weird choice. Nusrat turned up with a huge book of handwritten qawwali (sufi music) lyrics and sat in the far side of the control room while his band set up the harmoniums, tabla and dholaks in the recording booth. They were amazing players who practised eight hours a day as a spiritual activity. The singer and band were all deeply religious although the same could not be said of one of their team. He invited me upstairs for a cigarette and a chat and, to my great surprise, pulled out a half bottle of cognac from his pocket, took a big swig, then offered me some. Then he pulled a little pill box out of his pocket full of tiny packages called paan, put one in his mouth and pushed it into his cheek. I did the same as he explained that it was held in the cheek and swallowed. He said that betel juice produced a psychoactive stimulant when it reacted with your saliva. It tasted of perfume and he explained that was to mask the bitter taste of the opium. It was crazy; there I was, smoking cigarettes, drinking brandy, getting stoned on opium, about to record with a group of devout Muslims. Thankfully, they didn't realise and the recording never got released.

Another Asian music biz associate, Amrik Rai, had managed Cabaret Voltaire and various British dance acts. He put me together with two vocalists, Mal from the Cabs (I'd guested on their *Crackdown* album) and Ruth Joy from Krush, who'd recently had a Top 3 record with 'House Arrest'. We decided to record a version of the War electro-funk classic 'Galaxy' for Parlophone Records. As producer, I booked a three-piece horn section led by trumpet maestro Guy Barker and I hired ex-Amen Corner keyboardist Blue

Weaver to program the Fairlight III. It was a very strong line-up, but not strong enough to make a hit record. Parlophone even gave us a video budget for the single which was meant to be all summery and light. A stylist was duly hired. Ever since my early days of filming Soft Cell videos, I've always been deeply suspicious of stylists and this time was no different. My outfit was a really cool, red bomber jacket. Great, I thought initially, but then she wanted me to wear shorts and that was it. 'No way am I wearing shorts in a video. I don't even wear them in summer. If this record has legs, they're not gonna be mine.' (I did wear the red bomber jacket but insisted on wearing black jeans.)

The single was eventually released with mixes by Robert Gordon from Sheffield's Fon studios. The mixes were great, particularly the B-sides, which were basically Robert doing his own thing, but the idea of half of Cabaret Voltaire and half of Soft Cell cavorting around in beachwear with a white girl singer with dreadlocks was never gonna be a winner and the record duly bombed.

I also did a promotional record for *Prisoner Of Rio*, a film about Great Train Robber and occasional Sex Pistols singer Ronnie Biggs. The deal was unusual, not least because the vocalist was still on the UK's most-wanted list and also because the film people who asked me to do the track didn't have a clue about how to record or release a record. As luck would have it, my friend Lawrence Brennan owned a label based in São Paulo called Stiletto Records. They were the biggest indie label in Brazil as they licensed all the top UK indie labels including Mute and Factory. Their amazing roster of acts included Depeche Mode, New Order, Nick Cave, and Erasure and they had them all exclusively for Latin America, so Lawrence was pretty savvy when it came to indie record deals. He suggested we set up our own label for the project and we formed Pink Flamingo Records.

The film company paid for the recording, artwork, manufacture and distribution of the record and we got all the sales. The profits worked out at quite a few thousand pounds, but it was just a promotional exercise for the movie people. We set up a company bank account, Lawrence and I were joint signatories and we had quite a healthy balance for a newly formed indie label that only released one single. But without warning, Lawrence died of a heart attack or stroke and that was the end of Pink Flamingo Records. I couldn't even get the money out of the bank to give to his grieving widow because I wasn't allowed to sign cheques on my own, so the treasury got the lot. I seemed to be having a run of dreadful luck. Something had to change and, fortunately, it did.

Chapter 34

THE GRID

I HAD A GOOD VIBE WORKING WITH RICHARD NORRIS ON the *Jack The Tab* album and later that year he and I formed The Grid, the name suggested by his old friend Martin Callomon. Cally had just got a job in A&R and offered us a deal on the newly formed East West label, a subsidiary of Warner Bros.

We visited the label's swish office building in The Electric Lighting Station off Kensington High Street to sign the contracts and, after a spot of free lunch, were told we had carte blanche to do what we wanted as long as it fitted into the contemporary club genre. We were delighted as we were both really into a lot of the new stuff coming up through the clubs. Originally Gen was going to be in The Grid and I was signed as the producer but it soon became clear that Richard and I were a duo and Gen viewed the idea of working with a major label as a match made in corporate hell.

Initially we recorded a track called 'Islamatron' with engineer Martin Rex at Terminal 24 Studios in Amelia Street in south-east London for an East West compilation album called *Vaultage From The Electric Lighting Station – Winter 1988/89*. It was a sampler of new electronic dance acts. In early 1989 we released two promo twelve-inches to try and create a buzz in the clubs. The first, 'On The Grid', was a cover version of a track by American hi-NRG act Lime and we also recorded an original track called 'Intergalactica'. We recorded everything at Terminal 24, including a bizarre rendition of The Edwin Hawkins Singers' gospel hit, 'Oh Happy Day' and an electro version of U2's 'Where The Streets Have No Name', long before the Pet Shop Boys segued it with the Andy Williams/Boys Town Gang classic 'Can't Take My Eyes Off You'. Another strange track from that time that never made it to vinyl was the self-penned 'The Man With Everything', which contains one of my all-time favourite Grid lyrics, as performed by an Atari computer: 'Disco pimp – do you wanna hustle?' That was recorded at Fon Studios in Sheffield with a slightly bemused Robert Gordon producing.

By January 1990 we'd grown tired of Terminal 24 and relocated to Pacific Studios in Kingsland Road, east London. Hoxton wasn't quite the trendy place it is now and the only famous people I regularly spotted there back in those days were the artists Gilbert & George, who lived locally. There were no bearded hipsters or Vietnamese restaurants as yet, just a nice American-style bar and grill place next door called The Ringside. It was owned and run by a retired boxer called Vic Andretti, who, like a lot of East End pugilists, was a one-time friend of the Kray twins. He had old black-and-white photos of himself fighting in the ring with Ron and Reg sat ringside, looking on.

There were also lots of striptease pubs, the most famous called Browns, which used to get full of city boys. Nearby there was a wonderfully named curtain shop, Peter the Pleater, and loads of Asian wholesale shops selling either children's or ladies' underwear or shoes. The studio was in the basement of a shoe shop until it had its insurance fire. Thankfully, the arsonist was clever enough not to let the fire spread downstairs.

Despite being underground I never felt claustrophobic; quite the opposite, in fact. The studio had a decent-sized control room with a huge DDA desk and a very spacious live room, complete with a grand piano and a vocal booth. It was run by a guy from Hastings called Nick Hopkins, who'd previously been in the RAF. He hadn't been a fighter pilot, but rather I think he was involved in the communications division as he was very technically proficient. He engineered our first ever Grid remixes, 'Frontera Del Ensueno' by Rey De Copas for Pete Lawrence at Cooking Vinyl Records, and for Creation Records, 'Hairstyle Of The Devil' by Momus plus a quirky cover of New Order's 'Blue Monday' by Ed Ball's band, The Times, called 'Lundi Bleu'. Richard was a friend of Creation's Alan McGee and we had quite a few chats in the local strip pub with him and his business partner Dick Green about him managing The Grid. I think he did manage us for about three months but he was very busy with an unknown band from Manchester he'd just signed – they were called Oasis...

We continued getting more remix work. Stex were a funky soul group from London who for reasons known only to Stevo were signed to his Some Bizzare label. With my long history of working with Stevo, Richard Norris and I were invited to do some additional production and remix work on their single, 'Still Feel The Rain'. The added juicy carrot was that Stevo had persuaded guitar legend Johnny Marr to join us one Saturday afternoon in 1990. We were booked into John Henry's recording studio in King's Cross, whose rehearsal studios I'd previously used. I didn't even know they had a recording facility. I soon found out why – the tape machine kept breaking down and the desk wasn't patched in properly, and as it was a Saturday the only technical assistant available was the lady who worked behind the bar. It looked like it was going to be a disaster but, miraculously, everything started to work so when Johnny turned up he just plugged in his effects rack, tuned up and played some of his wonderful jangly guitar stuff. Then things got even better when a friend of the band, a tall, leggy black lady in a very short skirt, came into the studio holding a mirror like a platter filled with lines of very strong cocaine. Someone piped up, 'Oh, great, I didn't know there was a buffet.' The rest of the day sped by and, amazingly, we ended up with a great result.

I was also trying to focus on recording my first album and at the same time my marriage was finally falling apart. I was totally to blame as I was the one who was cheating, mostly because I felt trapped, restless and bored. The atmosphere was horrible, especially for our children, so I left home and went to stay with my other woman, Fiona, at her flat in Putney. When Gini went to visit her mother in Leicester, I got my mate with a van to help me and moved out of our St John's Wood place for good and returned to my flat in Marylebone.

Then I did what I usually did in times of crisis and immersed myself in work. In my free time I was also working in another studio called The Beat Farm in Berwick Street, Soho, playing some additional synthesiser for Genesis P. Orridge and Fred Giannelli's band, Psychic TV, on a track called 'I.C. Water', a tribute to the late Ian Curtis. The record turned out really well and came out on their own label, Temple Records. I also found time to co-write and play on a track called 'Humanity' with Indian writer/producer Biddu. He was a very charming man who'd enjoyed massive success during the disco boom of the early seventies, writing and producing multi-million-selling number one hits 'I Love To Love' by Tina Charles and 'Kung Fu Fighting' by Carl Douglas. He'd obviously made a fortune in the seventies, judging by his beautiful house in Kensington and the outfits he used to wear when he was conducting his band, the Biddu Orchestra. I believe he's now very big in the Bollywood scene.

When I was back in Pacific Studios with Richard, we did that classic thing where the band thinks the album's finished – we even had a wrap party in the studio with guests that included Alan McGee and Primal Scream, Boys Own and various bands, DJs and producers. Cally, our A&R man, said he thought we should write and record one more track. We were slightly nonplussed but reluctantly agreed and recorded a track called 'Floatation'. I had two nice John Barry-style piano chords and added a third on Richard's suggestion. I then suggested a clarinet solo. Nick, the engineer, knew a guy called Julian Stringle who played woodwind. We overdubbed Richard's lovely friend, Sacha Souter, who provided sultry vocals, and the track came together really easily. It was released in July 1990 but only got to number sixty in the main charts. More significantly, it went on to be considered an Ibiza classic, especially once Andrew Weatherall and Richard remixed it. Richard told me it was always a favourite of his friend and superstar DJ Paul Oakenfold. Later that year, the follow-up, 'A Beat Called Love' came out and peaked at a very disappointing number sixty-four; we realised our days at East West were probably numbered. As a final grand gesture we cut the first Grid album at Abbey Road Studios. In the lobby I was thrilled to see one of the original tape machines Sir George Martin had used to record The Beatles' *Sergeant Pepper's* album. It looked so primitive compared to the gear we used – I still find it incredible how they got those records to sound so good.

In the end the first Grid album, *Electric Head*, failed to make much of an impact on the charts. East West had just appointed a new MD, Max Hole, and he was having a good old spring-clean which meant that Cally, our only friend in the company, lost his job and we were dropped from their roster shortly after. I'm pleased to say that the *Electric Head* album was later licensed and reissued in deluxe form on Cherry Red Records.

★ ★ ★

The Grid wrote, recorded and produced a track in Mute Records' studios at 249 Harrow Road called 'Origins Of Dance' for a guy called Frazer. He used to bring in his weird Mexican hairless dog to the studio and it stared strangely at us throughout the session like the Sphinx. The track featured a specially pre-recorded voiceover by acid guru Timothy Leary, the man who popularised the phrase, 'Turn on, tune in, drop out' in 1967. It just so happened that Professor Leary was in Amsterdam on a lecture visit when we finished the track, so Richard, a huge fan of all things psychedelic, went to meet the Godfather of Acid. He was still a persona non grata in the UK even though it was years since he was caught plotting to put LSD into LA's water supply. I quite liked the idea of working with people who weren't allowed in the UK – Ronnie Biggs, Timothy Leary and, for a short time, Genesis P. Orridge.

I remember one time Gen had visited me in St John's Wood with his family for Sunday lunch and gave me a new seven-inch PTV single, 'Roman P.', which had a picture of *Tess Of The D'Urbervilles* on the cover. He proudly announced the sleeve was 'hyperdelic'. I stared at it for a while and he asked what I thought. I said, 'Yes, it really is hyperdelic. I took quarter of a tab of acid before you arrived.'

On the subject of LSD – my friends Rick and Terry got in touch via a mutual friend, Martin, to let me know they had re-recorded the track 'Sun Arise' with Rolf Harris and wanted Richard and I to help them do an acid mix at their studio, Kick, in Soho Square, where everyone dropped a tab. It wasn't quite the acid mix they'd bargained for when everyone started tripping off their heads. At one point we sampled the whole track and played it back with the keyboard modulation wheel on full. We thought we'd invented a new form of music, as it sounded totally amazing to us at the time. It didn't seem quite so inspired the next day and that was the last time I took acid in the studio. Things got more insane when we all piled into McDonald's on Oxford Street for breakfast at the crack of dawn – sun arise! My friend Martin was wearing a top hat and looked more and more like the Mad Hatter as he stood on his chair and announced that the yellow polystyrene container tasted better than the scrambled eggs. We kept getting lots of funny looks from the staff and the normal people en route to work. Luckily, paranoia got the better of us and we left before the police were called.

★ ★ ★

That summer I got a really nice surprise when I was asked if The Grid would do a remix for the Marc Almond single, 'Waifs And Strays'. Richard didn't mind and I was delighted as it was the first collaboration of sorts since we'd disbanded Soft Cell. We worked in Pacific Studios with our new engineer Nick at the controls and everyone seemed to be happy with the end result. I was very pleased because it felt like a door that had been shut for some time between Marc and I was now slightly ajar. Marc asked us to co-write some tracks for his *Tenement Symphony* album so we ended up writing three tracks together: 'My Hand Over My Heart', 'Meet Me In My Dreams' and 'I Have Never Seen Your Face'. Richard programmed the drum loops, I played some synth parts and Marc wrote the lyrics and vocal melodies. We recorded the initial tracks at Pacific Studios and then did additional work at Marcus, Matrix and, most notably, RAK Studios in north London. RAK was also a famous seventies record label, home to acts such as Hot Chocolate, Mud and Suzie Quatro. The whole empire was the domain of pop svengali and producer Mickie Most, whose London mansion boasted the largest privately owned swimming pool in the capital. I suddenly found myself thinking of Daniel Miller's imaginary electronic pop group The Silicon Teens, when he played and sang everything and credited himself as producer, Larry Least. One afternoon, we were overdubbing a saxophone solo on 'Meet Me In My Dreams' when Mickie popped into the studio for about five minutes. He just stood and glared at us somewhat disapprovingly, then left without saying a word – very strange.

Marc was also working with producer Trevor Horn with a much bigger budget than ours. The money showed when he did some additional production on our track, 'My Hand Over My Heart', flying in two programmers from Germany to try and recreate Richard's drum loop, then keeping the original, as it worked better. He also brought in the Art Of Noise's Anne Dudley to do a big orchestral arrangement. He recorded a sixty-piece section, including strings, brass, woodwind and percussion but decided it didn't sound big enough, so he double-tracked it, creating a hundred-and-twenty-piece orchestra. When the record came out we ended up with just drum programming and vocal production credits, as we'd recorded Marc's original performance, which was, as was often the case, the best take. It didn't become the monster hit we'd all hoped.

However, Soft Cell enjoyed a lot of back catalogue chart success the following year, 1991. Marc re-recorded the vocals for some of our hits and I did additional synth and drum machine overdubs with producer Julian Mendelsohn at SARM West Studios, in Basing Street. When freshly buffed album *Memorabilia – The Singles* was released it reached number eight in the UK charts. I personally prefer the original versions, as do Marc and most of our fans but the two singles 'Say Hello, Wave Goodbye '91' and 'Tainted Love '91' reached number thirty-eight and five, respectively (that money for old rope thing again).

The Grid, in the meantime, had been looking for a new record deal and we secured one with Virgin thanks to Boy George putting in a good word to MD Simon Draper for us. We'd done a remix for George's 'Bow Down Mister' for his band Jesus Loves You. One afternoon Richard and I were in the conference room at Virgin headquarters working on visuals for our live shows. The head of A&R popped in with a lady wearing a smart, beige trouser suit and big sunglasses. He introduced her: 'Hi, guys, this is Janet.' We said, 'Hello,' barely acknowledging her: thinking she was some new executive or something. Then it occurred to us Virgin had recently signed a US superstar – the woman we'd just been introduced to was none other than Janet Jackson!

We'd also found a new manager, David Enthoven, who had a company called E.G. Management. He was a completely charming gentleman, educated at Harrow but a rocker at heart. His pedigree was impeccable. He'd managed some of the most seminal acts of the seventies, such as Roxy Music, King Crimson, ELP and T. Rex. Apparently, he was the man who told Marc Bolan to stand up, rather than sit like a cross-legged hippy, when performing. Bolan did so, shortened their name from Tyrannosaurus Rex to T. Rex, swapped his acoustic for an electric guitar and became one of the biggest British pop stars of the early seventies, heralding the birth of glam rock. David was also the E in E.G. Records, the label he and his colleague John Gaydon set up that put out records by Roxy Music, King Crimson and Brian Eno. He understood the music industry from the band's and the label's perspective – quite a rare thing.

Just as we got our deal with Virgin, the owner of Pacific Studios decided to close the place down. That had been our base for quite some time, a home from home, so we had to find somewhere to write and record demos. Richard found a space in a business park in the Grand Union Centre opposite Virgin on Kensal Road, west London, where we built a small writing room based around my Seck sixteen-track mixing desk. I'd bought a few new midi synth modules too; a Waldorf Microwave, which was basically a rack-mounted PPG, an Oberheim Matrix 1000 and a funny little micro-synth, the Yamaha FB-01. We didn't last in the writing room very long as the business rates and rent proved excessive. The only track we wrote there became our first single for Virgin, a pumping dance tune called 'Boom!' that we recorded and mixed in Marcus Studios in Fulham with our engineer, Nick Hopkins.

We needed to find another studio to record the next Grid album and Richard asked if I knew anywhere. I'd recently done a session for Serge Gainsbourg's friend, singer Alain Bashung, with producer Nick Patrick at a studio called Eastcote, owned by Ian Dury & The Blockheads' keyboard player, Chaz Jankel and engineer/producer Philip Bagenal. The studio was also conveniently located in Kensal Road, across the road from Virgin headquarters and just round the corner from Richard's flat. It had a brilliant German engineer/programmer called Ingo Vauk. The studio was a favourite of Depeche Mode and it turned out to be perfect for The Grid too; it felt like being in a big flat and had daylight, which was quite a rare thing in a studio (although the view was only of the Pizza Express headquarters).

Recording the album *456* was my favourite studio experience since recording *Non-Stop Erotic Cabaret* in New York. The album was recorded upstairs at Eastcote with engineer Ingo Vauk. We then relocated to the once legendary, now non-existent Olympic Studios in Barnes with mix engineer Dare Mason, who did an amazing job. I liked that studio as you could see various rock luminaries including Bryan Ferry, Robin Trower and Prince recording in one of the other spaces, and the walls were covered in original drawings by Rolling Stone Ronnie Wood. Thanks to David, our manager, we got some very special guests on that album: Robert Fripp on guitar and Roxy Music's Andy Mackay on electronic woodwind, plus mixes by Phil Manzanera and Brian Eno. We also had soul legend and former Ikette P. P. Arnold on vocals and, from Zodiac Mindwarp, Zed (Zodiac) and Cobalt on vocals and guitar respectively. Other guests were Henry Cow/ Slapp Happy collaborator Dagmar Krause on abstract vocals and Alex Gifford, who we'd met at Peter Gabriel's Real World Studios during WOMAD recording week, on additional keyboards. Alex also became part of our touring band, playing sax and keyboards. He then went on to form The Propellerheads who wrote the wonderful song 'History Repeating' that they recorded with Shirley Bassey. That song even got used for a Jaguar commercial; it was all very impressive – if you're gonna work with a diva...

Throughout 1991 and 1992 we did a lot of Grid remixes for several well-known pop acts including 'Am I Right?' by Erasure, 'DJ Culture' by the Pet Shop Boys and 'Loose Fit' and 'Bob's Yer Uncle' by the Happy Mondays. We didn't meet or speak to the acts unless they had specific requests. Vince Clarke of Erasure called us at Snake Ranch Studios from his home in Holland to say he didn't mind what we did as long as we didn't use a Roland 909 drum machine as they were such a common feature on pretty much every dance track at the time (i.e. boring).

On a couple of occasions, we did a kind of cultural exchange, so no money changed hands; we remixed Brian Eno's 'Ali Click' from his *Nerve Net* album and Eno remixed our 'Heartbeat' off *456*. Similarly, we remixed a track called 'Darshan' by David Sylvian and Robert Fripp for free. Fripp hadn't charged us for playing on

456 and gave us a DAT full of Frippertronic loops, all in different scales and keys, to use as we saw fit, as long as he got credited for usage on any release. We couldn't afford to work on that basis with everyone as we had to make a living but as it was Fripp and Eno, we made an exception.

Richard and I were summoned to Factory Records in Manchester for a meeting with the Happy Mondays' A&R man, Phil Saxe. I liked Phil, not least because I knew he was a fellow northern soul fan. Manchester had acquired the rather ominous nickname 'Gunchester' because of the number of gang-related shootings in the city. There had even been trouble at Factory's nightclub, The Hacienda. But the company's offices were very New York slick and we saw the legendary suspended boardroom table that Tony Wilson had paid a fortune for. The Mondays' tracks were originally produced by Paul Oakenfold and Steve Osborne and the master tapes were a pleasure to work with, making it easy for us to get a couple of great remixes done. I read an interview with Shaun Ryder in one of the music mags in which he was asked about the mixes: 'It's 'im from Soft Cell but it sounds fuckin' great.' I was well chuffed.

Manchester played quite a part in our lives. Apart from remixing the Happy Mondays, we produced most of the album *Quality Street* for Manchester's World Of Twist on Circa Records, a subsiduary of Virgin. We recorded at Marcus; a residential studio in Fulham. The owner, who gave his studio its name, was Swedish and had some sort of early involvement with ABBA; he even had their little old sixteen-track mixer mounted on his office wall. The on-site restaurant and lounge bar were nice and sold Aquavit, the national Swedish liquor. It required discipline not to stay in there after lunch – we transgressed a couple of times but mostly kept it in check. We were already paying a grand a day, plus engineer (£150 a day), not to mention our fees and production costs, so we were on a very tight budget.

Sometimes just getting the various band members to do their bits was hard enough. Gordon King, the guitarist, once begged,

'Don't make me,' when he was due to play. I put it down to nerves or 'red light fever' as it's known – I've seen many singers and players rehearse a song perfectly over and over in rehearsal but then go to pieces the second they see the red recording light. I've even done it myself quite a few times. Then there was the time we wanted Tony Ogden to do the lead vocals on one track and someone remembered he'd gone to the launderette, even though he knew full well he was needed. I just kept thinking to myself, This is costing about £200 an hour and he's gone to wash his fucking undies – what a twat!

When we finally finished recording, we mixed the record with engineer Richard Evans, who we knew from Time Square Studios in Chiswick, and relocated to Peter Gabriel's Real World Studio in Box, Wiltshire. We'd spent some time there before when we wrote, recorded and released tracks with The Holmes Brothers, Sheila Chandra, Justin Adams and Jah Wobble, respectively, when participating in the WOMAD recording week. We'd also done demo sessions with Senegalese superstar, Baaba Maal, although nothing came of that. We knew Real World was a great sounding studio and a relaxing place to work. There were no distractions apart from the croquet lawn, Gordon the goose and the occasional sightings of guest luminaries such as Brian Eno, Daniel Lanois, Massive Attack or Van Morrison – who I accidentally mistook for a minicab driver when he knocked on the door during a WOMAD recording session. Real World was also where Richard first met and started working with Clash frontman Joe Strummer. Tony, the World Of Twist singer, a true urbanite, not unlike myself, would occasionally get stir crazy being surrounded by cows, trees and fields and drive back to Manchester to score drugs while we carried on working. To celebrate finishing the album, we had a drunken tennis tournament – not very rock'n'roll – and got Peter Gabriel, a.k.a. 'Mr Peter', to present an old trophy to the champion. Unfortunately, the album wasn't such a winner, only reaching a disappointing number fifty in the UK charts and, shortly after, the band broke up. I heard through the grapevine that Oasis's Gallagher brothers were fans and Liam's band, Beady Eye, even covered one of the tracks; sadly, not one of the ones we produced.

The early nineties were turbulent times for The Grid. In 1991 the LA riots followed several police officers getting caught on film beating Rodney King, and Richard Norris just happened to be over there on holiday at the time – he returned to the UK unscathed. In June the following year, Virgin was taken over by EMI, which meant lots of the great people we'd worked with were out of a job. The new MD, Paul Conroy, seemed like a decent guy, but we didn't exactly relish the idea of Virgin suddenly being part of EMI.

Chapter 35

DECONSTRUCTION TIME

THE NEW REGIME AT VIRGIN STILL WANTED TO TAKE UP THE option for another Grid album but after the EMI takeover they refused to pay the advance specified in our contract. They said if we didn't take their lower offer we were legally free to go, which is exactly what we did.

I'd recently had a tip-off from our friend and occasional record promoter Jonathan Richardson that Deconstruction Records were very interested in signing us. They were probably the biggest major dance label in the UK, with the clout of BMG behind them and we thought they would be perfect for us. We signed to Deconstruction on the same terms offered in the Virgin deal and also signed to their publishing company, M62 Music, in the BMG building by Putney bridge.

We also parted company with our manager, David Enthoven. It was totally amicable – we didn't feel he understood the dance music scene well enough. We weren't wrong and I think David would have agreed, and it didn't exactly harm his career. Shortly afterwards, he became Robbie Williams' manager and went on to broker his multi-million pound deals. The Grid were never going to achieve that level of commercial success.

Richard and I started 1993 working on *Evolver*, our first Grid album for Deconstruction Records, and our new manager was Pete Evans, who'd previously worked at Big Life Management. We were then asked by Billie Ray Martin to produce her and co-write *Four Ambient Tales*, to be released on Belgium's R&S label. We'd previously produced her hit single 'Your Loving Arms', which got to number six in the UK and number forty-six in the US. The US release was definitely helped by Junior Vasquez's excellent remix, although it was our pop mix that got played on UK radio. The ambient EP was recorded at Lotown Studios, around the corner from Richard's flat in Golborne Road, west London. It was a quirky little place run by Toby Andersen and Kadir Guirey, who'd been in the eighties London band Funkapolitan. My favourite feature was a platinum disc hung over the toilet, inscribed to producer Robert Stigwood for sales of the single 'Disco Duck' by Rick Dees & His Cast Of Idiots – shame it wasn't for one of his better-known productions, namely *Saturday Night Fever*.

The project we were working on was really interesting. It had four Grid electronic ambient backing tracks and featured the brilliant virtuoso B. J. Cole on his amazing pedal steel guitar, hooked up to a midi rack. It was a great combination, with lyrics penned and sung by Billie in her unique, sultry diva style. The recording sessions went really well and everyone was very happy – so far, so good. Then we relocated to a pokey little studio near the Young Vic Theatre, just off Blackfriars Road, south-east London.

We'd taken engineer Ingo Vauk with us and he was looking very nonplussed and shaking his head. I remember him saying something like, 'This has got to be the noisiest fucking studio in London!' That was the last thing we needed. We could cope with a certain level of noise on a loud dance track but it did not go well with an ambient record with lots of mellow, non-transient frequencies. We still had to record the vocals for four songs. We asked Billie if we could go to a better studio to get a better vocal sound but she was adamant that the recording budget was non- negotiable. Like it or lump it, we were stuck with that place. Somehow, by the skilful use of phase cancellation, noise-gating and low-pass filtering, Ingo miraculously managed to keep the noise to a minimum: what a star. Once the record was finally mastered in the cutting room and had gone through another noise reduction system it sounded surprisingly clean and warm.

The other thing that sticks in my mind about that year was meeting Leigh Bowery – performance artist, living sculpture and muse of painter Lucian Freud. Richard and I had been asked to do a remix of the track 'Useless Man' by Leigh's band, Minty. He decided he wanted to meet us first and we made a date at Richard's flat in Golborne Road, an area with a high Portuguese population, very close to the Trellick Tower, the west London block designed by Ernö Goldfinger. It was a lovely one-bedroom first floor flat, but it was above a Portuguese grocery store that sold some sort of dried fish that stank out the communal hallway. I didn't know what to expect from Leigh as we'd only seen pictures of him in his bizarre costumes. To our surprise he was wearing a fawn V-neck sweater, a light, checked cotton shirt and a pair of brown slacks and some men's work shoes. Perched on top of his shaved head was an obvious brown toupee. He sort of looked like a middle-aged Marks & Spencer's model except for the hole in both cheeks, each big enough to put your finger in. As Richard observed, Leigh looked more weird when he was trying to be normal.

We did the remix at Eastcote in Kensal Road with Ingo Vauk engineering – he'd actually recorded the original version, which was quite handy. I was at a bit of a loss because it wasn't a standard dance track and so it didn't need the usual funky synth bass groove. Richard had just bought a Novation Bass Station keyboard and suddenly started playing a filthy, buzzy bassline which was absolutely perfect. We looped up some tough beats and then sampled and chopped up Leigh's vocal – an obscene take on the Pepsi adverts: 'Lip-smacking, cock-sucking...' etc. The track got a great response in some of the more unusual clubs and I heard our mix on a Boy George DJ compilation playing in HMV in Oxford Street shortly after Leigh died.

Richard bought a very small Apple Mac, running Logic midi software and, as we didn't have our own studio, we wrote and programmed a track called 'Rollercoaster' in his flat. The track featured a Yamaha FB-01 synth as the lead instrument, with the portamento setting on maximum, creating an insane lead part that was impossible to be played by a human. I loved the track but I wasn't very confident about its commercial potential, so I was very pleasantly surprised when it reached number nineteen in the UK. Other highlights included headlining the Trance Europe Express tent at the Phoenix Festival on 16 July 1994. We were interviewed by Roger Morton from the *NME* and I told him, 'I've always been a lurker,' while Richard explained the difficulties of the 'one-fingered keyboard pogo'. An interesting interview, I'm sure, although Roger must have wondered about us: the last time we'd met him was in Peter Gabriel's duck pond during WOMAD recording week.

Chapter 36
SWAMP THING

'SWAMP THING' CAME ABOUT AFTER I'D BEEN OUT WITH my then girlfriend, Fiona, to a restaurant in Marylebone Lane and heard some music coming out of a nearby pub. It would go on to be The Grid's most successful single by far, selling over a million copies worldwide.

Fiona and I were walking past an Irish-themed pub called the O'Connor Don and we heard this amazing Irish-style music. I had to see who was playing so we went in for a few drinks and watched the band. They were playing what can only be described as Irish/bluegrass fusion. They had this amazing banjo player with long, dark hair and tinted glasses. I heard something in the rhythm of his playing that I could imagine working with a dance beat and bass sequencers.

When they stopped for a break I went over and introduced myself and asked him if he fancied coming to the studio to play some generic bluegrass riffs for a dance track. He eyed me with suspicion but agreed when I said he would get paid handsomely. By the following Tuesday the banjo player, Roger Dinsdale, was playing for us in Eastcote Studios. Richard Norris and Ingo looked at me as if I was insane but went along with it. We added beats, basslines and synth toplines, then chopped the banjo parts up and reassembled them and I think everyone agreed we'd made a killer track. Luckily the great British public agreed.

We performed 'Swamp Thing' on *Top Of The Pops* and the single got to number three, then dropped to number four, then went up to three again which surprised everybody. We were hoping it could go all the way – it was so tantalisingly close – but it wasn't to be. We still got nominated for the Brit for best single and went to the awards at Alexandra Palace. We knew beforehand that we hadn't won but that didn't stop us from having a great night.

Richard's friend, Graham Brown Martin, head of EXP Records, hired a stretch limo and we all met at the Halcyon hotel in Holland Park. I sat at the Deconstruction Records table with Pete Hadfield, Keith Blackhurst and Tom from the label and Heather Small from M People and her boyfriend, an English rugby league player, who shall remain nameless as he kept nicking my fags whenever Heather went off to perform or do an interview. Richard sat a few tables back with the guys from Blur and Alan McGee from Creation Records. I still love those kind of events and get excited when I see someone famous. The Brits was a star-spotter's paradise. Elton John and his band performed, as did Madonna, her unfeasibly large blonde hair extensions blowing behind her. Sitting at the table about six yards from me was none other than Prince. He looked every inch the megastar, dressed entirely in a yellowy peach colour – he wore a one-piece jumpsuit with matching chiffon scarf and five-inch stiletto boots. It was at the time he was in dispute with Warner Bros. and he had the word 'Slave' written on one side of his face in eyebrow pencil. I heard Pete say something like, 'What a cunt,' in his Manc accent, then he picked an orange out of the fruit bowl and, to my horror, threw it at Prince, narrowly missing his head. I don't think Prince noticed but his two very large bodyguards did. They thought I'd thrown it because they couldn't see Pete behind me and stared at me like a pair of hungry pit bulls – I thought I was gonna die. It was touch and go for a moment, then they muttered something into their headsets and the heat was off. One of the guys from Blur also spotted Prince and wrote on his own face, 'Dave'. I wish I'd thought of that – or maybe not, as I seriously doubt Prince's bouncers would have seen the funny side.

There was a huge party of about a thousand people after the show and everyone got totally shitfaced, myself included. At one point I was standing at the bar and Pogues frontman Shane MacGowan came over and started chatting. I'd briefly met him years earlier when Soft Cell played at Cabaret Futura, in the days when he still had all his teeth. He kept asking if I'd seen his girlfriend as he couldn't find her in the huge crowd. I explained that I'd never met her before and asked him what she looked like. He told me she was very pretty and had black hair and blue eyes – that narrows things down a bit, I thought. He said if I saw her, to tell her that he was looking for her. He thanked me for my concern, shook my hand and staggered off into the night.

Chapter 37

SOUTH-EAST ASIA

IN 1995, THE GRID EMBARKED ON A SMALL SOUTH-EAST Asian tour starting in Tokyo. The band comprised Richard Norris and me, Alex Gifford (keyboards and sax), Pablo Cook (percussion), Roger Dinsdale (banjo), Pete Evans (manager) and Fiona Alderson (my girlfriend).

I'd been having sleepless nights for about a month just thinking about the dreaded long-haul flights we had ahead of us for the next few weeks. My fear of flying had reached phobic proportions; thank God for vodka and diazepam. The thirteen-hour flight from Heathrow went incredibly smoothly but I was still greatly relieved when we were back on terra firma at Narita airport. We were met by our tour promoter, a really nice guy called Ray Hearn, an Australian. I remember being struck by how tatty everything looked on the approach to the city. Rusting crash barriers by the roadside and shabby old buildings behind them. Apparently, Tokyo hadn't had planning regulations so in the event of an earthquake, most of these structures would collapse although the huge modern skyscrapers are supposedly quake-proof. Our hotel was in an area called Shinjuku, which was much more how I had imagined Tokyo; neon lights and gigantic, high definition plasma screens everywhere. Ridley Scott was said to have wanted to film *Blade Runner* in this part of the city and it was very easy to understand why. It was like being in a sci-fi movie, a trashy electronic version of the future.

There were loads of people clutching armfuls of records waiting for us in the car park. Some of them had Grid records but most of them had Soft Cell records. This was both flattering and embarrassing as I was there as part of The Grid and it felt a little inappropriate to be signing records by my old band. Many of the Soft Cell fans had records already signed by Marc when he was there years before as a solo artist. I guess they just wanted my autograph to complete the set. I could hardly refuse as they had loyally waited so long.

There was a small bowl of fruit in our room with a welcome note signed by the MD of Sony/BMG Records, Japan. I thought that was a bit cheap as we had bought bottles of duty-free Johnny Walker to give to the company executives. Ray said that it was in fact a very special gift, as fresh fruit cost a fortune in Japan. As I discovered later in the bar on the sixtieth floor, drinks in Tokyo weren't cheap either. They sold draft Guinness which in taste was the same as anywhere else but in price was about £8 a pint – and that was nineties prices! We stuck to the cheaper option of Kirin and sake. Pablo, our percussionist, and I invented a new game we called the Bow Jam. We'd noticed that every time we spoke to a waiter they would bow and if you kept bowing back, Japanese etiquette required them to bow back, lower and lower each time, until they were practically headbutting the floor. We discovered we could keep this going for quite a while, until they got wise to us and retreated backwards through an open door – our record was ten bows.

Our first gig was in the Liquid Room in central Tokyo. We had to use a tiny elevator to get to the venue itself. We arrived in the afternoon to do the soundcheck and everything was set up perfectly. We had a bank of sixteen Sony monitors for our onstage video wall and it looked fantastic. The sound was crystal-clear and we were very happy. The Japanese crew were wonderful and they even marked the stage where every lead fell. Fiona asked for the bathroom and was directed to a door in the corner. She returned looking incredulous – the door led to the book section of a department store. I had to see this for myself so I walked out of the dark, smoky venue and sure enough it was like I was in W. H. Smiths – or Foyles... or Narnia, very bizarre. But space is scarce in Tokyo and has to be maximised. Our hotel, like a lot of the high-rise buildings, had a mini-golf course on the roof and an underground shopping mall that went down two storeys.

Apart from one really drunk American heckler who was politely asked to leave, the gig was a great success and a really encouraging start to the tour. Richard and I went to another club with the promoter and it was one of those brilliant, culturally confused moments that the Japanese do so well. There were loads of guys all dressed like identikit B-boys – NYC and LA baseball caps, Adidas or Nike Air trainers, Stussy and Mambo shirts and Avirex jackets, all the proper gear. But the music was heavy dub reggae. To top it all, they were all dancing like Michael Jackson in the video for 'Bad'!

The day after the show, a Sunday, Richard and I had to go to BMG headquarters to do some interviews for Japanese press and radio. We were told it would be conducted in the form of a press conference as it could be very time-consuming if we did individual interviews. We soon understood what they meant. Each question and answer had to be translated between Japanese and English. We ended up restricting every journalist to about six questions each, so they all effectively got a full interview, otherwise we could have been there for several hours. That interpreter could have had a right old laugh at our expense by changing our answers and we'd have been none the wiser.

Our next show was at a college in Osaka, which meant travelling on the Shinkansen or bullet train. The Japanese pride themselves on that train's punctuality. I love trains and have travelled all over the world on them, so I was really excited about my first trip. Just before I boarded, I got a message that my ex-wife's father, Neville, had just died. That came as a bit of a shock as I didn't even know he was ill. He was always very health-conscious, apparently as fit as a fiddle and he'd never been a smoker or a drinker. I did get a feeling of incredible sadness for Gini although we had been separated for many years. There wasn't a great deal I could do from the other side of the world just as we were starting a tour. Everyone seemed quietly relieved when I made it known that I wasn't going to get the next flight back to England for the funeral. I just sat back and enjoyed the amazing journey and had a few drinks in his honour as we raced across Japan. There was even a mini-shopping area on board with a choice of Japanese or western toilets. You could also rent an office – it was ultra high-tech. We went through seemingly endless rural areas full of paddy fields and I remember stopping in Kyoto and realising it was an anagram of Tokyo as well as being the former capital city. I felt very lucky to have that distraction.

Osaka had a totally different vibe to Tokyo, much less frenetic. I noticed huge cracks running up the outside of the hotel building. These were caused by the recent shockwaves from the Great Hanshin earthquake, nineteen miles away. The gig itself was in a college campus and was in a room full of seated, mostly bespectacled students so it didn't really rock. We returned to the Liquid Room in Tokyo to do our final show in Japan, which, like the first one, was great. Our promoter Ray took us all to a traditional Japanese restaurant afterwards. We were all asked to take off our shoes before being seated and the smell of several pairs of trainers was pretty bad until they were taken off somewhere by the waiter.

There were a couple of Yakuza (Japanese gangster) types sitting at the table next to us, with greased-back hair, wearing loud, spivvy-looking suits. One guy had a little finger missing which sort of confirmed who they were. They were drinking beers and sake and sweating profusely as they ate the potentially deadly blowfish or fugu. We didn't try that particular delicacy, but we did have other unusual dishes including sea urchin and, to my eternal shame, whale blubber. In all fairness, I didn't know what it was until I'd eaten half of it.

Behind us was a big party of about twelve elderly Japanese men and women chatting away and laughing. Ray, our Japanese-speaking promoter, suddenly hushed everyone at our table. 'They're talking and laughing about us because we're westerners. Watch this!' He turned to the table behind him and said something in Japanese – the people went deathly silent. He told us that he'd just let them know that we'd heard and understood everything they'd just said about us. They all looked totally mortified and left shortly afterwards, bowing continually as they hurried to the exit, while we sweetly smiled and laughed at them; it was hilarious.

The morning we left Tokyo wasn't quite so funny; a Japanese terrorist cult called Aum Shinrikyo carried out a series of sarin gas attacks on the Tokyo Metro which affected the subway station right by our hotel in Shinjuku. There were loads of armed police and militia everywhere in the city and on the road all the way to Narita airport. We knew something very serious had occurred but didn't find out what had really happened until we arrived in Thailand and switched on CNN.

Bangkok was an odd place, it has to be said. As we approached the city the pretty air stewardesses handed out immigration cards warning, 'Possession of drugs is punishable by death or life imprisonment!' We never carried substances overseas so there was no cause for concern on that count. Lots of Thai police officers with sniffer dogs waited in the airport, the very friendly-looking little dogs trotting around unleashed, sniffing everyone at their leisure. We'd been warned about this and told that the time to worry was if a dog sat down next to you. That was the cue for the police to move in and nick you. One particular dog was very interested in a leg belonging to Roger, our banjo player, and kept circling. The cops looked on hopefully, hands stroking revolvers. The rest of us backed off nervously because we knew how much spliff Roger smoked and he always wore the same black denims which were permeated with the stink of cannabis. Please don't sit down... I remember repeating over and over in my head until the dog finally moved on – it was a very tense moment.

We went out into the stifling heat and loaded our bags on the people carrier. It was night and was still sweltering. The traffic pollution was dreadful. The next day on walkabout I bought loads of fake stuff, T-shirts, CDs and other bits and pieces. Everything was fake, they didn't seem to have anything authentic. One thing that was a bit too real was a guy trying to sell a young boy for sex to me and my girlfriend and it was only ten o'clock in the morning. He even had a little book of semi-pornographic photographs of the child. Revolting man.

I didn't like the way Bangkok treated its elephants. They would chain their trunks up and drag them along the street and sell tourists slices of water melon to force-feed the poor creatures. I think my only fond memory of the place was hiring a tuk-tuk and being driven round the back streets of the city at night like being in a James Bond movie.

We only played one gig, in a club sponsored by Kahlúa. We had to do a TV appearance before the show as part of the deal and I ran into Bee, an old friend of mine from London who was something of a Thai pop star. He was the androgynous model draped over the timpani on the cover Marc designed for my solo album *In Strict Tempo*. I think he was still in touch with Peter 'Sleazy' Christopherson, from Throbbing Gristle and Coil, who also lived in the city. The club security was, oddly, provided by the Thai police. Apparently, they didn't get paid too well so they had to supplement their income by various other means. They all drove the latest BMWs and Mercedes and you can bet they weren't fakes. Each officer got a cash bung and a bottle of Johnny Walker Red Label whiskey in return for not closing down the club – an offer they could hardly refuse. I remember Pablo coming back from the toilet and nervously telling me there was one of our security men in there, swigging from his whiskey bottle and playing with his service revolver! We felt very secure, let me tell you.

We flew on to Changi airport for our show in Singapore city. It had a totally different vibe from Bangkok: very clean, ultra-modern and fairly right-wing. Smoking was banned in most places as was littering and, best of all, chewing gum was totally illegal. I think it was writer William Gibson who called it the most futuristic city in the world – it definitely had the look. On our first night, the promoter took us to an outdoor Malaysian restaurant by the bay in the middle of the skyscrapers of the financial district. It was just next to Harry's Bar where rogue trader Nick Leeson used to hang out. We had quite a few days in Singapore and spent most of the time in the twenty-fifth-storey swimming pool, drinking cocktails. I remember the corporate hotel restaurant advertised a weird meal called 'tunch', a hybrid of tea and lunch. I can't say I've ever had it before or since.

Everyone still had really sore throats from the polluted humidity of Bangkok but we did the show at Club Souk, which went very well. As it was so warm, the dressing room was outside, which was more bearable. Apart from the mosquitoes there were these amazing little bright green lizards running everywhere, it was very exotic. On the short walk back to our hotel banjo man Roger Dinsdale fell into a ditch and for the rest of the tour was known as Ditchdale.

The next afternoon, on our way to the airport we still had a few hours to kill. Rather than wait in a boring airport lounge we went to the famous Raffles Hotel. As this was the birthplace of the Singapore sling it seemed churlish not to quaff one or two at the famous long bar. We also had monkey nuts – you're allowed to drop their shells on the floor by the bar, the only place you can legally drop litter in Singapore.

After a two-hour stopover in Bali – which has to be the most chaotic airport I've ever been to – we flew on to Sydney. We'd had a huge hit with 'Swamp Thing' in Australia, reaching number three in their pop charts. The biggest gig of the tour was at the Hordern Pavilion, with an audience of about five thousand people. The last number of our set was obviously the big hit and during soundcheck Roger said he'd 'modified' his pickup. That made me very nervous and alarm bells started ringing. I come from the 'If it ain't broken, don't fix it' school but he assured me everything was cool. We did the gig, which was totally rocking. We had the audience eating out of our hands, then the grand finale, 'Swamp Thing'. The intro drums thundered in and then... total silence! Five thousand Aussies going mental and no fucking banjo! John, our sound guy saw what was happening and practically dived across the stage with a mic and saved the day.

It was rumoured that Mick Jagger came to the show and was sitting in a private director's box at the back of the arena. That may or may not have been true – The Rolling Stones were in Sydney at the time on their Voodoo Lounge tour and I'd seen a guy that looked like Mick doing a TV interview outside the Sydney Opera House earlier in the day. We were staying near Darling Bay at the Sebel Townhouse Hotel, which the Stones had apparently tried to book in its entirety for their entourage. I was politely told by the desk manager that there was a short delay as the previous occupant of my room was a member of the US thrash metal band, Slayer. He said, quite matter-of-factly, that I wouldn't have to wait too long as they'd already replaced the TV and most of the furniture and were just fixing the door back on its frame – how boringly old school rock'n'roll. I've never trashed a hotel room in my life – am I missing something?

One evening a man and woman got into the lift on the same floor as me and the guy spotted my laminate and asked me what band I was with. 'The Grid,' I replied.

He was Keith Richards' guitar technician. I was suitably impressed, but it got even better when he introduced his female friend with the immortal line, 'And this is my manager.'

'Hi, nice to meet you both,' I replied, somewhat astounded. Talk about rock'n'roll excess: the technicians had managers. Where did it end – did the fans have agents?

We'd pre-recorded an interview at the BMG offices in London with Molly Meldrum, of *Hey Hey, It's Saturday*, the biggest variety show on TV in Australia. We also did an interview at a radio station called Triple J as well as the usual music press. As we'd just had a platinum hit in Australia with 'Swamp Thing' we were put on the same bill as our Deconstruction Records label mates, M People, who were also having a lot of success.

We flew on to Tullamarine Airport to play a couple more dates in Melbourne. We had a dinner with the Australian record company MD and Keith Blackhurst, MD of Deconstruction Records, who'd just flown in from London. We all got presented with platinum discs; my first in Australia since Soft Cell were number one there – the next one for Deconstruction would be by Kylie. They weren't exactly discs, more pieces of platinum-coloured plastic in the shape of Australia, mounted on a framed board, but gratefully received nonetheless. The most memorable part of the evening was Keith in his really smart, very expensive-looking white trousers over which, somehow, Pablo the percussionist managed to spill an entire chocolate mousse – Keith was not amused.

We travelled on to New Zealand for the last leg of the short tour in Wellington and Auckland. I really liked New Zealand; very green compared to Australia but, by that stage, I had to concede that I was starting to get very homesick. I was feeling acutely aware that we were on the other side of the world and began to understand why so many Antipodeans visit Europe. I felt very alienated and so far from the rest of the world. The tour had gone really well, I'd been to some amazing new places and met some really great people but, I have to say, I was quite glad when it was over. I've always been more of a studio person and couldn't wait to be back in London. Since that mini-tour I have generally refused to fly. We'd taken about seventeen flights in six weeks and quite a few of them were thirteen-hour long-haul jobs. We even flew back the long way around, including a two-hour stopover in Los Angeles before a twelve-hour flight to Frankfurt and the one-hour forty-minute flight back to Heathrow. That return journey took twenty-nine hours, in total.

We put out a compilation album, *Music For Dancing*, not long after our return in 1995. Having recorded some demos at EXP studios that the record company weren't very receptive to, we decided to put The Grid on hold and pursue other projects – in Richard's case, working with Joe Strummer. I found myself in yet another musical quandary until Eastcote engineer Ingo Vauk and producer Nick Patrick said they were looking at Tim Simenon's Bomb The Bass studio and thinking of going into partnership. I asked if they could use a third partner, as Nick worked overseas half the time. They thought about it and agreed, then Nick dropped out completely and it was just me and Ingo. Luckily, I was still signed to Deconstruction Records and still managed by Pete Evans, who helped us to get work.

Our first client was a massive branding company called Fitch who were working on rebranding British Telecom and needed someone to design electronic ringtones and idents. We'd only just moved into the studio and the only mixer we had was the Seck sixteen-track which looked really pathetic. Somehow we got away with it in front of the US Fitch executive. It was a great little project – not least because they paid us a fortune for doing a few bleeps – and we were also invited to the BT research laboratory which was like something out of a James Bond movie.

The next job was wiring the studio – by hand. Fiona made endless cups of tea as Ingo and I spent a weekend wire stripping and soldering. Boy, was it satisfying when we plugged into our brand new twenty-four-track Soundcraft mixing console and every cable worked – not a dry joint in the house. We went for a well-deserved celebratory curry and a few pints of Cobra at the Durbar in Hereford Road, off Westbourne Grove.

Chapter 38
ABSOLUT

NINETEEN-NINETY-SEVEN WAS A VERY STRANGE YEAR FOR me. Our first big project in our new studio was writing and producing some tracks with Kylie Minogue for Deconstruction Records: 'Breathe', 'Limbo' and 'Through The Years'. The album was going to be called *The Impossible Princess*, when the unthinkable happened. On 31 August, Princess Diana died in a car crash in Paris, France.

The whole of the UK went into mourning, bordering on mass hysteria; there was no way we could use that album title. It was totally inappropriate. If I'm honest, I got slightly caught up in the hysteria myself and went to see all the wreaths and floral tributes outside Kensington Palace. I even joined the roadside crowds and watched the hearse and funeral cortege drive through London on Oxford Street, five minutes away from my flat in Marylebone. I'm no royalist but I had a morbid curiosity about the circumstances of her death. The conspiracy theorists were having a field day as, apart from the Queen, Diana was probably the most famous woman in the world.

Less than a fortnight later, on 12 September, Gini and I received our decree nisi after just one hearing in the high court. That came as a great relief, having suffered the indignity of my recent financial affairs being scrutinised by total strangers. The legal people had gone through all my bank statements and private documents with a fine toothcomb. It was like being psychologically raped. The thought of a long, protracted divorce battle filled me with dread. Not least because of the emotional strain but also, more painfully, the financial side of things. I was paying all the legal fees – Gini's and mine. On 5 February 1998, I received a court order from the aptly named District Judge Million regarding my financial settlement. Let me just say, it was bad but it could have been a lot worse. It was probably a good thing that my ex and I were not permitted to speak during the hearing as there could have been a few words. The decree absolute was issued on 24 February and I celebrated with Fiona in a bar off the Strand. Normally, I would have a pint of best bitter but on that occasion a bottle of Bollinger and several ice-cold Absolut vodkas felt more appropriate. The final court hearing and settlement had cost a lot but I was glad it was over. At the beginning of the new millennium, Fiona would give birth to our daughter, Georgie.

Back at work, 'Breathe', the single Ingo Vauk and I had co-written and produced for Kylie, featured mixes by New Yorker Todd Terry. Somewhat disappointingly, it only reached number fourteen in the UK – not a brilliant chart position by Kylie's standards. I think it came at a strange time in her career as she was developing as an artist and experimenting with new ideas. On the plus side it did get to number one in Israel and did well in Australia although I still regret that we weren't asked to write some pop dance stuff with her – like 'Can't Get You Out Of My Head' – rather than being given the Indie Kylie brief by Pete Hadfield at Deconstruction. I remember he kept saying to me, 'Think Butch Vig and Garbage'. Much as I respect Pete's A&R ability, I think he got that one totally wrong.

Other projects we worked on around that time were remixes for German band Faust – the so-called godfathers of krautrock. We got on very well with founder member Hans-Joachim Irmler, who invited us to do a couple of live shows with them as part of the band in Leicester and London, at the Royal Festival Hall. The London show was a very weird gig as someone in the audience got stabbed (not fatally) with a hunting knife. Some members of the audience thought it was part of the act, as there was so much mayhem going on onstage – angle grinders sparking all over the place and a cement mixer spewing out paper letters above the stage while everyone was making as much noise as possible. I had two Technics SL-1200 turntables going through some Moogerfooger filters and ring modulators as I mixed mangled bits of *The Faust Tapes* album into the overall wall of noise. All the little old lady usherettes were running around frantically until the police and an ambulance arrived.

We also did a remix of Leeds band Black Star Liner but by far the best paid and most prestigious remix was for David Bowie's 'Hallo Spaceboy', featuring Pet Shop Boys, at EXP Studios. The first mix took two days to set up and was the commercial side, then we did a random chaos mix in two hours and – surprise, surprise – David preferred the chaos mix. Unfortunately, we never got to meet the great man as he was living in Switzerland at the time, although we did get a nice thank-you letter from his agents, MainMan Management.

We'd been working on some ideas for songs with Ingo Vauk, my writing/production partner at our studio, when a songwriter/producer friend, Chris Braide, asked if I'd heard David Gray's cover version of 'Say Hello, Wave Goodbye' on an album called *White Ladder*. He said I should check it out as it was the biggest-selling album in Ireland. I thought, Wow, a cover version of one of our tunes on a ten-track album that's selling well. I rushed out and bought a copy and there it was, a really nice acoustic version of our song that segued into some Van Morrison lyrics and was selling bucketloads. It was number one here and eventually it sold seven million copies worldwide and stayed in the UK charts for three years. My dad's old quote, 'Money for old rope' immediately sprang to mind. I saw David perform his version on *Top Of The Pops 2* a couple of years later. It was released as the last single from his album but only reached number twenty-six in the UK charts. When I saw him live at Shepherd's Bush Empire, he didn't even play our song. However, I did get to meet him backstage after the show and he seemed like a very nice guy, riding on the wave of his amazing success.

Chapter 39
YEAR ZERO

THE FIFTH OF JULY 1999 WAS PROBABLY THE SADDEST DAY of my life. After several months in and out of treatment and a final attempted heart operation, my mum died in theatre at Victoria hospital, Blackpool. The cause of death was registered as acute myocardial infarction – heart disease, caused primarily by years of cigarettes.

I still find it hard to believe my own stupidity sometimes: smoking-related diseases killed both my adoptive parents and yet I still continued to smoke. I've always had a problem with addictions; if there is such a thing as an addictive personality, I have it in abundance. I was the same with alcohol, sex, drugs (and rock'n'roll), even the taste of certain food, occasionally. If I liked something, I wanted more. I was exactly the same when I bought clothes and shoes, always in Selfridges, and record and book collecting in little specialist shops – totally habitual, compulsive and impulsive. I always bought things in bulk, one was too many and a hundred never enough, yet once I got them home, some of my purchases would remain unopened for months. It was like I had a vacuum in my life and had to fill it with stuff to feel complete. This is known as the 'God-shaped hole' and I first heard the phrase when I was in rehab for a few months. Marc and I wrote a song about the term.

My GP at the ironically named Crypt health centre in Marylebone prescribed me an anti-depressant called Seroxat. I was still using various street drugs: coke, speed, weed, various uppers and downers and drinking very heavily, hanging out with west London gangsters and hookers on the Edgware Road. The cocktail of anti-depressants and illegal substances was playing psychological tiddlywinks with my head. I was a fucking emotional mess and was heading towards an early grave. I was also saddened to read that 'Tainted Love' composer Ed Cobb, who I'd met in London and Los Angeles a few years earlier, died of leukaemia on 9 September, just five days after what would have been my mum's 66th birthday. I even gave her my first gold disc for that song back in 1981.

I was doing seven-day benders and crashing for two days at a time, usually still wearing one of my 'binge suits' with a small bottle of Armani cologne tucked in the top pocket. I was always smartly dressed because I believed, in my fucked-up mind, that no matter what state you were in, you could always get into clubs if you wore a whistle and smelled nice. Stubble was still quite fashionable and I was never proved wrong. I had a kind of routine; I'd have a bath and wash off the toxic, greasy drug and alcohol sweat after a serious bender. Shit and shave, splash on some cologne and put on some fresh clothes, then go to my local bistro for a nice light meal, usually eggs benedict or smoked salmon and scrambled eggs with a few glasses of buck's fizz. Then, as I started to feel more human, the cycle would start all over again, usually a few lunchtime drinks with one of my dealer friends, then by the evening I'd be ready to party all over again. Fiona, my long-suffering partner, had left me a few months before as she'd had enough of watching my gradually deteriorating mental state as I spiralled out of control. I'd pop out to get the papers on Saturday morning and return on Tuesday night, still clutching them, like there was nothing wrong – I'm surprised she didn't kill me.

241

Finally, it all came on top one morning in December. After yet another marathon drink and drug session, I woke up, still fully clothed, with dried dribble all down my face and thought to myself, I'm gonna die if I don't stop. The only person I could think to phone was Fiona who, realising I needed help, kindly got me checked into rehab at a counselling centre in south Kensington. I got a cab there immediately, still stinking of fags and booze and still half-cut. I was told by a member of staff to join the group, sit down, shut up and listen. I went back the next morning at 9 a.m., washed, shaved and stone-cold sober. I continued to do that for the next four months. My only vices were cigarettes and about half a dozen double espressos a day from Nero during breaks. I did start drinking alcohol again after a while but, apart from the very occasional lapse, I've managed to keep myself 90 per cent drug-free for the last twenty-seven years.

Rehab was a real eye-opener. Apart from models with eating disorders and a few functioning alcoholics like me, there was a hedge fund manager and an architect who, unbelievably, were both crack addicts. There was a whole array of successful, middle-class, normal and respectable-looking men and women addicted to cocaine, heroin and all sorts of other substances. My illusions of suburbia were shattered and I was suddenly thinking of seventies films like *Valley Of The Dolls* and *The Stepford Wives*.

Without a doubt, the most disturbed people I met in rehab were the self-harmers. They showed me some of their horrific, self-inflicted scars hidden under their sleeves and that was when I really learned never to judge people by their appearances; you never know what demons may lurk beneath.

There were about twelve people in the group and each day one person had to stand up and tell their story, about how they ended up with a problem. Then there would be a question and answer session. It was helpful to hear about other people's experiences and find the things we had in common. We also had to keep written journals and answer a large questionnaire about everything that related to our addictions, such as obsessive compulsive disorder, behaviour issues and low self-esteem. The work also included a twelve-step programme that I never completed.

We all had to attend Alcoholics Anonymous and Narcotics Anonymous meetings on a daily basis. There was also Sex & Love Anonymous but none of our group attended their meetings as far as I was aware, although some of the guys in our group joked that it would be a great pick-up joint. The meetings are known as The Rooms and I was amazed at how many famous faces I used to see in them, particularly in the wealthier parts of London like Kensington, Chelsea and Notting Hill. I've also attended meetings in the less wealthy parts of town, including one that ended up with two old Irish alcoholics having a punch-up. I eventually stopped because I didn't feel like I was benefitting from them and some meetings were very Christian-orientated – they were more like bible classes. As a non-religious person, that put me right off. A word you hear a lot in those meetings is 'sharing' but quite often, one or two people would hog the floor and no one else could get a word in edgeways, which completely defeated the object.

I tried will power, but found it very difficult, so I got private sessions with a counsellor in Crouch End, north London. Once a week, I'd go to his house and he'd sit and listen while I talked about myself for fifty minutes – never an hour, always fifty minutes. I began to believe it was a complete waste of time and money and I'd go to the nearest local pub straight after seeing him. Once he walked past and saw me at the bar but pretended he hadn't and carried on walking. That convinced me he was more interested in my money than my problems, so I quit immediately. I also did a course of one-to-one sessions at an NHS clinic that proved equally fruitless. In my heart, I knew the harsh reality was it's all down to me – unless the addictions kill me first.

★ ★ ★

As the end of 1999 approached, everyone with a computer was panicking about the possible effect of 'Y2K' or the 'Millennium Bug' but, like the pathetic new year 'River of Fire' display on the Thames, it didn't happen. The clocks rolled forward into 2000 as per normal and instead of Y2K making everything reset to 1900 all we got was the 'I love you' virus that only affected PCs. We only had Apple Macs, so we were totally fine. The main thing I remember was having a totally miserable New Year's Eve as I wasn't drinking at the time – on the one night of the year when most people were out getting rat-arsed, I was teetotal. I spent the hour before midnight with a few friends, stone-cold sober, standing frozen on the south bank of the River Thames. I was surrounded by loads of pissheads and it made me think just how boring drunkards really are. The only thing was, they were all enjoying themselves and I really wasn't.

Chapter 40
COMEBACK #1

SOFT CELL WERE INVITED ON THE *TOP OF THE POPS 1981 Reunion* show in 2001 which, for some strange reason, was to be filmed during daytime in Pennington's nightclub in Bradford. This venue had previously been called 'Caesars' and we had played there live back in 1983.

Marc and I had separate, chauffeur-driven, matching titanium-coloured Mercedes pick us up from London. The drivers were both friendly, suited-and-booted, professional Millwall boys from Bermondsey and the journey went very smoothly – until we arrived in Bradford, that is. I arrived in a rundown part of the city and the satnav was completely useless. I'd heard there was a lot of racial tension in the area and there had been violent skirmishes with members of the extreme right. While we were stopped a large group of Asian kids were picking up stones and bricks and threatening to throw them at our cars. Presumably because we looked wealthy and we were white. The driver was having none of it and somehow managed to defuse the situation. It reminded me a lot of Leeds in the late seventies.

We finally found the venue and met up with Marc who had a huge gash on the side of his nose. I asked him if he'd been in a fight – knowing that was highly unlikely. He'd let his pet parrot out of its cage and it looked like it must have been bloody painful when it attacked him. But Marc is a very good make-up artist and you couldn't see any sign of a facial injury when we filmed our bit. We performed 'Tainted Love', which had been number one twenty years earlier, and our fee was the most we ever got paid by the BBC. We weren't promoting anything and as our track was top of the pile we had bargaining power – a very rare thing with the TV companies I've dealt with over the years.

On the morning of 9/11 I was sitting at my work station, editing a track on my Mac and Ingo was sitting on the far side of our studio doing some work on his machine. I had an old TV set in my bit that I always had on with the sound muted. I remember looking up and couldn't believe what I was seeing; the first airliner had just crashed into the World Trade Center in New York. 'Ingo, look at this. I don't fucking believe it!' He came running over, looking worried and was equally stunned. For a few minutes we thought it had been a tragic accident but when we saw another jet heading into the other tower, we knew something worse was happening. We turned up the sound and stared in disbelief: 'What the fuck is going on?'

We stopped work and decided to go to the pub and watch the news. It was late lunchtime in the UK and everyone in the Village Inn pub was in shock and drank their pints in silence. We listened to the news as they endlessly looped the footage of the two collisions. I remember saying to Ingo, 'I bet both towers will just collapse vertically, that's how they're designed,' and, sure enough, a few minutes later, that's exactly what happened, creating the huge dust clouds. A slightly sinister Chinese saying came into my mind: 'May you live in interesting times.'

On less significant days the Village Inn was an interesting mix of people – employees at the Pizza Express headquarters across the street, a few manual labourers and the occasional musician. Kensal Road was full of studios, the main one being the legendary Eastcote Studios where quite a lot of big bands recorded. It wasn't unusual on quiz night to see Depeche Mode or Blur with all the regulars.

That same year, Soft Cell had been invited to launch a new two-thousand-seater music venue called Ocean, in Hackney, east London. The venue was a converted Methodist hall and had received lottery funding of £23 million with a view to providing live entertainment as well as being involved in community arts projects. It was indeed a very big deal and we even got on the London TV evening news shows. But when we arrived for the soundcheck in the afternoon there were still gangs of workmen hammering and drilling away; the building work was way behind schedule but the venue had advertised and sold tickets for loads of gigs in advance. If they had cancelled shows they would have had a financial and legal nightmare with hordes of angry fans demanding refunds and bands' lawyers drafting lawsuits. So forget 'health and safety', the small matter of building work not being complete wasn't going to stop the venue from opening on time.

We were to play to an audience made up primarily of music industry types plus various bands and their agents. Some had come to check out this new music venue and, God knows, we needed more places in the capital for live music. Quite a few had come to check us out. Suggs from Madness was compere and came backstage to say 'Hello' but a stage manager came over to me and said, 'Are you ready to introduce them now, Suggs?' A weird case of mistaken identity but Suggs didn't go on to play keyboards for Soft Cell that night. I remember Marc and I waiting very nervously in the wings – we hadn't played in front of an audience together for seventeen years and we were going to debut some new songs.

We got a huge cheer as we walked on and, once we got through the first number – 'Memorabilia' – we relaxed and started to enjoy it too. What a relief. It's always very nerve-wracking playing to your peers. The next two nights were for ticket-holders only, with ticket touts and counterfeit merchandise-sellers lurking outside. The place was filled with two thousand fans going mad on both nights. I say two thousand, although I believe this venue had what's known as 'rubber walls' (i.e. the promoter printed a few hundred extra tickets that didn't go through the books). When we kicked off with 'Memorabilia' again the place went ballistic. I think a lot of the older fans couldn't quite believe we were back on stage together again. In fact, neither could we. They were great shows in an amazing venue. Sadly, at the time of writing, Ocean has been closed for a few years – so much for urban renewal.

Chapter 41

MONOCULTURE

SOFT CELL HAD A BIG YEAR FOR RELEASES IN 2002.

We had *The Very Best Of*, released on 16 April through Universal Records. That album featured all the singles, a couple of remixes, plus a few favourites of ours and two new tracks, 'Somebody, Somewhere, Sometime' and 'Divided Soul', which had started out as a soul-style groove that Ingo Vauk and I had written after listening to a few of my northern soul records in our studio one afternoon. I was reading the 1985 biography *Divided Soul – The Life of Marvin Gaye* by David Ritz. It was a fascinating insight into the life of one of my all-time favourite soul singers and the story was so strange, an odd mixture of religion, transvestitism, drug abuse and infanticide. I thought it had all the ingredients for one of Soft Cell's darker songs so I gave the book to Marc, knowing it would appeal. He didn't disappoint and wrote some great lyrics whilst borrowing the title of the book, which was perfect.

Our new studio album, *Cruelty Without Beauty*, was released on 8 October on Cooking Vinyl records. The first single off the album was 'Monoculture', a song Marc wrote about the dumbed-down culture we now appeared to live in. The word 'monoculture' is actually an agricultural term relating to growing the same crop repeatedly. We filmed the video one night in a privately owned kebab shop in Hounslow. We'd decked the place out like a burger joint and had Cell Burger cartons made in red and yellow to match our hideous red and yellow uniforms, complete with baseball caps. I flipped the burgers and injected them with something green and toxic-looking, while Marc served the customers freshly fried burgers and oven chips. We insisted that Stevo appeared in the video as a clown and I think he made a convincingly sinister John Wayne Gacy meets Ronald McDonald-type character – he was clearly made for the role.

I went to America twice in 2002. I travelled on Concorde the first time, taking only three hours and fifteen minutes. The second time, after spending summer playing Europe and Scandinavia, I went back to the US the slowest way, on a container ship across the Atlantic, taking eight days for what was a short and ill-fated US tour.

The first visit had been in spring. We were invited by NBC TV to appear on *The Today Show* live in New York. NBC wanted us to perform 'Tainted Love' and promised that we could also perform 'Monoculture'. Our main reason for going in the first place was to do the current single. I insisted on Concorde because of my phobia of flying and, surprisingly, my request was approved. Andy from Some Bizzare delivered my tickets by hand in a pub, to ensure I didn't bottle out and say they hadn't arrived. I made sure I arrived in good time at Heathrow and headed straight for the Concorde Lounge. That place was an alcoholic's paradise – a free, self-service bar with everything you could imagine available. I poured myself a very large vodka – nearly half a pint – and slimline tonic. 'Ah, I see we have another nervous flyer like myself,' chirped a fellow passenger as he filled a tumbler with Jack Daniel's and one ice cube. 'Cheers,' our glasses clinked. I should probably have booked the seat next to me for my liver. I had two more drinks like that before I got on the plane, then washed down a temazepam with the complimentary champagne on boarding, followed by several miniature bottles of wine with my meal once in flight. I slept well for most of the journey and arrived at JFK feeling a bit groggy with a mach-two hangover.

It was a great relief to pour myself into my waiting limo. I started to feel better as I sipped a complimentary bottle of Perrier and saw the Manhattan skyline come into view – the first time I'd seen it without the Twin Towers. I was staying at the Gramercy Park Hotel, which was a surprisingly dull experience. The suite I had was nice enough but there was no bar or restaurant and no atmosphere to speak of. It all seemed a bit odd for such a well-known Manhattan hotel to be so dowdy. Anita Sarko, my old New York flame, told me over dinner that the owner had recently leapt off the roof and committed suicide. Apparently, nowadays the hotel has one of the hippest and most exclusive bars in New York City.

Filming the TV show was quite a bizarre experience. It transpired that it was one of those 'Where are they now?' affairs, as we were largely perceived as a one-hit wonder in the USA. The Knack played their big hit, 'My Sharona', then we had to play 'Tainted Love' by the ice-skating rink outside the Rockefeller Center in Midtown Manhattan at nine in the morning. There were loads of NYPD officers and men-in-black with earpieces milling around to provide security. It reminded me of U2's video for 'Where The Streets Have No Name'. After each band played, the Kim Cattrall-lookalike presenter did a brief interview with the respective singers.

As Marc was doing his interview I stood behind my keyboard staring blankly at the stage floor. It gradually dawned on me that the stage designer had overlooked one important detail – the silver plastic floor covering was totally reflective and I was unwittingly staring at the reflection of the presenter's crotch. I think she realised when I did because she pressed her knees firmly together and looked daggers at me. I was wearing impenetrable sunglasses so she couldn't be entirely certain where I was gazing but I'm sure she had a pretty good idea.

After a leisurely week alone in New York it was time to take my return flight to London – fuelled by pills and alcohol, of course. I don't remember much about the flight apart from waking up at Heathrow airport; all the other passengers and flight crew had left and I was the only person on Concorde. I've woken up in some weird places before but I think that one takes the biscuit, waking up on Concorde.

★ ★ ★

Our European press and radio tour began on 16 June in Paris and moved on to Brussels, Amsterdam and Hamburg before returning to London on 22 June. Every interview was almost identical, the same boring questions, over and over. After some thirty-two interviews, I was very glad to be home for a few weeks before heading off to Italy to film our *Soft Cell – Live In Milan* DVD at the Rolling Stone club for release on Eagle Vision USA. We had a few other European dates lined up too and I'd agreed to travel with the crew on the tour bus so I didn't have to fly. I would also come back with money in my pocket as my expenses were less than Marc's, who flew everywhere. I slept some nights on the tour bus and saved money on overpriced hotel bills, although the smell of half-a-dozen blokes' feet, farts and breath in a confined space is not something you really want to wake up to every morning.

As we were filming a live video, I decided to dye my hair the night before we left as I was looking a bit grey. I got the wrong type – the sort that clearly says on the packet, 'Do not use on grey hair'. Obviously, I thought I knew better but my hair didn't end up as quite the natural black I'd hoped for. I decided I'd better wear my New York baseball cap when I turned up at our studio in Kensal Road the following morning, in the vain hope that no one would notice. I thought I'd got away with it; none of the crew said a word as they loaded our equipment onto the tour bus. That was until Andy, the guy who'd delivered my Concorde tickets, came over and asked me in a really loud voice, 'What's was wrong with your hair, Dave? Why is it blue?' It wasn't noticeable under the stage lights but I did get some very strange looks, walking round Milan in daylight. I don't think the fashion capital of Italy was quite ready for an eighties synth player with navy blue hair.

On 11 August we headlined the M'era Luna festival in Germany (and I didn't dye my hair). It was located at Hildesheim at a former British army airbase about thirty kilometres from Hanover. The main stage is in an enormous aircraft hanger and hosts a predominantly goth/industrial line-up. Previous headliners included Sisters Of Mercy, The Mission, Bauhaus, Nitzer Ebb, The Jesus & Mary Chain, New Model Army, Marilyn Manson, Fields Of Nephilim and, my personal favourites, Deutsch Amerikanische Freundschaft.

I really enjoyed the festivals because we played to big, enthusiastic crowds and finally made some real money, as we didn't have the usual expenses of travelling with a full road crew or have to truck sound and lighting rigs. We played all over east and west Europe and also Scandinavia, where we entertained one of our biggest audiences with some 25,000 Swedes.

Chapter 42

THE (NOT SO) FANTASTIC VOYAGE

AFTER TRAVELLING TO THE USA AND BACK THE FASTEST way – on Concorde – earlier in the year, it was time to take the slowest route.

My next big adventure was sailing both ways across the Atlantic Ocean on a container ship in winter (not exactly Rod Stewart's *Atlantic Crossing*). I kept a diary of the outward journey, which reads as follows…

Saturday 9 November
Terry, my driver/keyboard tech arrived promptly at 7.30 a.m. at my home in Kennington in the hired blue Mondeo. He was going to drive us to Hamburg by way of the Dover to Calais ferry (or fag-and-booze-cruise). We got to the port about nine-ish and it was very busy. Once on board there were queues everywhere – the bar, the shop and the restaurant. In fact, some people were still queueing for their full English breakfast when we arrived in Calais.

Once off the ferry, it was a ten-hour drive via Belgium, Holland and, finally, Germany. Once we got onto the autobahn we averaged about a hundred miles an hour so we made good time. We'd been told by the travel agent that the Holiday Inn we were booked in was just off the Reeperbahn in Hamburg. That wasn't the case – in fact, it was the first hotel we passed when we arrived in the city. We had to drive around trying to find it again, adding about another hour to our journey, but we finally got there.

Tired and hungry, we checked into our rooms then went down to the hotel restaurant to find the buffet selection being put away by a fat, unfriendly German lady who said we would have to eat a la carte as the buffet was finished. One of the other two, vacant-looking, waitresses brought over some menus. The waitresses then disappeared, so we adjourned to the bar where, as luck would have it, there was a selection of German bar snacks; sausages, frikadelle, rollmops, pretzels and pickled cucumbers; not exactly what we had in mind but after a few glasses of Riesling and a glass of Jever beer that Terry said was "orrible', we retired for the night.

Sunday 10 November
Met Terry for the Holiday Inn buffet breakfast at 10.30 a.m. – the closest thing to food we've eaten so far on our trip to Hamburg. I must say, I felt a lot better for a good night's sleep and a shower after sitting in a car for twelve hours. We checked out and asked the very helpful girl at the reception desk if she knew where I could buy a Euro charger for my Nokia. 'Nowhere is open on a Sunday, sir,' she replied, then disappeared for a minute. She returned with a box full of phone chargers that people had left in their rooms. None of them fit but we gave her top marks for trying.

'OK, Terry, there's only one place to go where the shops are open in Hamburg on a Sunday. *Der Bahnhof*,' I said, all worldly-wise, so off we went to Hamburg train station. I got an adapter for my phone plus a *Sunday Times* (minus magazine), chocolate bar, a biro and a slice of pizza. We had a quick drink, me a beer, Terry a coffee, then I bought two hundred Marlboro Lights and a bottle of apfelkorn. We set off to find the docks, which took a similar number of attempts as we had made to find the Holiday Inn, but find it we did and, before we knew it, we were surrounded by thousands of containers and those weird vehicles that lift them and move them. 'It's like something out of *Star Wars*,' exclaimed Terry.

We found where I was supposed to be and I was in the spooky sea mist of Hamburg dock, the place from which my ship would depart.

'I think I'm more excited about this than you are, Dave,' chirped Terry.

'Yes, you are, I'm totally nonplussed,' I replied in my dourest northern accent.

The truth was, I was starting to feel a bit nervous. When you get up close to one of those ships you realise just how big they are and if something were to go wrong, it really would be on a *Titanic* scale. We went up the gang-ladder (sorry, they don't use planks any more) and Terry carried one of my bags as an excuse to get on board and that was it: he had to head back to England and I was on the ship.

I was introduced to the other two passengers, an elderly German couple called Dieter and Erna who live in Canada. We were shown to our respective cabins. I was going to be having three meals a day with these two people for the next eight days so I tried to get on with them. After dinner, I went to my cabin and sort of semi-unpacked and sipped my way through my apfelkorn. I was in passenger cabin number two on poop deck number five. Poop deck took on a whole new meaning when I realised I was on a ship with an Indian captain and an almost exclusively Indian crew who ate curry for every meal, as did we passengers. The ship was registered in Bermuda (don't mention triangles) so it had a Bermudan flag, although it was actually owned by Canadian Maritime and was under the command of Captain Singh. It was called the *Canmar Courage*; it occurred to me that maybe they should have changed it to the *Canmar Curry*.

Monday 11 November
We finally departed at 1.45 a.m. I watched the activity of Hamburg docks and the harbour lights fade into the distance during my first night on board. I woke up several hours later and looked at my

watch: Shit, I've missed breakfast, I thought. I went down for lunch at noon to be reminded by the friendly Indian cook, 'You are early, did you forget to put your watch back by one hour?' Of course, I had, and had arrived an hour early for lunch; worse things happen at sea I suppose. I was bang on time for dinner though – chicken nuggets, curried veg, dahl and chapatis. That evening I started reading *The Old Man And The Sea* by Ernest Hemingway, as it seemed like an appropriate choice for my voyage. I should probably have taken *Moby Dick* as well.

Tuesday 12 November
Three more curries today and I nearly finished the Hemingway. I couldn't see land any more, we were totally surrounded by water. I bought a litre bottle of duty-free vodka from the steward.

Wednesday 13 November
Breakfast, 7.30 a.m. and the chef managed to slip in a curried rice and potato kedgeree type thing. Once again, curried breakfast, lunch and dinner. I saw a spectacular double rainbow, wow! Sat in the huge lounge on my own and finished watching *Lara Croft: Tomb Raider* on video. Being in that big room alone reminded me of the deserted hotel bar in Kubrick's film, *The Shining* – very creepy.

Thursday 14 November
7.40 a.m. samosas for breakfast today. It was curry for lunch again but, amazingly, dinner was curry-free: steak and fries, although it was served with a chapati. Time was really dragging, nothing to do apart from read, eat curry, smoke, drink, watch videos, listen to music and sleep. I got back into long periods of reading rather than my usual sporadic bursts when I'm on land with loads of distractions. God, I missed the distractions.

Friday 15 November
Missed breakfast and had a long, vodka assisted lie-in. Overcooked fish and curry for lunch. Discussed the price of phone calls and

car parking with my two elderly fellow travellers. Even they were getting cabin fever. The steward brought some fresh supplies up to my cabin. The prices were unbelievable: three cases of Beck's (seventy-two bottles), two litres of Smirnoff and two hundred cigarettes: total cost, $51. I gave him sixty dollars, so he got a nine-dollar tip. Even so, it was still a bargain.

Apart from the arrival of my new supplies, an otherwise quiet day. Watched a few films and really got into my new book, *Therapy*, by David Lodge. I even laughed out loud, possibly the first sign of madness.

I really hated night-time on the ship. We went through the back end of a hurricane so we were bouncing around like a cork and the ship was making hideous screeching sounds like the dinosaurs escaping from the container marked 'Property of Jurassic Park'. That night I just chain-smoked, chain-drank and chain-read until I fell asleep.

Saturday 16 November
Missed breakfast again and had another vodka sleep.

I couldn't sleep when it was really stormy so I read and drank until I finally nodded off. I started watching Tom Hanks in *Castaway*; I had a vague idea what he felt like. Once again it was time for lunch so I decided to watch the rest later – after yet another curry. One of my fellow passengers, the elderly German lady, was convinced she heard the bells of Atlantis last night as opposed to the escaped velociraptors I heard. Her husband looked at us both – slightly concerned.

At 3.15 p.m. there was a knock on my cabin door – it was the steward with my illicit bottle of Napoleon brandy. It's funny how things are always available for the right amount of dollars. I'd just finished my second litre of Smirnoff, so it was good timing. At least I got to sleep through the stormy night. I was just thinking about the saying about drinking enough to sink a battleship – obviously not as much as required to sink a cargo ship.

Sunday 17 November

Land ahoy! According to my basic geography, it must have been St John's on the east coast of Canada. That bit was plain sailing. I was so excited to see land. I had a shit, shave and shower and was fully dressed with a cup of Brooke Bond Taj Mahal in my hand by 7 a.m. It said on the box of teabags 'Dip, dip, dip,' which I kept repeating out loud as I paced around my cabin like an over-excited child. I probably wouldn't actually be on land for another thirty-six hours but it was nice to be able to see it at least. The ocean was very calm so that made a nice change after some of the turbulence we'd been through.

I spoke to the chief engineer who said we should be in Montreal by eight-ish on Tuesday morning, so it was in fact about another forty-eight hours before we'd be on land: bugger! I still hadn't seen any dolphins and all the whales had migrated to warmer waters, and the only iceberg we'd seen was the lettuce in last night's salad.

I couldn't wait to get off the ship, it was so boring and lonely. I was alone twenty-two and a half hours a day. I've never been imprisoned but this felt like I was in solitary confinement. The only company I had for an hour and a half was for breakfast, lunch and dinner, when I sat in the dining room with my German pensioner friends and the captain and various crew members. I didn't like being that isolated, my thoughts started to wander down some very dark alleys. I had cabin fever, big time. Crikey, it just started snowing, mind you, I suppose we were in Newfoundland.

Monday 18 November

Looked out of my porthole at 7.40 a.m. and everything was covered in snow. All the containers were covered in about ten inches of snow and resembled huge slabs of Christmas cake... hmm, roll on Christmas. I never thought I'd hear myself say that but it meant I'd be back in England. There was a blizzard going on, it was foggy, with huge waves and a very strong tailwind so at least we were moving faster. I think the term rock'n'roll must be a seafaring term because one of the crew told me that when you sailed into the wind, the ship rocked back and forth and when the wind was behind you, the ship rolled from side to side.

I went up to the bridge with Dieter the German and the waves were thirty foot high – quite scary. Then the captain ominously informed us that the Atlantic was the most unpredictable ocean in the world.

After I finished my lunchtime curry, I got back to my cabin and spotted more land; I figured that had to be Anticosti Island in the gulf of the St Lawrence River. We headed upstream to Montreal via Quebec. A pilot boarded our ship to guide us as the water level in the St Lawrence was very low and we didn't want to run aground. Our estimated time of arrival was 10 a.m. My phone started working again and I was on the Rodgers Network which I presumed must have been Canadian. Quebec City looked beautiful at night from the river – but, mind you, the South Bronx would have looked appealing after a week in the Atlantic on a cargo ship in November.

Tuesday 19 November
I arrived in Montreal after eight days at sea, said 'Goodbye' to my elderly German companions and the captain on the snowy quayside and met Terry, who'd flown in from London with our Mancunian tour bus driver, at the entrance to the docks. My legs were really wobbly; I'd got sea legs from the ship's movement and I felt really strange for about an hour. I had a bit of immigration bureaucracy to deal with on the Canadian/US border and was confronted by a Canadian customs officer, armed with a ginger crewcut and a gun. After a bit of form-filling, rubber-stamping and a six-dollar fee, I was free to go. I felt like an extra in the Coen brothers' *Fargo*: the snowy landscape around the immigration office was really similar.

We were all starving so we stopped off at a drive-in Burger King as there was no alternative for miles apart from McDonald's. Full of fast food, we set off for upstate New York. I was leaning forward talking to Terry in the steering compartment when the driver suddenly and inexplicably did an emergency stop which sent me flying, face and fingers forward into the cockpit. I pulled myself up and had a massive bruise on my right hand and a big scratch on my neck and I felt like I'd broken three fingers. The driver apologised profusely, obviously thinking, Christ, I've broken the keyboard player's fingers before the tour's even started, they're gonna sue my ass. Once things settled down, we decided to drive directly to Washington rather than via New Jersey to pick up a trailer. Obviously, the driver wanted to get rid of his dangerous cargo (me) as soon as possible. We got to the hotel, had a couple of beers then called it a day.

Wednesday 20 November
I woke up feeling rather fuzzy and got a phone call from Gary Westman, our US tour manager. He said Terry, my keyboard tech, was not in his room, nor was his luggage and no one had slept in his bed. A bit strange I thought as I went back to sleep. A bit later, I got another phone call, this time from Vicki Wickham, Marc's US manager in New York, who was looking after Soft Cell for the mini-tour. She was also worried that Terry was missing and then informed me that six out of eleven shows had been cancelled. The day was not going well: I had a pounding headache, my hand hurt like hell and I was starting to get a bit worried about my missing keyboard tech. Just as I got out of the shower, my phone rang again; that time it was the hotel manager, again asking the same question about the missing Terry.

Sometime later, yet another phone call. This was the tour manager again who told me that the situation was getting really serious. He explained that we were in the capital city of post-9/11 America and if we didn't locate Terry very soon, the hotel was required by law to report him missing to the FBI and the police. By that time, I was breaking into a cold sweat, the situation was getting fucking scary. I was the last person to see Terry before he disappeared and I had a bruised hand and a scratched neck. The injuries came from my fall in the coach but they were not going to look too good if my suite was soon to be full of FBI agents and cops asking me questions. I couldn't really remember anything about arriving at the hotel and started running around the hotel trying to find him myself. Then I spotted Terry in the lobby, leaving by the front exit.

'Terry!' I yelled at the top of my voice, terrifying a few of the guests in the process. 'Where the fuck have you been?'

'Oh, I overslept, they put me in Marc's room by mistake,' he replied, blissfully unaware of the anguish he'd just caused me and three managers (in fairness, it was the hotel's incompetence that actually caused the problem).

'Well, thank fuck I found you anyway; I'll see you at soundcheck in a couple of hours,' I said as he jumped in a taxi. I took a stroll around Washington for an hour and was shocked that there was so much poverty in the US capital. There were gangs of guys, all wearing similar bandanas, leaning on big old cars and some of the slums looked like shanty towns that could have been in Soweto; yet in the near distance was Capitol Hill.

I arrived at the 9.30 Club mid-afternoon, drank about a litre of Diet Coke and had some of the sandwiches and pizza that had been laid on. As I was tuning up my synthesisers there was the unmistakable sound of several gunshots from just outside the club, followed by wailing police sirens. It sounded like a US TV cop show, except it was for real and a young black guy had just been 'shot to death', as they say in America – and it was only three in the afternoon. I was having one of the heaviest days of my life and wondering what else could go wrong. But the show went without a hitch and the enthusiastic crowd loved it.

A long-term fan handed me his business card afterwards and invited me to go to his place of work, which just happened to be the White House. Sadly, I couldn't make it as we were heading off to the relative sanity of New York the following day.

Thursday 21 November

As the tour had been considerably shortened and to cut costs, it was decided we didn't need the tour bus and some of us would travel to New York by train.

I was disappointed and surprised that certain dates had been cancelled – in particular, the show in San Francisco, as Soft Cell obviously have a large gay following. The last time Marc and I had toured America, back in the eighties, we played a great gig there and San Francisco remained one of my favourite US cities. I still remember our disappointment after we went to the bay to see the Golden Gate Bridge and were told Alcatraz was closed because it was November. We had to settle for the shrunken heads in Ripley's Believe It Or Not! and take a cab ride down the famous sloping street that Steve McQueen raced in the film *Bullit* and that also featured in the Barbra Streisand film, *What's Up, Doc?*

Anyway, back to the current tour... Terry, Gary, Ingo, Martin (our crew) and I got the commuter train to the Big Apple. We arrived at Pennsylvania Station a few hours later and the place was teeming with armed guards and police. The amount of security in large public spaces in the US since 9/11 is incredible and I guess Penn Station is right next door to Madison Square Garden.

I checked into the Milburn hotel on West 76th Street between 2nd Avenue and Broadway. I had my own mini-apartment with a lounge, bedroom, bathroom and kitchenette – absolutely perfect.

Friday 22 and Saturday 23 November
Two days off, wandered around New York on my own. Discovered a great local Irish bar, the Dublin House on West 79th Street, which claimed to have the 'best jukebox in New York'. They also poured an excellent pint of Guinness.

Sunday 24 November
Show day – the Roxy, NYC. I walked fifty-eight blocks from the hotel to the venue at 515 West 18th Street for the soundcheck. I used to go to the Roxy back in the early eighties and watch all the rap artists so I was very familiar with the venue. It had more of a nightclub than a traditional rock-gig vibe and had a good compact stage which I preferred – Marc wasn't quarter of a mile away. The soundcheck went well and Ingo and I shared a cab back uptown

with Vicki Wickham. Ingo and I went for a Japanese meal before the gig. The show went really well, with a very enthusiastic New York crowd and we did a meet-and-greet (or shake-and-fake, depending on your mood) with fans after the show. Later I met up with this guy Phil, a DJ/fashion photographer/coke dealer, for a few drinks then headed back to my hotel to watch Manhattan Cable and sleep.

Monday 25 and Tuesday 26 November
Hung out in various bars in the very trendy Meatpacking District with my coke dealer friend for a couple of days.

Wednesday 27 November
It rained all day so I stayed in, despite it being my last shopping day in New York. I hate shopping for the sake of it and was getting bored with my own company. Terry, Gary and I met up in the evening and went to the Irish bar for a few drinks, then I went on to Big Nick's diner and had steak and onion, two eggs over easy, mashed potatoes and gravy. The steak was in the middle of a big, oval-shaped platter with the eggs on the right and the mash and gravy on the left. My main objective when eating was to make sure that the eggs and the gravy didn't come into contact pre-digestion. It was all washed down with a glass of chilled Chardonnay. The meal, including tip, only cost $15.

Thursday 28 November
New York to Chicago – a thousand miles.

Due to the Thanksgiving parade, half the streets our cab wanted to go down to get back to Penn Station were closed, so it took twice as long and cost twice as much as usual. We eventually made it and were soon trundling out of New York via Philadelphia on a tatty old Amtrak train, headed for Chicago.

The sleeper compartments had their own toilet and sink and a mini-TV monitor which played the films *Mr. Deeds* and *Men In Black II*, plus various National Geographic programmes about grizzly bears and episodes of *Whose Line Is It Anyway?* presented by Drew Carey. The buffet car was OK: I had a burger, fries and a beer. The smoking carriage was right at the back end of the train, which meant about a quarter of a mile walk every time I went for a cigarette. Walking up and down the wobbly train really fucked my leg joints up, especially after my eight days crossing the Atlantic. My hip and knee joints were absolutely killing me.

Friday 29 November
Chicago to Los Angeles – 2,265 miles.

Our show in Chicago was cancelled so we had a short stopover before the two-day journey. We arrived on the early morning train and there was no breakfast, just black coffee and a can of warm orange juice. Terry and I got off the train and checked in our bags ready for the afternoon departure to Los Angeles (which would arrive on Sunday morning). We came out of Union Station right by the Sears Tower, the tallest building in the US, and found a place that was doing breakfast for just $2.99. We chanced it and it was really good. I had the 'three-egg scrambler', with gammon steak, fried potatoes and flat-baked bread (which I couldn't finish). Terry had the same eggs, but bacon patties, fried potatoes and flat-baked bread (which he did eat). It all came with as much black coffee as you could drink. Fully stuffed, we then waddled around Chicago for a couple of hours. We went to the Harley Davidson shop which was full of bike leathers, belts, boots, T-shirts and, best of all, a whole range of motorbike clothing for dogs – jackets, T-shirts and, my personal favourite, peaked leather caps – for dogs? Only in America.

Then it was time to get back on the train again.

Saturday 30 November/Sunday 1 December
Travelled all day Saturday and woke up in California at 5 a.m. Pacific Time on Sunday morning. Had breakfast at 5.30 a.m. then went back to my cabin to watch the California sunrise. Arrived at Grand Union Station, Los Angeles at 9.40 a.m. and was met

by Gary, our tour manager. We drove to Le Parc Hotel in West Hollywood, where I had a suite for the week.

The first thing I did was wash some socks, undies and jeans in the sink in my kitchenette – Hollywood glamour. Later on I met Ingo in Santa Monica. He'd driven to LA from San Francisco in a hire car and it was quite good being able to drive around a bit. We went to a sports bar/burger joint I'd heard about. All the waitresses were pneumatic California girls, wearing hotpants and tight-fitting T-shirts with a picture of an owl and the word Hooters printed on the chest. A blonde-haired, blue-eyed waitress, who looked no more than 18 years old, came skipping over to our table to take our order. We both ordered burgers and fries and two beers and were stunned when she asked for ID to prove we were over 21. I was in my early forties with grey hair and Ingo was a bald thirty-something.

I don't know if it was my English accent but, somehow or other, somebody in there recognised me. Just as we finished eating, three waitresses danced over to our table, singing 'Tainted Love' at the top of their voices – at which point, we beat a hasty retreat.

Monday 2–Thursday 5 December
Three shows at venues in Anaheim, Santa Barbara and Santa Fe were all OK, nothing to report. I was just enjoying the California sunshine rather than the New York rain and having free time to walk around the corner to Sunset Boulevard, past the Viper Room, where River Phoenix died. I spent hours in the world-famous Tower Records store and bought three compilation CDs – *The Best Of Steppenwolf*, *The Best Of The Edgar Winter Group* and *The Best Of The New York Dolls*.

Friday 6/Saturday 7 December
My last day in Los Angeles.

I caught the evening train from Grand Union Station, bound for Chicago. They had a big piece of one of the Twin Towers in the entrance hall, as a memorial to all those who died on 9/11. Spent the evening checking out my new CDs, drank a bottle of wine and went to sleep.

Woke up the next morning still in California and later in the day we reached Albuquerque, New Mexico and were allowed off the train for a couple of hours. The train station was right by Route 66, the freeway that goes all the way to Chicago. I found a bar on the famous street, had a few beers and bought a Carhart denim shirt and a Native American Indian dreamcatcher from a store on the way back to the train. Next stop – the Windy City.

Sunday 8/Monday 9 December
Arrived in Chicago early Sunday evening. I felt really ill and my legs were killing me. Got the overnight train to New York, found my cabin and slept right through.

Tuesday 10 December
Met Gary, the tour manager, at Penn Station and boarded the next train, yet another old Amtrak, called *Adirondack* (I hadn't even noticed that they had names until then). We had an eight-hour journey ahead of us. Gary said the scenery was fabulous as the train went all the way along the banks of the Hudson River. We arrived at Montreal Station and it was about a quarter of a mile walk to the main concourse; apparently that was to stop the diesel fumes from trains smoking out the station. I hobbled along and a porter loaded our bags into the trunk of a cab.

When we told the driver which hotel we wanted to go to he complained, 'But it's just there, across the street,' at which point Gary stepped in.

'He's got bad legs, just take us there please,' Gary said.

The Hilton Montreal Bonaventure was a hideous corporate place that had a sort of corrugated concrete and jagged stone theme, inside and out. Gary revealed a hitherto unseen dark side when we met in the bar later and he said, 'I was just thinking, if ya wanted to fuck someone up real bad, ya could just push them into a wall.' It was true, you could seriously slash yourself to bits if you bumped into the wall. That kind of summed up the unwelcoming feeling I got from the hotel and I had weird dreams all night.

Wednesday 11 December

I took a stroll around downtown Montreal and bought a few bits for my voyage. I had to show the pharmacist my UK passport to buy some codeine phosphate painkillers for my knees; Gary said those pills were illegal in the US. I got some bandages – 'Amtrak knee' was a bugger. I bought a mental CD – *In A Metal Mood: No More Mr Nice Guy* by Pat Boone – absolutely priceless, in which the crooner covered hard rock classics in a lounge style. It even had a sticker on it that bore the legend, 'Value with a vengeance' – it certainly was. Got back to the hotel and had some Quebec pea soup for lunch; I expected it to be green like the English version but it was actually light brown and very tasty.

We arrived at the docks at 4.15 p.m., said hi to some of the crew that I knew from my last trip, including Captain Singh, who informed me that this time I was the only passenger and we wouldn't be departing until the early hours of Friday 13th. Normally that would have sent me into a complete headspin but I'd gotten (whoops, that's a bit American, Dave) so used to freaky things happening and being on my own for prolonged periods that it didn't bother me – or maybe the codeine was kicking in. I was stuck in Montreal docks for the night and the whole of the next day – great.

Montreal's a weird place, everybody spoke French, but they sold souvenirs with pictures of the Queen on them (the Queen's picture was even on the twenty dollar bill) and yet looked at you suspiciously if you told them you were English. There were loads of strip clubs and lingerie shops on the main shopping street as well as endless underground shopping malls – and I don't mean 'underground shopping' as a covert activity but that physically the buildings went down two or three storeys below ground level, as they did in Tokyo. The hotel lobby was actually on the seventeenth floor. When I found that out, I realised why the window in my room couldn't be opened more than three inches. Just think of all the accidental suicides.

Thursday 12 December
Woke up late in my cabin, missed breakfast – probably the combined effect of Pernod and codeine. The steward burst into my room at 11.50 a.m.; I looked up from my bed while he excitedly told me that lunch was in ten minutes. He wouldn't leave until I agreed to be there (heaven forbid I should miss a curry). Got dressed, went for lunch – which was indeed a curry – then went back to my cabin. Had a really boring afternoon on my own. Went for dinner, another curry, went back to my cabin and had a really boring evening. Ran out of vodka at midnight and went to bed.

Friday 13 December
Departed from Montreal at approximately 1.30 a.m., worried about it being the thirteenth and thinking it could be a bad omen but, in this day and age, after 9/11, who knows? I relaxed and put on *In A Metal Mood* and read Pat Boone's autobiographical sleevenotes which started with the immortal line, 'Some of my early million sellers...'

★ ★ ★

At that point, I gave up keeping a diary and just counted the days until I was back in my favourite place in the world – London.

Chapter 43

PISSING IN THE PARK

IN 2003 SOFT CELL WERE INVITED TO HEADLINE GAY PRIDE in Hyde Park on 26 July. It had a potential audience of sixty thousand people, which would have been our biggest ever. Other acts on the bill were Liberty X, Appleton, Mis-Teeq, Blue, Dead Or Alive and DJs Judge Jules and Boy George. I was even introduced to Jimmy Somerville backstage.

The only problem was the English summer weather: it absolutely pissed down, all day. In the end, we probably played to an audience of about thirty thousand loyal drowned rats. It wasn't a real gig, anyway, as all the music was on playback and only Marc's mic was live. We played about five numbers before it was decided it was too dangerous to carry on. There was water everywhere, even dripping off the lighting rig above us onto my synth – fortunately it wasn't switched on. Marc, on the other hand, was seriously at risk of electrocution, holding a wet, live microphone on a waterlogged stage. It was a great relief when we finished and I headed back to my friend Dave's Land Rover with my girlfriend Lou, who was to become the mother of our son, Elliot, in the not too distant future.

We joined the huge queue of vehicles waiting to leave the park. The traffic was very tightly controlled and we were stuck there for about an hour. One of the side doors of the people carrier ahead of us slid open and a woman got out. She was very tall and wore a tight-fitting mini-dress and very high heels. She stunned us all when she ran to the nearest tree, pulled her skirt up and stood and had a piss. When she turned around we realised that 'she' was actually Dead Or Alive singer, Pete Burns.

That year we released our cover version of 'The Night' on Cooking Vinyl and reached number thirty-nine in the UK, which wasn't bad, considering we'd been away so long and there was no video and very little promotion. I remember my friend Daryl Easlea from Universal Records saying to me that this should have been the comeback single. In retrospect I think he may have had a point. If we'd spent the video budget on this track rather than on 'Monoculture' we may have made more of an impact on the charts. We performed the song alongside 'Torch' on *Top Of The Pops 2* but we didn't get very much radio play.

Soft Cell Live was released on 7 October on Cooking Vinyl. MD Martin Goldschmidt, being the astute businessman that he is, had kindly upped the advance for *Cruelty Without Beauty* with the proviso that we also gave him a live album. I was in charge of the production and financial details of both albums. I had to make sure everybody got paid – session musicians, studios, engineers (the people who actually did something creative). My main problem was my manager who only seemed to care about his commission. To meet his demands I had to renegotiate the deal and that was the biggest irony – technically that was what he was paid to do, negotiate. Suffice to say, I convinced the record company to part with a total of a 125 grand.

The live album, produced by Ingo Vauk and me, was recorded on our digital mobile system during our short tour of major UK cities earlier in the year, with the customary one-off date in Brussels. We recorded every show and once we returned to London, went straight back to our studio in Notting Hill to go through hours and hours of recordings on the Pro Tools system. We eventually whittled it down to a compilation of five shows

– Birmingham, Brussels, Leeds, London and Manchester. There were no overdubs added to the vocals or music, just equalisation and stereo-imaging. We did have to cross-fade and match some of the crowd sounds as the ambience and acoustics of each venue varied quite a bit. I must give full credit to Ingo for his technical wizardry on that live album. There was quite a lot of faffing about to get the whole thing to run smoothly but it does and, amazingly, sounds like one gig.

A shot from the festival just outside Venice that Soft Cell headlined in 2004.
We wouldn't play together again until 2018.
DAVE CHAMBERS

Promoting our 2002 single 'Monoculture' complete with mock-up padded cell.
DAVE CHAMBERS

y live rig for the three shows at Ocean, Hackney, London, 2001.

The Grid have a tea break. With Richard Norris in his back
garden, Notting Hill, London, 2008.
DAVE CHAMBERS

Onstage with The Grid
at the Glade Festival,
2008. The backdrop
projection was by
Kieran Evans.
DAVE CHAMBERS

With Richard Norris and Sir Tom Jones after a Grid show in Melbourne, Australia, 1995.

Having a 'production meeting' with Martin Rushent at his local in Pangbourne, Berkshire, 2010.
DAVE CHAMBERS

Filming the BBC 4 documentary at Leeds Warehouse, 2018, met with fond memories of playing our first paying gig there.
DAVE CHAMBERS

At BBC Radio 2 before appearing on Graham Norton's show, 2018. I had to have my photo with the legendary Elton John piano.
DAVE CHAMBERS

A good luck kiss backstage with Scarlet West, just before the O2 show, September 2018.
DAVE CHAMBERS

the O2 I came to realise just how big that place looks from the stage!

Onstage at the O2, which was very enjoyable. I felt surprisingly relaxed.
DAVE CHAMBERS

After the O2 show. 'I think that
went really well,' said Marc.

At the Soft Cell book launch/my 60th birthday party, with Lloyd Lewis Kristian, Marc Almond and Chris Smith, May 2019. Still signing books, even on my birthday!
SOURCE

In the tape surgery. Soft Cell photoshoot,

Our 'blue plaque' in Leeds. I am

Chapter 44

PERIL IN VENICE

IN THE SUMMER OF 2004 WE HEADLINED A SMALL FESTIVAL outside Venice with a capacity audience of six thousand. As I wasn't flying, getting there turned out to be quite an adventure in itself.

I went with Dave Chambers, Stevo and his girlfriend, Wendy, who was going to share the driving with Dave. We hired a people carrier from our usual firm at the Elephant & Castle, then loaded up my gear and set off from my house in Kennington to get the ferry from Dover to Calais and across the continent. We stopped occasionally for a beer and fuel, a change of driver, leg-stretching and for an al fresco meal at a restaurant by Lake Como, overlooking Mussolini's old house built into the rocks and accessible only by water. The place was like a scene from a James Bond movie – loads of speedboats and light amphibious aircraft landing on the water, surrounded by beautiful mountains.

Another stop was at a log cabin bar in Switzerland. It was a typically idyllic Alpine scene – longhorn cows with bells around their necks drinking in a stream with pine trees everywhere. I could imagine Julie Andrews yodelling over the hilltop. Geography was never my strong point and it had never really occurred to me just how many Alps there were. I suppose I thought there were about three or four. That day, I lost count and by the time we finally got the ferry to Venice I didn't want to see another Alp as long as I lived. A lot of the journey took us on narrow mountain roads with sheer drops and crash barriers that looked like they were made of dental floss. We were in a right-hand drive vehicle, I was in the front passenger seat and I spent much of the journey gazing a thousand feet down at the ravine, the drop beginning about a foot from where I sat.

When we arrived in Venice, the annual film festival was in full swing. Spielberg was in town and the only available accommodation was a shabby guest house. Stevo and Wendy were in a double room and Dave and I had a twin. Even at night, the city was baking hot, as was our room and the air conditioning didn't work. Unwisely, we left the window open, the stench of the nearby Grand Canal only becoming bearable after several drinks in a local bar. We slept soundly until the next morning.

'Fucking hell,' we both exclaimed as we woke up, scratching the enormous bites that covered every bit of our pale, exposed flesh. It hadn't occurred to us that being right by one of the most foul-smelling canals in the world there would be a very large population of extremely vicious mosquitos. Once we'd located some calamine lotion and covered ourselves in it, we returned to the bar next door for gin and tonics – purely medicinal, as we both needed plenty of quinine to avert malaria.

The venue for the show was on the mainland, which meant getting the ferry back to our car and driving several kilometres to meet Marc. The road was totally congested and we got pulled over by the police, which turned out to be a blessing because – once we'd explained that we were English and were involved in a local concert – they were very helpful. It was also a bonus that Wendy was not only a very attractive woman with long black hair and piercing blue eyes but she also spoke fluent Italian. Her considerable charms were not wasted on the Italian bike cops and she soon had them eating out of her hand. They almost fell over themselves to help us. Before we knew it, they'd cleared one lane of the autostrada and were giving us a police escort to the gig in return for a few CDs and T-shirts.

We made it to the show with plenty of time to set up and soundcheck, when the next problem presented itself. Ingo, who normally did our front of house live sound, had family commitments in Germany and I'd persuaded my friend Ian Tregoning to do our sound even though he'd never worked with us before. I don't know if he'd ever done live sound before as he normally engineered and co-produced the band Yello in the studio. We had severe technical problems with our hard disk machine with the backing tracks and as Ian was not used to the system I had to call Ingo in Germany and get him to try and solve the problem over the phone. As any computer helpline worker will tell you, that was not the easiest job in the world – especially when the call was between an English mobile in Italy to another in Germany with the occasional loss of signal.

I also had Stevo laughing at his own jokes behind me in his loud East End voice. My stress levels went through the roof. 'Will you shut the fuck up!' I yelled at him. 'Do you want the bloody gig to happen or not? We have half an hour to sort things out, then six thousand people are going to arrive and we haven't even soundchecked yet. If you don't shut your big gob, I'm going to have a spotlight put on you and announce over the PA system that it's all your fault the show is cancelled. Just remember what they did to Mussolini!'

Amazingly, silence finally prevailed, as the notion of being lynched by a huge crowd of furious, ticket-wielding Italians finally sunk in. I heard Ingo chuckle on the other end of the phone as he continued to talk us down and we resolved the problem, no thanks to Stevo.

Chapter 45
CRITICAL

ON MONDAY MORNING, 18 OCTOBER 2004, MY PHONE starting going into overdrive. I received about thirty messages in quick succession, all asking the same question: 'Is Marc going to be all right?' Even my lawyers and accountants phoned to ask what had happened. I had no idea what they were talking about but they all kept referring to an accident.

I turned on the TV but the breakfast news had just finished so I put on Ceefax teletext and there it was: 'Soft Cell singer in critical condition after motorbike crash.' Marc had been involved in a collision with a car in Cannon Street, near St Paul's Cathedral. I started shaking and went into shock, I knew nothing more than what I'd seen. I just remember thinking out loud, 'Oh, my God, is he going to die?' It was a truly horrible feeling, I just felt totally helpless. I'd known Marc on and off for twenty-five years and we'd survived all sorts of scrapes together; I just couldn't believe what was happening.

I eventually spoke to Marc's manager, who had been driving the bike, with Marc riding pillion. Dave Chambers and I went to visit him in hospital, where he was being treated for severe leg injuries. We never got to see Marc and he apparently spent about two weeks in a coma, with bad head injuries amongst other things. Thankfully, the pearly gates didn't open and, once he was transferred to a private hospital, he slowly seemed to make a full recovery. The last time I had worked with him was when Richard and I recorded his vocals for two unreleased tracks for The Grid at Eastcote Studios and he seemed to be in great shape. Since then, I'm glad to say, he seems to have gone from strength to strength, receiving an OBE and an Ivor Novello award and various other accolades in recognition of his work in both music and charities – from one critical list to another, as it were. At the time of writing, I'm very happy to be working together again on material for a new Soft Cell album. Marc has always been my favourite lyricist to work with. He seems to get my occasionally unusual musical moods and melodies better than anyone else.

Chapter 46

SOS

I ALWAYS HATED NOT HAVING WORK TO RELEASE AND 2005/06 was one of those lean periods. *The Bedsit Tapes* – yet another compilation, cobbled together by Stevo from my personal archives of early Soft Cell demos – was all that broke the drought.

The CD was mastered from knackered old cassette tapes that had been gathering dust in my loft for years. It was strictly lo-fi, for collectors and completists only. Somewhat appropriately, it was released on Some Bizzare, which seemed to have become little more than a dusty catalogue label, mostly trading on past glories.

But 2006 wasn't all doom and gloom as I had some very good news from the US. On Valentine's Day, Rihanna released a single called 'SOS'. The track was largely based around an instrumental sample of our version of 'Tainted Love', which meant they had to pay us a royalty on every record and download. The record went to number one globally, topping the US charts for three weeks, where it sold over a million copies. It was officially recognised as the biggest-selling single in the world at the time. Funnily enough, our version of 'Tainted Love' only got to number eight in the Billboard 100. So in a way, we did eventually hit the US top spot – albeit by proxy.

I've never actually met Rihanna but had a few near misses, so to speak. We were invited to do a cameo appearance with her on an MTV Europe Music Awards show but couldn't make it due to prior commitments. Then there was the time I was watching TV in my house as she was being interviewed live on a morning show at Cactus TV, whose studios were at the end of my street. She said she'd really like to meet us but I didn't really fancy just turning up unannounced. My closest encounter with her was one afternoon in a Caribbean restaurant called Savannah Jerk, on Wardour Street, Soho. There was a group of mostly American flunkies at the next table surrounding this very striking-looking young woman. My two friends and I twigged that she had to be either an actress or a singer but couldn't quite place her. After they left, the waiter revealed, 'That was Rihanna. She likes to eat here whenever she's in London.' I guess we're just not destined to meet.

Chapter 47
MOTHER AND CHILD REUNION

MANY YEARS AFTER I WAS BORN AND ADOPTED, THE LAW was changed, allowing parents who'd given up their children to track down their long-lost offspring. Previously, only the child could try to relocate the parent but not vice versa. That was something I'd never even considered doing but my birth mother felt otherwise and, via an agency in Liverpool, finally traced me to London, where I've lived for the past thirty-seven years.

After writing the occasional polite letter and chatting on the phone, I finally agreed to meet her in Chester, where she still lived. Even though it had been over forty years since I'd last laid eyes on her I recognised her at once. The same eyes and mouth as mine and something about her aura and demeanour betrayed her. Her husband, a pleasant Irishman I'd also spoken to on the phone, was by her side. I imagine it must have been very weird for him when I suddenly materialised. I got the distinct feeling she'd probably talked about me incessantly and driven him mad with it. That said, he was incredibly protective of her; they had, after all, spent most of their adult lives together – a life in which I'd played no part.

As a man, my interest was always more about my natural father than my mother but I didn't feel I could ask any of the questions I'd wanted to all my life. For years, all sorts of imaginary and occasionally grotesque scenarios had run through my warped mind. Had they been lovers in a long-term, caring relationship? Was I the result of a one-night stand and a burst condom? Could I have been the lust child of a careless prostitute or, worse still, was my mother a rape victim? It was totally inappropriate to ask any of that, of course, especially with her devoted husband acting as a human shield between her and my morbid curiosity.

At midday, we went to a pub that was one of the many black-and-white mock-Tudor-style buildings in the city centre. I was politely informed that they no longer smoked tobacco or drank alcohol, both of them giving me slightly disapproving looks as I lit a Camel Light and sipped my pint of cider. Had it been a problem in the past? I wondered. Were they going to get all born-again preachy on me? I sensed from their behaviour that maybe one or both were recovering alcoholics. That may explain some of my addictive genes – it takes one to know one, as they say.

Once I'd established that I was returning to London later that day and would not be sleeping in their spare room that night as they'd wrongly assumed (Christ, I barely knew them), we continued with more small talk. The microwaved pub grub arrived quickly and they nearly choked on their baked potatoes when I told them what I did for a living. Both of them were quite taken aback when they realised they'd probably seen me on TV and heard me in the background on the radio without ever realising I was her long-lost son. For me, the most illuminating moments of the day were seeing the house where I spent my first year with my mother and her aunt and my surprise when my birth mother told me that she and her husband have three middle-aged daughters. We are semi-related by blood – I have three younger half-sisters I've never met – as far as I'm aware.

Chapter 48

WILDERNESS YEARS
PART TWO

AFTER MUCH INDECISION AND ARGUING WITH STEVO, *Heat – The Remixes* was released in 2008. Stevo had wanted to use all his unknown acts to do mixes and promote his label and the record ended up belying its title. It was a very lukewarm effort; some all right, some not bad, but mostly average. I didn't even like my own mixes.

We'd approached Pet Shop Boys and Scissor Sisters, who'd both said they were interested, but there was no real budget so we couldn't get any big names on board. If I am totally honest, I think the end result was a complete waste of everybody's time and it was hardly groundbreaking compared to its eighties predecessor, *Non Stop Ecstatic Dancing*.

The other bad news was the Astoria in London's Charing Cross Road finally shut down in 2009 and was later demolished by developers. Yet another great venue bit the dust. I've performed there on two occasions. Once as half of The Grid and once at G.A.Y. as half of Soft Cell. The Soft Cell gig was basically a half-hour playback of all the hits with live vocals. A piece of piss for us and they paid very handsomely – God, I love the pink pound.

In 2010 I was very flattered when A-ha performed a live version of 'Say Hello, Wave Goodbye' in September at the BBC's Maida Vale studios for the Ken Bruce show on Radio 2. I have to say, Morten Harket has an incredible voice.

The following year started badly for me. On 30 January I was very saddened to hear the news that one of my all-time musical heroes, John Barry, had died. I have collected his records since 1981, when Anni Hogan kept playing a double greatest hits album at our shared Leeds house. In total, I must have over a hundred vinyl albums and singles by him, including a very rare bootleg of the soundtrack to Nic Roeg's *Walkabout*, signed by the composer. Back in 1982, I was lucky enough to spend an evening in his company. I remember the day very clearly because I was in a small studio next door to the deaf school in Nottingham, recording an album with a local electronic band called Sense. They had an album deal with the Parisian disco label Carrere, with me on production duties. I was due to head back to London later in the evening when I got a phone call from one of my friends in our office above Trident Studios. He knew I was a massive J. B. fan (John Barry and James Bond) and could barely contain his excitement when he told me they were recording the demo for the theme for the next James Bond film, *Octopussy*, and my hero was going to be in the studio later. I cut short my session and was on the next train to London St Pancras like a shot. When I arrived at the studio they'd just finished recording a Tim Rice song called 'All Time High' with vocalist Rita Coolidge. She was sitting next to John Barry and producer Phil Ramone, who I knew already.

The first things I noticed about John were his deep-voiced Yorkshire accent and how thin he was. He had a quietly serious, stern manner about him that oozed sophistication and he was definitely not a person I would have liked to have got on the wrong side of. When I enthusiastically asked him how the session had gone, he matter-of-factly said he was quite pleased with the recordings. I supposed that, at his level, doing a Bond score was just another job. His main concern seemed to be getting some brandy to drink while he smoked his Havana cigars. As we were in Soho, central London, on a Sunday night, that was a bit of a problem as all the shops were closed. We did eventually manage to order a couple of bottles of Armagnac, at highly inflated prices, from a nearby restaurant, so everyone was happy. The other James Bond-related person I was really thrilled to meet that day was producer Albert R. 'Cubby' Broccoli. I always remembered being intrigued by his name as the credits rolled on the Bond films I'd watched in the cinema as a child.

Some years later in the late nineties I twice saw John Barry conducting his orchestra at the Royal Albert Hall. The first time he was introduced by his good friend Michael Caine and on the second occasion by Sir George Martin, presumably another old pal. I remember spotting Robbie Williams at the first show; I guess he must have been a fan too, as he used the string part of 'You Only Live Twice' on his track 'Millennium'. I even saw Damon Albarn at the second gig.

I found myself again at a creative loose end as there were no plans for Soft Cell after Marc's bike accident. I kept myself busy musically with my friends Rick Mulhall and Terry Neale who had a nice studio in Richmond called Kick. They had a very successful business writing and producing music for children's animated TV programmes. On Thursdays and Fridays they'd down their glockenspiels and xylophones in exchange for theremins, synths and electronic drum kits and we'd meet up for our weekly jamming/writing sessions, mostly in what I would call an electro-punk style. I think it also doubled up as therapy for them after a week of major-key tinkling. We had more than an album's worth of backing tracks but as yet, no vocalist. Then David Hoyle's manager, Dr Steve Warren, a psychologist friend of mine with connections to the Royal Vauxhall Tavern, said he knew a female performer called Celine Hispiche, a polari/vaudeville performer who'd recently done a guest appearance with Marc at Wilton's Music Hall. I was told she'd also expressed an interest in meeting and maybe working with me.

I played Celine the stuff I'd been working on with Rick and Terry and asked her if she would be the singer/front person of our fledgling band, originally called Nitewreckers then Nitewreckage. It was quite an odd juxtaposition – music hall/Poly Styrene-meets-electro – but I've always loved experimenting with elements not traditionally associated together – with varying degrees of success. Northern soul + electro = 'Tainted Love', bluegrass + electro = 'Swamp Thing', both million-sellers.

We began to write lyrics for an album's worth of tracks at our weekly band rehearsals at Kick Studios. Celine managed to get us a deal with a music biz friend of hers called Derek Savage, who'd previously worked with Hazel O'Connor and The Stranglers and was now in the property business. We played at our launch party at Derek's rehearsal studios under the arches of Waterloo Station with guest DJ Richard Norris and our album, *Take Your Money And Run*, was released on his indie label, Alaska Sounds, on 6 June 2011. They say it's cold in Alaska and the reception to our album certainly was.

The single, 'Popabawa', got a great review in *The Guardian* and DJ Mark Moore of S'Express gave us a good namecheck in one of the gay free sheets, but two small reviews didn't make an ounce of difference when the overall press and radio promotion were virtually non-existent. I thought of the thousands of great records that had slipped through the net over the years, while loads of the crap ones became hugely successful and I genuinely believe ours was a really good record. But if you don't have promotion, you don't stand a cat in hell's chance. I've worked on dozens of records in my thirty-odd years as a professional musician and producer and I know it takes just as much time and effort to write, play and record the flops as it does to create the hits. I don't consider that record to be anywhere near my personal best, or worst, come to that. It had some great material on it and as a band, we each gave it one hundred per cent, but it was destined to fail.

We had a very striking photographic image taken by our friend, David Chambers and we all agreed that we wanted to use it as the album sleeve. The record company decided, without proper consultation, to use an artist friend of theirs who did some nondescript, wishy-washy doodles that none of the band liked. As the label were paying for everything (except our time), we didn't have a say in it and at that point my interest in the project ran out. The whole thing no longer represented our original idea – far too much interference for my liking. I even forfeited my producer credit, as a display of solidarity with the band.

What saddened me the most about that ill-fated album was not its lack of success, more that it was one of the last projects our associate producer – and all-round studio genius – Martin Rushent worked on. He was an old friend of Derek, who'd brought him in to finesse our tracks. I first met Martin after we'd signed the deal and Derek treated us all to a night out in the West End, starting with dinner at the Ivy followed by the musical *Jersey Boys* and finishing up guzzling red wine in the Groucho Club.

I didn't always see eye-to-eye with Martin when we worked at his Pangbourne farmhouse studio, although most of our disputes were usually resolved once I bowed to his 'superior judgement' (his words) and bought him dinner and a few glasses of red wine in the local gastro pub. Sadly, Martin died on 4 June, aged 62, and Nitewreckage disbanded shortly afterwards.

We'd had some good times as a band and my personal highlights comprised playing a benefit for The Colony Room Club at the 100 Club on Oxford Street and the M'era Luna festival in Germany. The only thing that let M'era Luna down was that we weren't headlining as I had with Soft Cell.

★ ★ ★

One of my first childhood pop heroes, Davy Jones of The Monkees, died at the beginning of 2012 and May that year brought two very sad days for disco music. On Thursday 17 May Donna Summer died, followed on the Sunday by Robin Gibb of the Bee Gees. I never met them but their music had a profound effect on me as a teenager. I'd never really thought about my own music featuring in the soundtracks to people's lives until 2018, when someone handed me a copy of the *Mail*'s *Sunday Live* magazine with a piece by Piers Morgan. I'm a fan of his anyway, so I read it and was, indeed, truly flattered. According to the article, he was at a private dinner party with Simon and Yasmin Le Bon when they were playing an eighties pop quiz game and all concurred that Soft Cell's 'Tainted Love' summed up the summer of 1981. That was thirty-seven years ago – God, I suddenly felt very old, a feeling that was confirmed when my friend Mat Fox, a musician and avid crossword-doer, spotted a clue in the giant puzzle in *The Independent* around the same time: '1980s British electronic pop music duo comprising Marc Almond and David Ball.' It felt oddly embarrassing to be a clue in my friend's crossword. It was both flattering, because it confirmed our minor contribution to popular culture, but also slightly depressing as it gently consigned us to the history books. Funnily enough, quite a few Soft Cell-related questions have cropped up on radio and TV quiz shows, not to mention pub quiz machines. We've been answers on *Eggheads*, PopMaster and even *Mastermind*. The contestants have always got the answers right – so far. The same couldn't be said when Pablo Cook, percussionist with The Grid, did the line-up round on *Never Mind The Buzzcocks* and the team picked out the wrong person. When I saw him an old catchphrase of his sprang to mind – 'What are you doing boy?' A phrase I've frequently begun to ask myself, with the addition of the word 'old'.

I must say I was very chuffed by an ITV poll of number one records of the last sixty years – although it did cross my mind that I'd been alive for fifty-nine of the 2018 poll's years. The Soft Cell version of 'Tainted Love' was number eighteen but what really made my week was when Gary Crowley played our track 'Torch' on his show on BBC Radio London as a tenuous connection to the 2012 Olympics. The idea of Soft Cell having anything to do with sport was inconceivable.

No sooner had the London Paralympics come to an end in 2012 than I read the obituaries of two of my other heroes: Neil Armstrong the astronaut, and music legend Hal David, one of my favourite US male pop lyricists of all time. Years earlier, I'd had the pleasure of meeting Hal at the Ivor Novello Awards. I was very pleased when Marc received the 2013 Inspiration Award at the Novellos although I've never even been nominated. And Marc's manager for the US, Vicki Wickham, got an OBE, as did Marc himself. As Mat Fox once said to me, 'Never mind, Dave, you'll probably get a ward in St Thomas' one day.'

I got invited to the Ivors a couple of times by Pete Hadfield and Keith Blackhurst, who owned Deconstruction Records. It was always a star-studded occasion and, as a music fan, I loved going to those kind of events, especially for the late morning champagne reception when the Bentleys full of A-listers began arriving outside the Grosvenor Hotel on Park Lane. Elton John and Rod Stewart were the most notable guests I spotted, Rod looking very LA in a suit with no socks under his Gucci loafers. I was sitting chatting with Richard Norris from The Grid and Tom from Decon when Sting came over to our table and started talking with Keith. When he'd gone, we were all suitably impressed.

'How the fuck do you know Sting?' I asked, knowing everyone else at our table was wondering exactly the same thing.

'Oh, sometimes we go skiing together,' came his smooth-talking Scouse reply.

Hal David was given a well-deserved lifetime achievement award by the Novellos and, to my surprise, I saw him standing on his own afterwards. I seized the opportunity and introduced myself. At the risk of sounding like a slightly tipsy, gushing fan (which I was), I told him I just wanted to say 'thank you' for the music (oh dear) that he and Burt Bacharach had written. I'm sure he'd probably heard it a million times before but he seemed very happy when I said they'd made some of the best pop music of all time. I think he could tell I really meant it and he shook my hand firmly and smiled benignly. The truth is, I really did mean it. I have every composition they ever released in my collection. It was indeed an honour to meet a musical legend and a true genius.

Chapter 49
CATWALKS

I ONCE PLAYED AT THE IN & OUT CLUB IN ST JAMES'S during London fashion week when I was asked by Paul and Jim from Candy Records to be the warm-up DJ for the late Leigh Bowery's band Minty, fronted by Matthew Glamorre. John Cale from The Velvet Underground recited some poetry that no one listened to in one room while I played dark ambience next door, as requested.

I was foraging through my records when people started cheering inexplicably – not the normal reaction I expected, considering the subterranean music I was playing. It was only when I looked up that all became clear. Nicola Bowery, Leigh's nubile young widow, was modelling the emperor's new clothes; dancing stark naked around the stage, right in front of me.

Apart from co-writing the music for a show in Marylebone at the American College in London, one of my other encounters with fashion shows was as a guest of my make-up artist friend and old flame, Gemma. It was at a show at the Natural History Museum. I got really excited, not so much about clothes but the surreal experience of sitting right opposite Ronnie Corbett, whose legs were so short that his feet didn't touch the floor as he sat and watched the parade of tall, leggy models.

I've always loved playing music in unusual venues. I was once invited to DJ at Tate Britain by my friend David Crawforth, the curator of the Beaconsfield Gallery in south London. He asked me to play New York-style disco as he knew I had all the original twelve-inch records, having misspent a considerable amount of my time in Manhattan's nightclubs in the early eighties, taking drugs and collecting records with equal enthusiasm – a true vinyl junkie. It was very odd playing disco in a roomful of old masters worth millions. Amazingly, nothing got damaged.

I was asked to London fashion week again by my old axe-wielding friend Cobalt Stargazer. He played guitar on The Grid's 456 album and we'd recorded an unreleased studio album together with Ingo Vauk and Elton Jackson under the name of Mi7. I'd also done a guest spot, playing a synth solo vs heavy metal guitar solo battle, with his hard rock band, Zodiac Mindwarp, at the Camden Underworld – I think we agreed it was a draw. His band Rooster features his partner Sara J. Stockbridge, actor, author and former muse of fashion designer Vivienne Westwood. Rooster was to play live to accompany the models on the catwalk and I was asked if I would do some additional electronic sounds with my Korg Kaoss Pad – an offer I couldn't resist, especially as the show was at the Foreign Office.

Rehearsals began at 6 p.m. on Saturday evening and we arrived in Cobalt and Sara's big old Jaguar XJ6, which was checked for explosives by one of the guards, while the registration number and various other details were verified before we were let in. The place was a vast construction in stone and marble with a very high ceiling that made the acoustics incredibly lively. That wasn't too much of a problem on the ground floor as they'd installed a nearfield surround sound system with twelve speakers focused on the catwalk. Everything went very well and we were done in about an hour which was lucky for me as I had to go to a party afterwards.

The following day we piled into the Jag and headed off to Whitehall for another run-through at midday. There were some men doing maintenance on the hydraulic security barricade at the entrance to the Foreign Office and we were told to take the next left. We all looked at each other in disbelief as it dawned on us that the next left was in fact Downing Street. But we had no problem as the armed police opened the gates for us and pointed us in the direction of another security area where an officer checked under the car and bonnet again for explosives.

Showtime was at 2 p.m., when the all-important critics and corporate buyers were seated. I can never get over how painfully thin the models look at these events. My dad's old saying, 'I've seen more meat on a butcher's pencil,' came to mind – but then again, he'd never seen how fat their bank accounts were. The whole event was filmed and looked great. Vivienne Westwood, wearing a black hat, big knickers, grey tights and a T-shirt, sported an unusual monocle and moustache drawn on her face in black make-up. At the end of the show, she was draped in a voluminous metallic bronze fabric banner that was unfurled by two stick insect models to reveal the slogan 'Climate Revolution'. She then took her bow, with much applause from the invited audience. We celebrated with a few glasses of complimentary champagne then took a taxi back to reality. A few days later I enjoyed much schadenfreude when a Tory politician with a bike and an attitude had a problem with the police on the gates at number ten after allegedly calling them 'plebs'. I thought it was the musicians who were supposed to be the troublemakers.

★ ★ ★

I finally quit cigarettes on 18 April 2012 and, after extensive medical tests (endoscopy, X-rays, CT, MRI scans, etc.), on 5 June 2013, I was officially diagnosed with COPD (chronic obstructive pulmonary disease), which is associated with chronic bronchitis and emphysema. The only people who get it are smokers and miners and, as I've never been near a pit in my life, it was my bad habits to blame. Nearly forty years of heavy smoking had finally caught up with me. I just felt extremely lucky that I wasn't diagnosed with the lung cancer that killed my dad when he was 52 – a year younger than I was when I stopped. My mother's death from heart disease was also related to her years of smoking. I've never understood why I smoked but I think I became addicted when I was a child by breathing my parents' smoke. I also have quite a self-destructive nature and I think there's always been a bit of me that has a death wish (cue Soft Cell – 'Mr Self Destruct'). I quit illegal substances several years ago and the only chemicals I take nowadays, apart from alcohol, are prescribed but, to be quite honest, apart from painkillers, I don't really get a buzz off inhalers, antibiotics and steroids.

At the ripe old age of 59, as I write this in 2018, I have become more and more aware of people, who have been part of my life in one way or another, dying off. My old friend, record producer Phil Ramone, died not long ago and a woman I never met but who still affected much of my adult life, namely, Margaret Thatcher, finally died on 8 April 2013. I did once unintentionally have a drink with her daughter, Carol, in a bar in the West End. I was never a supporter of Maggie although, like her *Spitting Image* puppet, I think she had more balls than most of her male colleagues. When she came to power in 1979, it was just as Marc and I formed Soft Cell, so her passing really felt like the end of an era. What made it really strange was watching her funeral. When it finished on TV I went out, heading up to Kennington Lane. Two police motorcycle outriders drew up, blowing whistles to stop the traffic at the busy crossing. The same black hearse I'd seen ten minutes earlier on TV, with the Union Jack draped over the coffin, was whisked past me and several other incredulous bystanders on the way to Mortlake Crematorium. The last time I'd seen a coffin with a flag was when I watched Princess Diana's hearse drive through town a few years earlier – with considerably more people lining the pavements. I thought to myself, Who needs reality TV when you live in a city like London?

Chapter 50
COLLABORATIONS 2014–18

IN 2014 I WAS BACK IN THE STUDIO WORKING ON THE
music and co-production for two albums – one with The Grid
and Robert Fripp, although Robert was not physically present.
Richard had some DATs of loops Robert had created and imported
them into Logic Audio on his Mac to work on in his studio in
Stoke Newington in north London and Lewes in Sussex. That
album was finally approaching release in 2018, when I attended
a 5.1 surround-sound playback session at Opus Productions,
Shepherd's Bush with Richard Norris and my girlfriend. I think
it's been worth the wait.

I was co-producing another album in London and Dublin
with my friend Riccardo Mulhall and assistant, Paddy Kennedy,
working with Gavin Friday. This ended up sitting on the shelf, but
hopefully one day it will get released. Anni Hogan's album, *Lost
In Blue*, that I co-wrote and co-produced with Anni and Riccardo
Mulhall, finally came out on Coldspring Records, with a limited
edition on blue vinyl for collectors. It features guests Lydia Lunch,
Wolfgang Flür, Richard Strange, Enrico Tomasso, Scarlet West,
La Celine, Gavin Friday, Kid Congo Powers, MC & The 7 Pedals,
Joanna Neale, David Coulter and Derek Forbes. BBC 6 Music's

Marc Riley gave it its first few airplays and the general reaction has been very positive.

One album that has come out as a very limited edition was a Grid/Moog album, released by Paul Smith on Moog Sound Lab Records in 2018. This was all recorded under laboratory conditions with top-of-the range kit, including Bowers & Wilkins 802 monitors, an Elektron Machinedrum, a Roland Space Echo RE-201, an EMS VCS 3, a four-unit Voyager polyphonic tower, a five-unit Slim Phatty polyphonic tower and a rack of twenty-four Moogerfoogers and Logic Audio with a Prism Atlas analogue-to-digital converter, in the music department of the University of Surrey on the mighty Moog Modular System 55 (like the one Keith Emerson used). We were nobly assisted by modular synth wizard Finlay Shakespeare of Future Sounds and Professor Tony Myatt of University of Surrey.

I also co-wrote and co-produced an album called *Photosynthesis* with pianist Jon Savage (not the journalist) released on Coldspring Records in 2017. Stylistically, this was what is known as dark ambience and I am currently working on a sequel as it was well received by the press and fans alike. I am also working on various other projects with Jon Savage at Orange Girl's Studio, Loughton, Essex (basically, Jon's garage).

On the back of the success of Marc's 2016 box set, the number seven chart position of *The Very Best of Marc Almond & Soft Cell* album in 2017 and a very productive meeting with Marc and me, a Soft Cell ten-disc box set was scheduled for release in 2018. This was co-ordinated by Chris Smith, my manager at Renegade Music and Mark Wood and Chas Chandler at UMG. The other really big news for Soft Cell fans was at 8.25 a.m. on 21 February 2018 when Marc Almond appeared on Chris Evans' Radio 2 breakfast show, with an audience of nine million, to announce our one-off show at the London O2 Arena on 30 September.

There was incredible reaction from the press, social media and, most importantly, the fans. It's only when you make this sort of announcement that you realise the power of the internet. Within a couple of hours, more than ten thousand people had responded.

Some were jubilant, but others complained about various things – that we weren't doing a tour (which was mainly due to various health problems), we weren't playing anywhere apart from London, the venue was apparently shit, the tickets were overpriced and I was accused, personally, of setting prices to allow for an enormous fee for me. Then there were the usual blaggers, people I haven't seen for years, wanting to get on the guest list, people I may have once met in a pub asking for passes for the after-show party, plus an array of opportunists offering various services including DJing, support act, stage manager, roadie-ing, video directing, film crew, security guard, dancer etc. I felt like a careers advisor or someone at the job centre.

Marc even appeared in a brief interview on ITV's *News At Ten* – we were a news item on national television! I found it all quite insane; it was hard to believe they were talking about our little duo who, back in the late seventies, were playing to forty or fewer drunken, hostile people in some of the rougher nightclubs in west Yorkshire. I've always had mixed feelings about performing live as, unlike Marc, the stage is not my natural habitat, so suddenly to be getting ready to perform to potentially one of the biggest audiences of my life was very daunting. We'd played to big crowds before at various festivals but this was an audience of people who just wanted to see us. I was getting the fear... my feelings swinging from giddiness to sheer terror with occasional thoughts of, It's going to be great to What if the equipment breaks down? It was the way I always feel before a gig multiplied by a hundred.

The year 2018 will definitely go down as a landmark on many levels. Marc went to Buckingham Palace in February to receive his OBE from Prince William. It's all quite fantastic, who would have ever imagined that? I'm sure Marc and I would have laughed our heads off if someone had suggested that in the old days when we sat in the back of a rusty old Ford Transit on a wet Thursday night after playing a gig in Hull or Bradford. Another surprising thing – Marc and I have been writing and recording some new material in 2018. I never thought that was going to happen in a million years but it's going really well and it still sounds like Soft Cell, thanks largely to Rick Mulhall, my writing and production partner, and thanks also to my manager Chris Smith's boundless enthusiasm. I've also been re-recording some very early Soft Cell tracks with Jon Savage which has been great fun to do and will see the light of day in some format or other.

The UK had Record Store Day on 21 April, when Universal released a limited edition twelve-inch of my 'Say Hello, Wave Goodbye – Lateral Mix' and 'Youth – Wasted On The Young Mix'. I always thought that 'Youth is wasted on the young' was an Oscar Wilde quote but apparently it is attributed to George Bernard Shaw. Putting the sleeve together was quite interesting as Universal had picked an old photo of Marc and I from the eighties when I still had my moustache. I complained that they always did that and, much to my surprise, they offered me a 'digital shave' and photoshopped it out. Who said the camera never lies?

Marc and I were guests on Graham Norton's show on Radio 2. We hadn't done an interview together for about fifteen years so I was a bit nervous, particularly knowing that millions of people listen to Graham's show – no pressure at all. As it turned out, Graham Norton was a really lovely guy who made us feel totally at ease and the interview came out really well. Marc and I were both very relaxed. What was really weird was walking from Oxford Circus down Portland Place to Wogan House at the BBC. I'd met Chris, my manager, in All Bar One for a quick drink to steady the nerves and as we turned into the entrance of Radio 2 it was like I became a different person. I'd just walked anonymously down the street and suddenly there were fifty people clutching records, autograph books and pieces of paper asking for my signature and selfies. I've never been comfortable with the fame thing but it felt like I'd just gone through some kind of portal to a parallel universe – and in the background was the big O2 show, looming large.

I did a photoshoot at Chris Smith's farmhouse in Oxfordshire with Dave Chambers which included burning an old Revox B77 and Chris waving a chainsaw around while wearing my ice hockey mask! I did another – more normal – shoot in J. J. Park studios in Shoreditch with Marc, loads of neons and photographer Mike Owen. I'm pleased to say that both shoots produced very good results. Then there was programming the set, arranging backing vocals and horn parts, working out the visual projections for the giant LED screen and putting together the onstage backing group which comprised two female and two male backing singers, Grid percussionist Pablo Cook, our original live sax player Gary Barnacle and his friend Jack on French horn and trumpet. We had to find companies interested in buying the film rights and sorting out a film crew. Then we had to sort out the rehearsals and my synthesiser rig. Oh, and just to add to the pressure, the venue was sold out! People kept asking me if I was excited about the show and my reply was always 'No, I get really bad panic attacks when I think about it.' I kept having recurring nightmares of various scenarios where everything went wrong and would wake up in a cold sweat.

I've never been very keen on the performance element of what I do but, unfortunately, it's an occupational hazard. Sometimes it even feels like someone else is playing the role of being me, like an out-of-body experience and I'm looking down on myself – it's weird. As we got closer to the date, there seemed to be more and more to do, which was great – at least the interest was still there. BBC 4 were making a one-hour documentary about us which was great fun, in spite of my initial reticence.

In July we rolled into Leeds to commence filming the following day at Leeds Warehouse, where it all began (our first paid gig – £40). We did a semi-playback of two very early numbers, 'A Man Could Get Lost' and 'Bleak Is My Favourite Cliché', using the original equipment – Korg 800 DV and SB-100 synths, plus a Revox B77 reel-to-reel machine and a (remade) Soft Cell neon sign. Not forgetting Marc, authentically positioned with his straight mic stand – he hates boom stands (for those of you that know the difference). We did some filming in the Fenton pub next to Leeds Polytechnic, an old haunt from our student days, where we decided to use a reel-to-reel tape machine onstage and, unwittingly, became Britain's first ever synthpop duo.

The next phases of the documentary were shot in various locations back in London. We did some in a place called the Lucky Pig cocktail lounge in Fitzrovia, Marc did more in L'Escargot in Soho and I did some stuff playing records in Chris Smith's riverside office in Mortlake, conveniently located next to Rick Stein's restaurant, where the sashimi is to die for!

I had to do another interview for the documentary, one of those classic album formats, set in a wonderful studio in Holborn called Fiction Studios, presumably because it's full of books and bookcases and run by a lovely librarian/sound engineer called Nathan. I had to play some of the live synth parts on 'Say Hello, Wave Goodbye', 'Memorabilia' and 'Bedsitter', which was fun as I hadn't played them for over fifteen years. In between all this activity I did interviews for *Uncut*, *Boyz*, *Classic Pop*, The Electricity Club and still found time to write and record some new material with Rick and also with Jon.

Our new single was premiered on Chris Evans' Radio 2 show in August with a short phone interview with Marc. Not a bad start – nine million listeners!

Chapter 51
TWISTED WHEELS

WE FILMED A VIDEO FOR SOFT CELL'S 'NORTHERN LIGHTS' in Manchester. My girlfriend Scarlet and I got the train to Leeds in late August and changed for Manchester and the legendary Twisted Wheel club, as Marc mentions it in our song.

The song basically paid homage to our northern roots and to the influence of northern soul on our music and outlook. Amazingly, all the old guard of the scene turned out en masse and really appreciated that we were effectively saying 'thank you' to them and their music. When we first recorded 'Tainted Love', a lot of the soul boys hated us but we did it out of love for that music and inadvertently created a whole new following for younger people who became curious about northern soul because of that cover and 'What' and 'The Night'. I feel vindicated that the owner of the Twisted Wheel shook my hand and asked me for a seven-inch vinyl version (what else?) of 'Northern Lights' to play in his club.

The following morning Scarlet and I woke up in our lovely big bed at the Malmaison hotel and went down for breakfast. We didn't have to check out until midday so everything was very relaxed. The journey went fine until suddenly there was a slight bump from the driver's cabin just ahead of our carriage, then the sound of something sticky and crunchy under the wheels. Scarlet thought we must have run over a stray cow as there was a field of them next to the train. We came to a halt so the driver and crew could inspect what we had hit. It turned out to be human – a person who had decided to end it all, and the sound was that of several tons of steel on wheels travelling at speed crushing a human body – something I'll never forget. Eventually the air ambulance arrived as the young train driver was completely traumatised, followed by the police and forensics. The policemen carried little yellow body-bags while the forensic guys in white, disposable boiler suits looked at all the wheels while they picked out bits of human remains. It was like someone using a toothpick after eating barbecue ribs. Two and a half hours later we were free to go. Keep the faith.

The following week we were off for band rehearsals at the Fulham Bar And Grill, just near Chelsea football ground, Stamford Bridge, thanks to my friend, proprietor Bren McGee. The rehearsal was just for the horns and percussion supplied by Gary Barnacle, Jack Birchwood and Pablo Cook, respectively, with our sound engineer Philip Larsen operating the hard drive and mixer while I acted as arranger and conductor to get everything really tight.

We had a launch to celebrate our signature beer collaboration, the Soft Cell 'Say Hello, Wave Goodbye' edition of a West Berkshire Brewery drink, at the Southwark Tavern in London Bridge. Scarlet DJed, playing Soft Cell all evening, as it was also a launch for the *Keychains And Snowstorms* box set. The venue was perfect, as it was in the basement which had real cells where they used to keep prisoners overnight before they went to prisons or the gallows the following day. It was absolutely rammed and everyone said they had a great time, not least because we gave away seven hundred pints of free beer. If that hadn't worked I doubt anything would. It was a really great night and everyone was on top form.

After all this fun it was time for work on the show to commence. Full rehearsals with Marc and four backing singers ensued with two days at Cato Music studios in Wandsworth. It was also confirmed we were going to appear on *Later With Jools Holland*, a day of rehearsals followed by a day of filming – a killer week! Come 1 October it would be holiday time.

Chapter 52

ENDGAME

AFTER ALL THIS FUN IT WAS ALMOST TIME FOR WORK TO begin. On Sunday 23, the week before the O2 show, I went to an open day at Space Gallery on the Old Kent Road to meet some of my art friends, in particular Michael Corkrey, who'd invited me and my friend Jason Vincent. We bought some alcohol and I think we may have overdone it; I managed to trip over and 'sprain' my ankle really badly, just before my busiest week of the year.

We were booked to appear on *Later With Jools Holland*, which entailed a day's rehearsal without Jools on Monday, followed by filming in Maidstone Studios, Kent, on Tuesday. Other acts on the show were Jess Glynne, Idles, King Princess and Ralph McTell, with us being the last act. Show day definitely felt more intense, not least because Jools was on the set so it all felt a lot more real. After the camera rehearsal, we all went to the canteen for dinner and a few beers, before all the bands jammed with Jools and rehearsed a groove which was quite a laugh – kind of atonal funk.

The pre-recorded Saturday show was filmed in front of a studio audience that evening. We performed 'Northern Lights', had an interview with Jools and then closed the show with 'Say Hello,

Wave Goodbye'. There was a fifteen-minute break while they reset cameras and lights, and then we were live from 10 until 10.30 p.m., opening with 'Northern Lights' and finishing with 'Bedsitter'. After the show a lot of people said how touched they were when Marc came over to my keyboard area and I turned and smiled at him. I must point out that the producer asked me to do this, so my spontaneity was somewhat rehearsed – not that I don't have great affection for Marc anyway!

The next day I headed back to London for two days of band and technical rehearsals with Marc, percussion, horns and four backing singers at Cato Music studios in Wandsworth, preparing for the O2 gig that Sunday. At that point my 'sprained' ankle had swelled up massively; I could hardly get my shoe on and walking was a real struggle. Fortunately, our archivist, Lloyd Lewis Kristian, who has some medical training, was there so he came to the rescue with painkillers, an ice pack and a support bandage, which really helped. It later transpired, after several X-rays at Guy's Hospital, that my ankle was fractured, perfect timing just before the biggest gig of my life. The old theatrical adage 'break a leg' came to my mind. At least I had an excuse to sit down throughout most of the show, in case anyone was wondering.

On Friday I took it easy and rested my ankle although I did venture out to my local barbers on Saturday for a pre-gig haircut. Then, suddenly, it was the big day. I went to bed at about midnight and got up at six as I couldn't sleep. Funnily enough I didn't have one of my weird pre-gig dreams that I'd been having on and off for the last few months. Scarlet, Dave Chambers and I were picked up at 12.30 p.m. and taken to the Intercontinental Hotel next to the O2. We had a great room on the twelfth floor with two views: the River Thames on one side and the O2 on the other. It looked enormous that close; it was hard to believe that in a few hours the place would be packed out with people that had come just to see Soft Cell. We'd certainly come a long way from playing the common room at Leeds Polytechnic.

Around 4 p.m. Chris Smith came to collect us for the soundcheck, which was later than it should have been. I walked into the arena and was immediately blown away by the size of it with all the house lights on. I'd only been there twice – for a Leonard Cohen and a U2 gig – and it looked completely different, especially with thousands of people packed in there. We located my dressing room which was quite big but very dull, with a TV that didn't work and a shower with no towels. Fortunately, there was a fridge full of beer, wine and vodka, plus a load of soft drinks. Some plates of chicken and potato finger food arrived so everyone tucked in as no one had had lunch. Then Chris's phone rang and I knew it was bad news. Apparently my main polyphonic keyboard, a Korg Prologue, had been badly damaged by a clumsy roadie who had dropped a keyboard stand on it, smashing the low octave plastic keys and rendering it useless. In my younger days I would have hit the roof and threatened to call off the gig, but I thought better of it and just said to the people looking after the sound, 'What are you going to do about it?'

As it was a Sunday it was not the easiest of times to hire a keyboard for a gig starting in about three and a half hours. Luckily they managed to locate a Roland Juno 60 synthesiser, which I'd never used before, but it did the job. Eventually we did a rather rushed soundcheck as the venue was so far behind. Unfortunately, a few fans who had bought tickets that included watching part of the soundcheck completely missed it as it was so slow to get through security. Some of my friends on my guest list didn't even get in and someone told me that Marc Almond's mother even had difficulty at the ticket office. She did eventually get in and was spotted later on singing along to 'Sex Dwarf' whilst sitting a few seats away from non other than Sir Andrew Lloyd Webber!

After the soundcheck Scarlet and Dave went back to my dressing room and Dave said there was a backstage canteen where we could get hot food. We went and had a look and they had a choice of roast beef, chicken or nut roast. I said to the serving lady I'd have the roast beef.

She then asked me, 'Where's your meal ticket?' I had no idea what she was talking about and proceeded to explain to her that I was the artist and would be performing that evening. She was having none of it, so I indignantly stormed off, as would most people in that situation. Her supervisor must have seen what happened as she followed us down the corridor, apologising for the misunderstanding, but there was no way I was going back in there after that treatment. I was gradually starting to get more and more pissed off with that place but once I had a look from backstage as the crowds began filling the seats, all bad thoughts disappeared.

Before I knew it, the moment of reckoning arrived. I had on my black shirt, black jeans and suit jacket with a T.G. badge that Genesis P. Orridge once gave me on the lapel and was ready to rock. Strangely enough, I didn't feel nervous at all, just very exhilarated and when I walked on stage and a whole arena of people cheered it felt amazing.

The gig went pretty well by our standards even though there were a few false starts when I think Marc couldn't hear the drums properly as his monitors weren't in the right place. Also he didn't have a set list which is usually taped on the floor by the mic stand by a crew member.

My monitors sounded absolutely shit, all the levels were wrong and it was difficult to hear what I was playing, but everyone said it sounded great out front, which is what really matters, I guess.

That's the problem with doing a one-off show really, because if you are touring with the same crew every night, everyone knows how everything is meant to be set up. At least we knew the visuals looked great but, as it's all preprogrammed, there's not much that can go wrong, unless something fuses or blows up. Anyway, the final strains of 'Say Hello, Wave Goodbye' faded away seconds before the deadline of 10.30 p.m.; the fine for overrunning was good incentive to finish on time. I was glad it was over when we came off, I felt mentally exhausted and despite Chris Smith's attempts to persuade us otherwise, Scarlet and I didn't attend the after-show party. All three floors of the All Bar One were totally rammed and the thought of all those people after playing a huge gig just didn't appeal so we retreated to our room to admire our window views of the night-time London sky.

EPILOGUE
60+

IT'S BEWILDERING TO THINK WHEN WE FIRST FORMED Soft Cell in that little sound room in college it would end up in the O2. Another thing that still bewilders me after forty years in the music business is the logic behind the Radio 2 playlist selection. It was announced by Marc live on The Chris Evans Breakfast Show that we were performing at the almost sold out O2. Chris also played an exclusive of our new single, 'Northern Lights', on a later show and we did an interview on Graham Norton's radio show, our first interview together for fifteen years. We had major features in most music magazines and the *Daily Telegraph* plus generally favourable reviews of the live show in every paper, and our box set, *Keychains and Snowstorms*, was number one in the Amazon pre-sales chart. We had also been filming a documentary with BBC 4 over the last few months but, guess what, we still couldn't get on the Radio 2 playlist, because someone in that old boy's establishment said we 'sounded too eighties', whatever that meant.

Then all the madness was over. Christmas came and went – I had a very nice Christmas dinner cooked by my good friend Dave Chambers – and I stayed in for New Year's Eve, watching the fireworks over the River Thames from my balcony. On Saturday 2 February I did my first live performance of the year at the University of Surrey's Institute of Sound Recording in Guildford, as part of the Moog Symposium with Richard Norris. It was basically a live Grid Moog filter remix, totally improvised. There's a great feeling of freedom doing improv and luckily it worked out really well. It was a much more intimate performance than my last show at the O2.

We are reviewing all our Grid back catalogue in 2019, but the start of the year has focused on Soft Cell archive work; all our albums are being released on high grade vinyl, including *Cruelty Without Beauty* (ironically never previously released on vinyl despite being on Cooking Vinyl Records). We also released a DVD of the Soft Cell O2 show, and a coffee-table book, *To Show You I Was There*, packed with rare and unseen Soft Cell photographs and test shots, which comes with a free vinyl EP *Magick Mutants* as a belated follow up to *Mutant Moments*. Like the original, it features my sleeve artwork. I've also done an online DJ set for Big Mouth on Soho Radio and for Boogaloo Radio, which were good fun. Boogaloo Radio was broadcast from a shed at the back of a north London pub that Shane MacGowan used to live above and I think Pete Doherty was a regular too – very rock'n'roll.

Suddenly it was my 60th birthday, which almost coincided with the publication date for *To Show You I've Been There*. So, my manager, Chris Smith, ever the marketing man, put on a combined launch/birthday party at The Phoenix Arts Club beneath The Phoenix Theatre on Charing Cross Road. Although it's one of my favourite late-night venues in the West End, I initially had reservations about my birthday celebrations being turned into a semi-public event, as I am usually a fairly private person. But loads of old friends and people I've worked with over the years came so it turned out OK and I think everyone had a great time, including yours truly. So, at the ripe old age of 60, I have just signed a new recording deal with BMG, which is very exciting, and commenced work with Marc on a new Soft Cell album due for release in early spring 2021. Watch this space!

EQUIPMENT LIST

ARP Odyssey Synthesiser
Arturia Beatstep Pro Sequencer
Alesis HR-16 Drum Machine
Alesis MMT-8 Sequencer
Alesis Nanosynth
Alesis Air FX Contactless Effects Unit
Akai MiniAK Virtual Phrase Synthesiser
Akai S1100 Sampler
Akai MPC Live
Akai MPK Mini Controller Keyboard
Bliptronic 5000 Matrix Synthesiser (x 2)
Casio VZ-10M Synthrack
Casio SK-1 Toy Sampling Keyboard (Circuit Bent)
Control Synthesis Deep Bass Nine Synthrack
Dunlop Cry Baby Wah Wah Pedal
Dubreq Stylophone (x 3)
Electro-Harmonix Pedals: Electric Mistress Deluxe Flanger,
Deluxe Memory Man Delay, Mel9 Tape Replay Machine, Synth9
Synthesiser Machine, Bass Micro Synthesiser
Nano Looper 360 (x 2)
E-mu Proteus Orchestral Synthrack
E-mu Proteus 2000 Synthrack

Eurorack 3-Tier Modular Synthesiser Modules: Doepfer A-118
Noise, A-140 ADSR, A-110 VCO, A-160 1 Clock Divider, A-161
Clock Sequencer
Soundhack Echophon
Studio Electronics: Oscillation, SE88, Amp, Levels
Mutable Instruments: Peaks (x 2), Streams, Braids, Clouds
Tiptop Z3000 Smart VC Oscillator
Tiptop Z2040 LP-VCF
Spectral Multiband Resonator
VCA Matrix
Korg 800DV Synthesiser
Korg SB-100 Synthe-Bass
Korg Prophecy Synthesiser
Korg Prologue Synthesiser
Korg MS-10 Synthesiser
Korg MS-20 Synthesiser
Korg SQ-1 Sequencer (x 2)
Korg Kaossilator Pro Synthesiser
Korg Kaoss Pad Synthesiser
Korg Kaossilator Dynamic Phrase Synthesiser
Korg Kaoss Pad Dynamic Effect Sampler KP3+
Landlord FX Banging Hangover Reverb
Landlord FX Happy Hour Looper
Minimoog Synthesiser
Moog DFAM Analog Synthesiser
Moog Mother-32 Semi-Modular Synthesiser (x 2)
Moogerfooger Lowpass Filter
Moogerfooger Ring Modulator
Moogerfooger Phaser
MXR Heavy Metal Distortion Pedal
MXR Distortion Pedal
MXR Pitch Transposer Rack
MXR 32 Band Graphic Equaliser Rack
Novation Bass Station Synthrack
Novation 495L MkII Controller Keyboard

Oberheim Matrix-1000 Synthrack
Oberheim DMX Drum Machine
PPG Wave 2.2 Synthesiser
Roland SH-101 Synthesiser
Roland System-1M Synthrack
Roland System-100M Modular
Roland System-500 Modular
Roland CR-78 Drum Machine
Roland TR-8 Drum Machine
Roland TR-707 Drum Machine
Roland MKS-70 Synthrack
Roland SVC-350 Vocoder Rack
Roli Seaboard Block Expressive Keyboard
Sequential Circuits Prophet 5 (Rev 3) Synthesiser
Sherman Filterbank
Texas Instruments Speak & Math (Circuit Bent)
Volca Kick Module
Volca Bass Module
Volca Beats Module
Volca Keys Module
Waldorf Microwave Synthrack
Yamaha CS-5 Synthesiser
Yamaha QS-300 Synthesiser
Yamaha SPX-90 Digital Delay Rack

ACKNOWLEDGEMENTS

Special thanks to Chris Smith at Renegade, Doug Kean at Gunn Media, Lloyd Lewis Kristian, Marc Almond, Richard Norris, Riccardo Mulhall, Jon & Anna Savage and the boys, Archie & Theo, David Chambers, Ritchie Franklin, Peter Ashworth, Charlotte & Ronnie Harris and Stuart Kirkham. Thanks to everyone involved in the O2 show, especially the fans for your continual loyal support. Thanks to Omnibus Press, Warner Chappell Music, UMG, BMG, Korg Synthesizers, Red Dog Music & Macari's London. Cheers to everyone at The Black Prince (Kennington) plus The Coach & Horses and The Phoenix (Soho). Bon appetit to The Coriander (Vauxhall), Yoshi (Hammersmith) and Melanie's (Soho). Very special thanks to Scarlet West.